PATHWAYS
THIRD EDITION
Listening, Speaking, and Critical Thinking

JOHN HUGHES

Australia • Brazil • Canada • Mexico • Singapore • United Kingdom • United States

---

National Geographic Learning,
a Cengage Company

Pathways 1: Listening, Speaking, and Critical Thinking, 3rd Edition
John Hughes

Publisher: Sherrise Roehr

Executive Editor: Laura Le Dréan

Senior Development Editor: Andrew Gitzy

Director of Global Marketing: Ian Martin

Heads of Regional Marketing:

   Charlotte Ellis (Europe, Middle East and Africa)

   Justin Kaley (Asia and Greater China)

   Irina Pereyra (Latin America)

   Joy MacFarland (US and Canada)

Product Marketing Manager: Tracy Bailie

Content Project Manager: Samantha Bertschmann

Media Researcher: Leila Hishmeh

Senior Designer: Heather Marshall

Operations Support: Hayley Chwazik-Gee

Manufacturing Planner: Terry Isabella

Composition: MPS North America LLC

Printed in Singapore

Print Number: 01 Print Year: 2024

© 2025 Cengage Learning, Inc.

WCN: 03-300-327

ALL RIGHTS RESERVED. No part of this work covered by the copyright herein may be reproduced or distributed in any form or by any means, except as permitted by U.S. copyright law, without the prior written permission of the copyright owner

"National Geographic", "National Geographic Society" and the Yellow Border Design are registered trademarks of the National Geographic Society ® Marcas Registradas

> For permission to use material from this text or product, submit all requests online at **cengage.com/permissions**
> Further permissions questions can be emailed to
> **permissionrequest@cengage.com**

Student's Book:
ISBN: 978-0-357-97874-0
Student's Book with the Spark platform
ISBN: 978-0-357-97873-3

National Geographic Learning
5191 Natorp Blvd,
Mason, OH 45040
USA

Locate your local office at **international.cengage.com/region**

Visit National Geographic Learning online at **ELTNGL.com**
Visit our corporate website at **www.cengage.com**

Scope and Sequence

Unit Title & Theme	Listenings & Videos	Listening & Note Taking
1 **EXPLORING WORK** *page 1* **ACADEMIC TRACK:** Career Studies / Social Science	**Lesson A** An Interview with Annie Griffiths **VIDEO** Working in the Wild **Lesson B** What Does It Take to Be an Explorer?♦	• Listen for Repeated Words and Ideas • Use Linear Notes and Mind Maps
2 **GOOD TIMES, GOOD FEELINGS** *page 21* **ACADEMIC TRACK:** Psychology	**Lesson A** Remembering the Past* **VIDEO** A Shared Memory **Lesson B** What Do We Remember?	• Understand a Speaker's Purpose • Use a Split Page to Take Notes
3 **THE MARKETING MACHINE** *page 41* **ACADEMIC TRACK:** Business / Marketing	**Lesson A** Mascots and Marketing **VIDEO** Advertising Just for You **Lesson B** Graphic Design*	• Listen for Examples
4 **WILD WEATHER** *page 61* **ACADEMIC TRACK:** Environmental Science	**Lesson A** Strange Weather* **VIDEO** Understanding Tornadoes **Lesson B** The Future of Sports	• Listen for Definitions • Abbreviate Numbers and Measurements
5 **FOOD ON THE MOVE** *page 81* **ACADEMIC TRACK:** Cultural Studies	**Lesson A** Food Fact or Fiction?♦ **VIDEO** How We Taste Food **Lesson B** Ugly Food	• Listen for Reasons • Use a T-Chart

* With slideshow
♦ With animation

Speaking & Pronunciation	Grammar & Vocabulary	Critical Thinking	Final Tasks
• Say That You Don't Understand • Take Turns • Final -s / -es Sounds	• Simple Present • Adverbs and Expressions of Frequency • Word Families	• Make Inferences	**Option 1** Role-play a conversation about dream jobs **Option 2** Discuss what makes a good job
• Give Reasons • Structure a Presentation • Simple Past -ed Endings	• Simple Past and Time Clauses • Abstract Nouns	• Recognize Assumptions	**Option 1** Play two truths and a lie **Option 2** Present a special object or photo
• Ask for and Give Clarification • Brainstorm with a Group • Aspirated /k/, /p/, and /t/	• Simple Present and Present Continuous • Noun Suffixes -ment and -tion	• Analyze Graphics	**Option 1** Design a mascot **Option 2** Present an advertisement
• Express Likes and Dislikes • Use Slides • Syllable Stress	• Count and Noncount Nouns • A, an, some, any, a lot of • Verb + Gerund or Infinitive • Synonyms	• Remember and Apply What You Know	**Option 1** Present tips for doing an activity **Option 2** Present a process
• Tell a Story • Use an Effective Hook and a Call to Action • Long and Short Vowel Sounds	• A lot of, much, many, few, little, enough • Compound Words	• Recognize a Speaker's Point of View	**Option 1** Do a food survey **Option 2** Present an argument about food

Scope and Sequence

	Unit Title & Theme	Listenings & Videos	Listening & Note Taking
	6 **HOUSING FOR THE FUTURE** page 101 **ACADEMIC TRACK:** Engineering / Urban Planning	**Lesson A** Housing Solutions* **VIDEO** Steel Container Buildings **Lesson B** How to Build a New City	• Use Context Clues • Use Diagrams and Flowcharts
	7 **THE HUMAN BODY** page 121 **ACADEMIC TRACK:** Health / Biology	**Lesson A** How Humans Are Changing **VIDEO** Brain Connections **Lesson B** The Benefits of Bacteria♦	• Understand Time Periods • Use an Outline
	8 **LEARN TO LOVE ART** page 141 **ACADEMIC TRACK:** Arts / Music	**Lesson A** Temporary Art* **VIDEO** Making Art from Recycled Glass **Lesson B** Jake Shimabukuro	• Recognize Opinions
	9 **OUR RELATIONSHIP WITH NATURE** page 161 **ACADEMIC TRACK:** Science / Anthropology	**Lesson A** The Penguins at Simon's Town* **VIDEO** Falcon Farmers **Lesson B** Kariba Town, Zimbabwe	• Recognize Cause and Effect
	10 **HOW WE COMMUNICATE** page 181 **ACADEMIC TRACK:** Communication / Sociology	**Lesson A** Solving Communication Problems **VIDEO** A School for Communication **Lesson B** The Importance of Gestures♦	• Listen for Key Words

Appendix page 201

* With slideshow
♦ With animation

Speaking & Pronunciation	Grammar & Vocabulary	Critical Thinking	Final Tasks
• Ask for and Give Opinions • Encourage Other People in a Discussion • Sentence Stress	• Conjunctions *and, but, or, so* • Adjective Suffixes	• Rank Options	**Option 1** Present a house and sell it **Option 2** Plan a new city
• Talk about Possibilities • Participate in a Group Discussion • Recognize Reduced Forms	• *Will* for Predictions; Adverbs of Certainty • *Will* and *Be Going To* • Choose the Correct Meaning	• Question and Check What You Hear	**Option 1** Survey classmates about the future **Option 2** Discuss pros and cons of future situations
• Express Degrees of Uncertainty • Debate an Idea • Recognize Connected Speech	• Modals of Present Possibility • Modals and Questions for Suggestions • Collocations with Prepositions	• Synthesize	**Option 1** Describe an image or book **Option 2** Have a class debate
• Compare and Contrast • Plan Your Presentation • Recognize Reduced Words	• Comparative Adjectives • Superlative Adjectives • Collocations	• Analyze Arguments	**Option 1** Play a vocabulary game **Option 2** Give a presentation about the natural world
• Explain and Check • Invite and Answer Questions from the Audience • Consonant Clusters	• Present Perfect • Present Perfect and Simple Past • Phrasal Verbs	• Recognize Cultural Differences	**Option 1** Explain a piece of technology **Option 2** Present a form of communication

Welcome to *Pathways Listening, Speaking, and Critical Thinking*, Third Edition

NEW AND UPDATED

Compelling photography and infographics in **Explore the Theme** draw students into the unit, develop their visual and information literacy skills, and get them speaking.

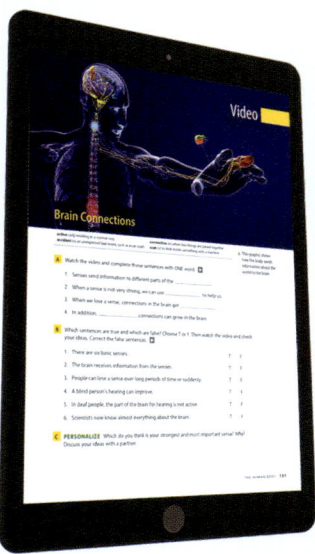

A **multimedia approach** featuring videos, slideshows, and animations supports listening comprehension while making content accessible and engaging.

Updated Speaking Activities give more guided instruction and language support, building fluency, accuracy, and learner independence.

Academic competency skills like collaboration, communication, and problem-solving help students develop the skills and behaviors needed to succeed in school and their lives.

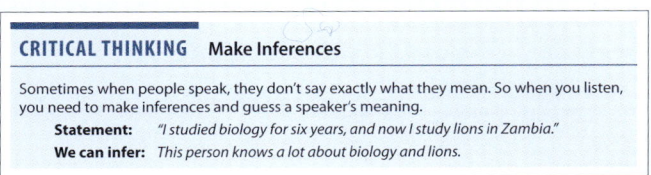

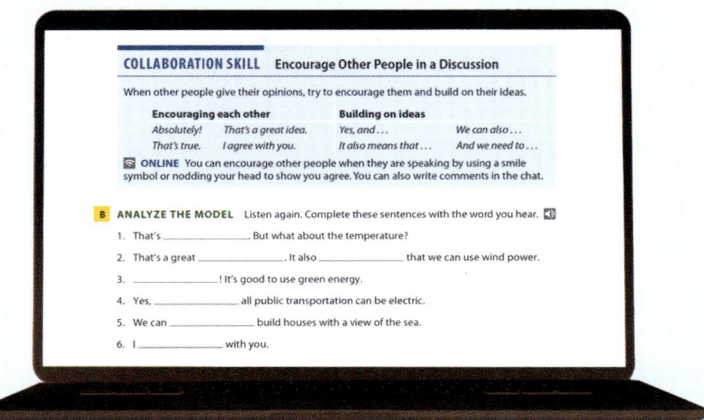

Assessment

Pathways Listening, Speaking, and Critical Thinking supports teachers and learners with various forms of assessment, with the goal of helping students achieve real-world success.

A **new Review section** provides additional opportunities for formative assessment and encourages students to take control of their learning journey through guided self-assessment.

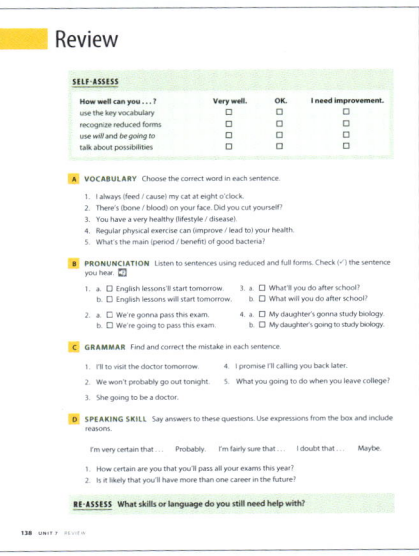

The **Final Tasks** section with two options provides flexibility for various learning environments and another opportunity for formative assessment.

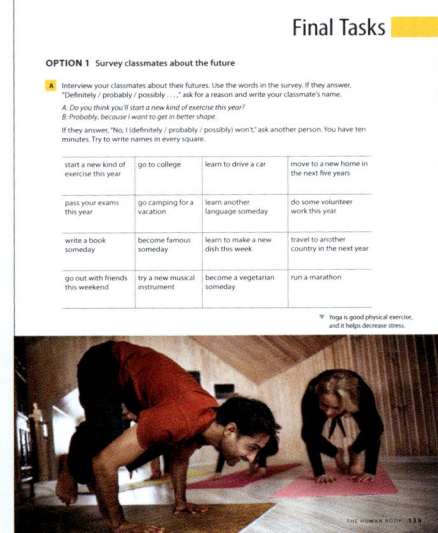

Opportunities for online assessment on the **new Spark platform** include:
- The National Geographic Learning Online Placement Test, which places students into the correct level of *Pathways*
- Interactive Online Practice activities and online tests from the Assessment Suite, for formative and summative assessment
- A Course Gradebook that tracks student and class performance against learning objectives, providing teachers with actionable insights to support student's progress

spark

Bring the world to the classroom and the classroom to life with the Spark platform — where you can prepare, teach and assess your classes all in one place!

Manage your course and teach great classes with integrated digital teaching and learning tools. Spark brings together everything you need on an all-in-one platform with a single log-in.

Track student and class performance on independent online practice and assessment. The Course Gradebook helps you turn information into insights to make the most of valuable classroom time.

Set up classes and roster students quickly and easily on Spark. Seamless integration options and point-of-use support helps you focus on what matters most: student success.

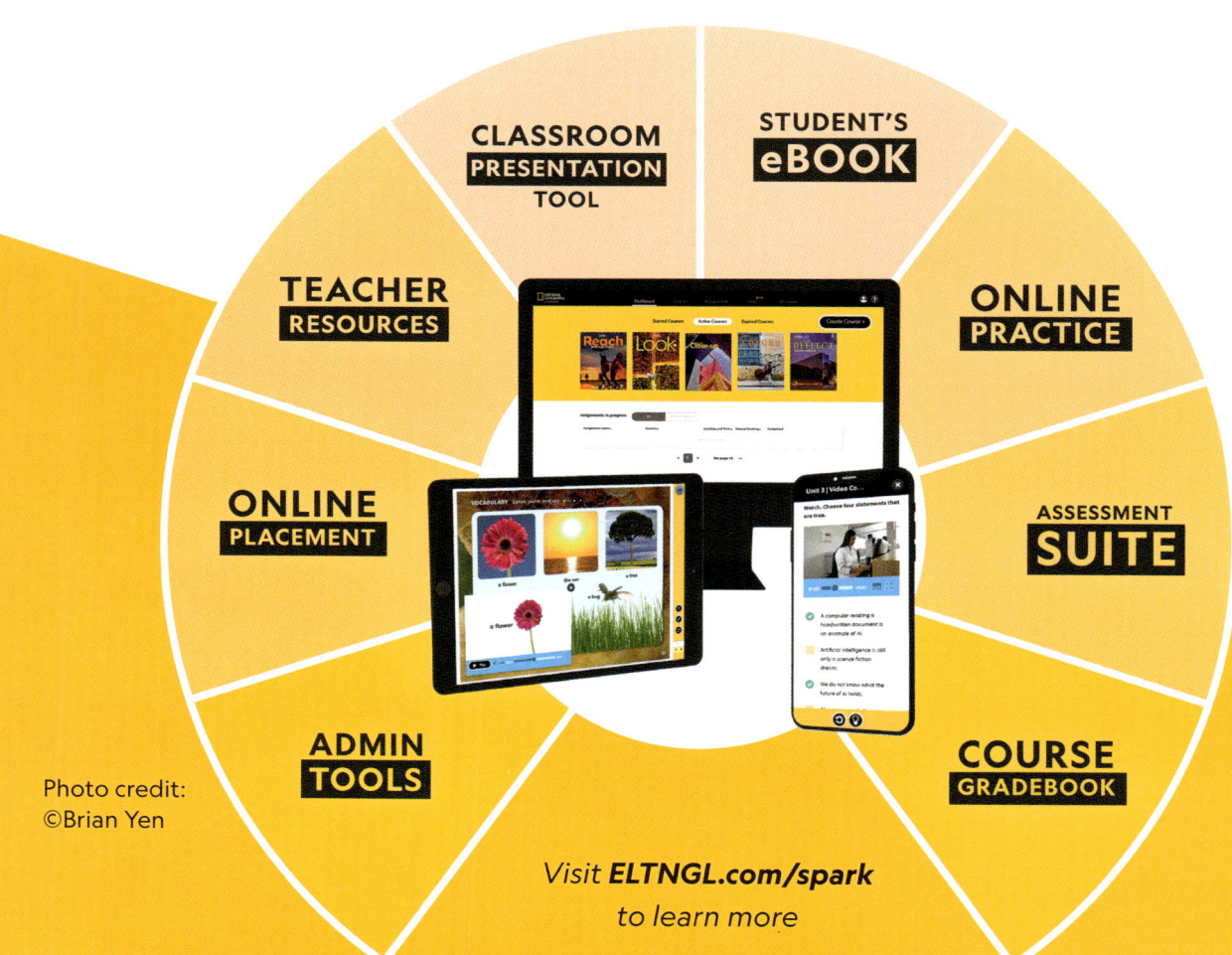

- CLASSROOM PRESENTATION TOOL
- STUDENT'S eBOOK
- TEACHER RESOURCES
- ONLINE PRACTICE
- ONLINE PLACEMENT
- ASSESSMENT SUITE
- ADMIN TOOLS
- COURSE GRADEBOOK

Photo credit: ©Brian Yen

Visit **ELTNGL.com/spark** to learn more

EXPLORING WORK 1

A zookeeper at the Tennoji Zoo in Osaka, Japan, works with a hippo named Tetsuo.

IN THIS UNIT, YOU WILL:
- Listen to an interview with a National Geographic Explorer
- Watch a video about working in the wild
- Watch or listen to a presentation about how to become an explorer
- Role-play a conversation about dream jobs
  OR Discuss what makes a good job

THINK AND DISCUSS:
1. What is the man in the photo doing? Where does he work?
2. Do you want a job like this? Explain.
3. Is it important to have a good job? Explain.

EXPLORE THE THEME

Read the information. Then discuss the questions.

1. Which three job pros do Gen Z employees talk about the most?
2. Do you agree? What are your top three job pros?
3. What other things do you think are important in a job?

A job pro is something you like about a job. These are the most common job pros that Gen Zers talked about in reviews of their jobs.

Work environment **4.3%**
Flexible hours **4.2%**
Good pay **3.5%**
Great people **2.9%**
Flexible schedule **2.5%**
Great work **1.6%**
Easy job **1.6%**
Employee discount **1.5%**
Free food **1.4%**

MOST COMMON JOB PROS FOR GEN Z*

*Gen Z are people born between 1997 and 2012.

Source: Glassdoor Economic Research

This is the office for Selgascano Architecture in Mallorca, Spain. Studies say that workers are happier in offices with plants and sunlight.

A Vocabulary

A Listen and repeat. Check (✓) any words you already know. 🔊

| adventure (n) | creative (adj) | experience (n) | opportunity (n) | skill (n) |
| communicate (v) | dangerous (adj) | explore (v) | ordinary (adj) | view (n) |

B **MEANING FROM CONTEXT** Read and listen to the article. Think about the meaning of the words in blue. Write each word next to its definition below. 🔊

MEET THE EXPLORERS

Different people have different **views** about "big cats," such as lions and jaguars. Some people think the animals are beautiful, but other people are afraid of them because they can be **dangerous**. Thandiwe Mweetwa and Ricardo Samuel Moreno are biologists, and they love to **explore** the natural world. They both work with big cats and teach **ordinary** people about them.

Thandiwe is from Zambia, and she helps lions in her country. Sometimes people kill these animals because they want to protect their farm animals. So Thandiwe **communicates** with people in the villages and shares her **experiences** so they learn about the lions. She also works to give more **opportunities** to other women scientists.

Ricardo is from Panama, and he often goes on **adventures** in the jungle. Sometimes he tries to photograph jaguars. It's difficult, and it takes special **skills**. He has to find **creative** ways to photograph them. For example, he uses special cameras in the trees; when a jaguar walks past the cameras, the cameras take photos of the animal.

▼ Thandiwe Mweetwa

▼ Ricardo Samuel Moreno

1. _____ (n) a chance to do something
2. _____ (adj) having the ability to make things or think of new ideas
3. _____ (adj) likely to cause harm or injury
4. _____ (v) to travel to different places and learn about things
5. _____ (n) an opinion or a way of seeing things

4 UNIT 1 LESSON A

6. _____ (n) an exciting time or event

7. _____ (n) something that happens to you

8. _____ (v) to share information with others

9. _____ (n) something you are able to do well

10. _____ (adj) not different or unusual

VOCABULARY SKILL   Word Families

A word family is a group of words with the same base word. We add prefixes and suffixes to make word forms in the family.

create (v)   creat**ive** (adj)   creat**ively** (adv)   creat**ion** (n)

When you learn a new word, try to learn the other forms as well. You can write down the form after the word using these abbreviations: (v) for verb, (adj) for adjective, (adv) for adverb, and (n) for noun.

C Work with a partner. Write the different forms of these words. Use a dictionary to help you.

1. communicate (v)   _____ (n)

2. _____ (n)   dangerous (adj)

3. _____ (v)   photographer (n)

4. adventure (n)   _____ (adj)

5. _____ (v)   explorer (n)

6. skillful (adj)   _____ (n)

D Choose the correct form of the word to complete these conversations. Then listen and check your answers. 🔊

1. A: Do you like to do (danger / dangerous) things?

   B: Sure! I like surfing and skydiving!

2. A: Do you take a lot of (photographs / photographers)?

   B: Yes, I do. I have thousands on my phone.

3. A: What (skillful / skills) do you have?

   B: I speak two languages, and I can play the guitar.

4. A: Who do you (communicate / communication) with every day?

   B: My family and also my teachers at school.

5. A: When you go on vacation, do you prefer to have (adventurous / adventures) someplace or to relax on the beach?

   B: I like to relax on the beach!

E **PERSONALIZE** Work with a partner and take turns. Ask the questions in exercise D. Answer the questions so they are true for you.

A Listening An Interview with Annie Griffiths

Critical Thinking | **A** **BRAINSTORM** Look at the photo by Annie Griffiths and read about her. With a partner, think of two questions to ask Annie.

Women from the UAE Cycling Girls club, Dubai, UAE

Annie Griffiths is a National Geographic Explorer and photographer. She travels around the world and takes photographs of people and wildlife.

LISTENING SKILL   Listen for Repeated Words and Ideas

Speakers often repeat certain words (and their word forms) when they talk about a topic. They sometimes use synonyms or similar phrases for the key words and ideas. These repeated words help you identify the main idea and the most important information.

> Some people think "**big cats**," such as **lions and jaguars**, are beautiful, but other people believe the **cats** are dangerous. Thandiwe Mweetwa works with **big cats**....

B Listen to the interview with Annie Griffiths. You will hear these nine words. Check (✓) a word each time you hear it. Which FIVE words are repeated several times? 🔊

_____ photographer   _____ places   _____ travel

_____ wildlife   _____ world   _____ communicate

_____ dangerous   _____ people   _____ friends

6 UNIT 1 LESSON A

C **MAIN IDEAS** Think about the repeated words in exercise B. Check (✓) the main idea of the interview.

1. ☐ Annie Griffiths' work is dangerous sometimes.
2. ☐ Annie Griffiths travels around the world as a photographer.
3. ☐ Annie Griffiths knows how to communicate with the people she meets.

D **DETAILS** Listen again and complete these sentences with ONE or TWO words. 🔊

1. Annie travels to places such as Africa, Australia, the Middle East, and North and South _____.
2. Annie loves many places, so it's hard to choose a _____.
3. She takes photos of ordinary people, and she also loves taking pictures of _____ and landscapes.
4. When Annie talks to people or acts a little silly, they feel more _____.
5. It's important for photographers to be creative and see things in _____.

CRITICAL THINKING   Make Inferences

Sometimes when people speak, they don't say exactly what they mean. So when you listen, you need to make inferences and guess a speaker's meaning.

Statement: "I studied biology for six years, and now I study lions in Zambia."
We can infer: This person knows a lot about biology and lions.

E Think about the interview with Annie. Can you infer these statements? Choose Y for *Yes* or N for *No*. | Critical Thinking

1. Annie prefers to visit dangerous places.   Y   N
2. Annie likes her life of adventure.   Y   N
3. Annie knows how to make friends with strangers.   Y   N
4. Annie thinks everyone has the skills to be a photographer.   Y   N

F **FOCUSED LISTENING** Listen to part of the interview with Annie Griffiths. Complete the questions with the words you hear. 🔊

1. _____ favorite part of the world?
2. And _____ like to travel and explore the world so much?
3. But _____ communicate with people in so many places?
4. So _____ advice _____ for someone who wants to become a photographer?

G **RECALL** Work with a partner. Role-play an interview between a journalist and Annie. | Critical Thinking

Journalist: You can use the questions in exercise F and also think of some new questions.
Annie: Use the information from the interview to answer the questions in your own words.

A Speaking

> **GRAMMAR FOR SPEAKING** Simple Present Statements
>
> We use the **simple present** to express:
> - habits or routines: They **work** with animals.
> - things that are always true: She **enjoys** her job.
>
> | | | | |
> |---|---|---|---|
> | **Affirmative** | I /You/We/They | **live** | |
> | | He/She/It | **lives** | in Zambia. |
> | **Negative** | I/You/We/They | **don't live** | |
> | | He/She/It | **doesn't live** | |
>
> Note the verbs *be* and *have* are irregular: I **am**   You/We/They **are**   He/She/It **is**
>
> I/You/We/They **have**   He/She/It **has**

For spelling of verbs ending in -s/-es, see the Appendix.

A Complete these sentences about work. Use the simple present and contractions.

1. Explorers often _____ to different places around the world. (travel)
2. My father is a doctor. He _____ very long hours. (work)
3. I _____ a lot of work, and I get long breaks. (not have)
4. My brother is a soldier. He _____ much vacation time in the army. (not get)
5. Waiters _____ good pay, but they sometimes get big tips. (not receive)
6. My aunt is an artist. She works long hours, but every day _____ different! (be)

B Take turns reading the sentences in exercise A with a partner. Then describe each job using an adjective in the box.

| badly paid | creative | dangerous | exciting | easy | hard |

> *Explorers often travel to different places around the world. I think it's an exciting job!*

Critical Thinking **C** **EVALUATE** Work with a group. Choose FOUR jobs. Discuss the pros (good things) and cons (bad things) of each job.

Jobs		Pros and Cons	
artist	engineer	boring / interesting	normal / long hours
builder	photographer	creative	opportunities to learn / travel
businessperson	scientist	dangerous	well paid / badly paid
chef	teacher	difficult / easy	
doctor	veterinarian	exciting	

A: I think a doctor works long hours.
B: That's true, but a doctor is well paid, so that's good.

8 UNIT 1 LESSON A

PRONUNCIATION Final -s/-es Sounds

🔊 For most verbs ending in -s/-es and plural nouns, the -s/-es ending doesn't add an extra syllable.

work → work**s**   re•ceive → re•ceive**s**   opp•or•tun•i•ty → opp•or•tun•i•**ties**

When a noun or verb ends with a /s/, /ʃ/, /z/, /dʒ/, or /tʃ/ sound, you pronounce the -s or -es ending with the sound /əz/ or /ɪz/. This adds an extra syllable.

dance → danc•**es**   ex•er•cise → ex•er•cis•**es**   watch → watch•**es**

D Read the sentences and underline any verbs and nouns ending with -s or -es. Write the number of syllables above each word. Then listen and check your answers. 🔊

1. Annie communicates (4) with other photographers.
2. My son watches animals in the park.
3. She goes to different places and has amazing experiences.
4. My uncle drives buses for a living.
5. There are 16 doctors and 37 nurses at the hospital.
6. The students have three exercises.

GRAMMAR FOR SPEAKING Adverbs and Expressions of Frequency

We often use **adverbs of frequency** with the simple present. Notice the word order.
- After the verb *be*: He'**s always** late.
- Before all other verbs: She **always** carries a camera.

always	usually	often	sometimes	not often	never
100% ←					→ 0%

We also use **expressions of frequency** with the simple present. An expression of frequency answers the question *How often?*

A: *How often do you* go to school?   **once/twice/three times a** week/month/year
B: *I have class* **five days a week**.   **every** day/week/year/afternoon

▼ Construction workers work on a new building.

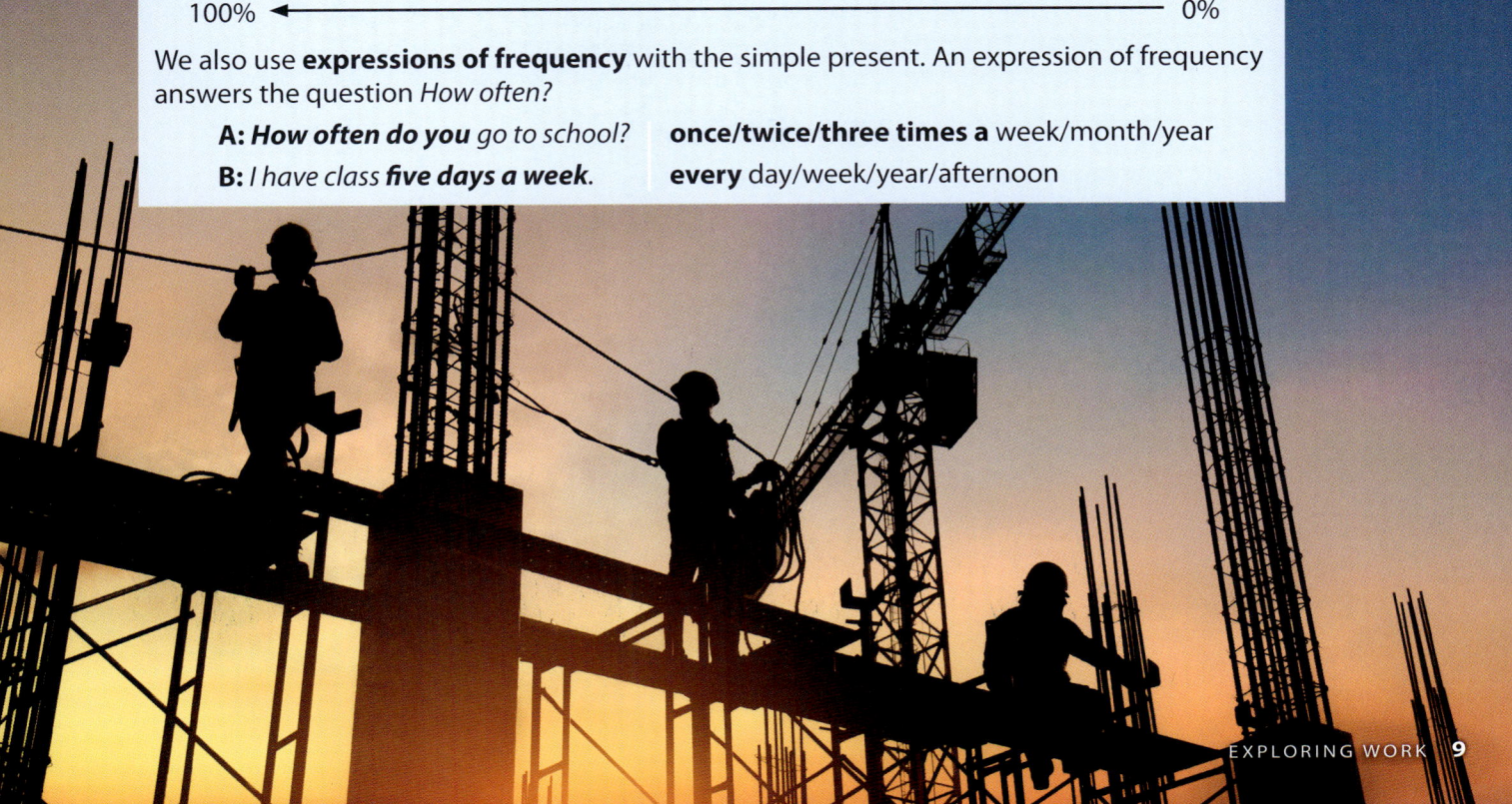

E Write SIX true sentences about people you know. Use ideas from the chart or your own ideas. Remember to change the verb and use the correct word order.

Person	Adverb	Verb phrase	
My mother / father	always	watch TV	at (+ *time*)
My brother / sister	usually	exercise at the gym	in the morning / afternoon / evening
My best friend	often	wake up	at night
	sometimes	do homework	on the weekends
My teacher	not often	finish work	during the week
My friend [name]	never	play sports	after work / school / class
		work in an office	

> *My mother always wakes up at seven o'clock during the week.*

F Share your sentences from exercise E with a partner. Pronounce the *-s* ending with an extra syllable where necessary.

G Work with a partner and take turns. Ask questions with *How often do you . . . ?* and a verb phrase from exercise E (or your own ideas). Answer the question with an expression of frequency.

A: How often do you watch TV?
B: About three times a week.

H Read the short description of a job. Then choose the correct adverbs and expressions of frequency in the sentences below.

A DAY IN THE LIFE OF A "DIGITAL NOMAD"

My name is Henry, and I work for a software company. Every day, I start work at eight. I design and write computer programs. I can work from anywhere in the world, so this month I'm in Seoul. Every four or five weeks, I move to a new city or country. My boss lives in Montreal, but as long as we talk on Mondays and Fridays, she's happy.

1. He **always / never** starts works at eight.
2. He moves to a new country about **once a month / twice a year**.
3. He speaks to his boss **every week / twice a week**.

Critical Thinking

I CREATE Follow these steps.

1. Choose a job and write a similar "day in the life" description (four or five sentences). Describe what you do, but don't write the name of the job.
2. Work with a group. Take turns reading your job descriptions. Try to guess everyone's jobs.

Video

▲ Holly Akello at the CTC Conservation Center in the Butambala District, Uganda

Working in the Wild

in the field (expression) in nature or the real world
look after (v phr) to take care of something / someone
increase (v) to go up; to rise
population (n) the number of animals in a group

A Watch the video about Holly Akello and an organization called Gorilla Doctors. Are these things true for Holly, the Gorilla Doctors, or both? Write the letters in the chart. ▶

a. want to help animals
b. look after different kinds of animals
c. look after one kind of animal
d. feed the animals
e. want to increase the number of animals
f. need special skills

Holly	Both	Gorilla Doctors

B Watch again. Choose the correct answers. For some questions, both answers are correct. ▶

1. Where does Holly work?   a. In Uganda.   b. At a conservation center.
2. Which animal(s) does she look after? a. Lions.   b. Snakes.
3. Why isn't she afraid of the animals? a. She feeds them. b. She understands them.
4. What do the Gorilla Doctors do?   a. Study the gorillas. b. Count the gorillas.
5. What do they give names to?   a. The babies.   b. The gorilla families.
6. Who do the Gorilla Doctors teach about the animals? a. Other doctors. b. Schoolchildren.

C PERSONALIZE Discuss these questions with a partner.

1. In the future, do you want to work with animals? Why? Why not?
2. Imagine you are going to interview a person for a job at the conservation center in Uganda. What can you ask at the interview? Write down three questions.

EXPLORING WORK 11

B Vocabulary

A Listen and repeat. Check (✓) any words you already know. 🔊

apply (v)	enthusiastic (adj)	interview (n)	perfect (adj)	responsible for (adj phr)
candidate (n)	equipment (n)	manage (v)	positive (adj)	training (n)

B **MEANING FROM CONTEXT** Listen and write the words you hear. Then think about each word's meaning. 🔊

PART-TIME BARISTAS NEEDED

The university café needs an ¹_____ student to work part-time. Are you the ²_____ person for the job? Baristas are ³_____ making drinks and cleaning the ⁴_____, tables, and chairs. Sometimes you will also need to ⁵_____ the café on your own. Anyone can ⁶_____ because we provide ⁷_____. The successful ⁸_____ is ⁹_____ and wants to learn new skills. Find out more about the job and ask for an ¹⁰_____ by email: info@unicafe.edu.

▲ A barista makes coffee for customers in his café.

C Read comments about working at the university café. Cross out the **bold** words in each sentence and write a word from exercise A.

1. "Builders use a lot of **tools and machines** _____ for their jobs."
2. "Only one **person** _____ has emailed about the job so far."
3. "I think I'm the **best** _____ person for the job."
4. "Why did you **ask** _____ for this job?"
5. "I'm so **excited and happy** _____ about my new job. I can't wait to start!"

D Read and complete part of a conversation with the OTHER five words from exercise A. Listen and check. Then practice the conversation with a partner. 🔊

INTERVIEWER: Thank you for coming to this job ¹_____. I have a few questions. Do you have any experience working in a café?

CANDIDATE: No, I don't. But the job advertisement says you provide ²_____.

INTERVIEWER: That's true. We can train you to use the equipment and make coffee, but it's harder to train people to be friendly! We want to hire very ³_____ people.

CANDIDATE: Oh well, I'm very friendly, and I love to learn new skills.

INTERVIEWER: That's good to know.

CANDIDATE: In my last job in a shop, I was ⁴_____ helping customers. And sometimes I had to ⁵_____ the shop when my manager was away.

INTERVIEWER: That's very interesting. Do you have any questions for me?

E **CREATE** Work with a partner and prepare for a job interview. Then do the interview. | Critical Thinking

Student A: You are a candidate for the job in the advertisement. Make notes about:
- your work experience and skills (e.g., do you know how to make coffee?)
- your personality (e.g., are you positive and enthusiastic?)

Student B: You are the interviewer. Prepare five questions for the candidate. Find out about:
- the person's work experience and skills
- the person's personality

B Listening What Does It Take to Be an Explorer?

Critical Thinking

A PREDICT You are going to hear part of a presentation about how to become an explorer. Write down FIVE words you think you will hear. Then compare your words with a partner.

_____

_____

B MAIN IDEAS Watch or listen to the presentation. How can you prepare to be an explorer? Check (✓) the speaker's four main ideas.

1. ☐ Study and explore wildlife.
2. ☐ Study your main interests.
3. ☐ Learn about photography.
4. ☐ Buy an expensive camera.
5. ☐ Learn other languages.
6. ☐ Find out about new things and ask questions.
7. ☐ Try some dangerous activities.

C Did you hear any of your words from exercise A?

D DETAILS Read the statements. Then watch or listen again and choose T for *True* or F for *False*.

	T	F
1. The presenter is talking about this topic for the first time.	T	F
2. People often don't know how to become explorers.	T	F
3. Most explorers climb mountains and dive in oceans.	T	F
4. Andrea Hernandez is an explorer and a filmmaker.	T	F
5. Many explorers know how to take good photographs of their adventures.	T	F
6. Explorers shouldn't make mistakes when they speak a local language.	T	F
7. Explorers usually travel to dangerous places.	T	F
8. You can prepare and get experience in your town or city.	T	F

NOTE-TAKING SKILL Use Linear Notes and Mind Maps

When you take notes, it's important to write down key words; these are often repeated words. You also need to organize your notes.

You can write notes in a list with subheads, numbers, and bullet points.

> How to become an explorer (topic)
> 1. Choose your interest. (subtopic)
>   - history?
>   - wildlife?

Or you can write notes using a mind map.

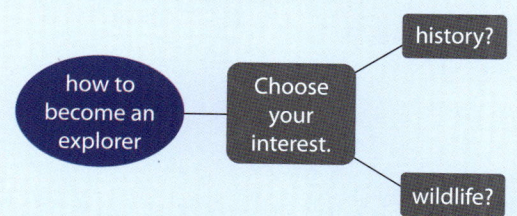

Some people also draw little pictures or use symbols in their notes. There is no correct way to take notes. Use a strategy that works for you.

E **EXPLAIN** Discuss these questions with the class.

Critical Thinking

1. When do you have to take notes? In class? When you watch a video for homework?
2. How do you decide which words to write down?
3. How do you organize your notes? Do you write lists, use mind maps, or do something else?

F Listen to part of the presentation again. Take notes about how to become an explorer. Use some of the strategies from the Note-Taking Skill. 🔊

G Compare your notes with a partner and answer these questions.
- Did you write down similar key words?
- How similar or different are your note-taking strategies?

▼ Bertie Gregory swims through a school of fish with his camera.

EXPLORING WORK 15

B Speaking

See Speaking Phrases in the Appendix.

SPEAKING SKILL Say That You Don't Understand

Here are some expressions to say you don't understand what someone says.

I'm sorry?	I'm not sure what you mean.	Can you explain (that)?
I don't understand.	I'm not sure I follow.	Can you repeat that/say that again?

ONLINE When you speak online, it can be more difficult to follow what people are saying. You may have to ask for an explanation more often.

A Listen to part of a conversation between a career advisor and a student. Check (✓) the FOUR expressions you hear. 🔊

1. ☐ I'm sorry?
2. ☐ Can you explain?
3. ☐ I'm not sure what you mean.
4. ☐ I'm not sure I follow.
5. ☐ I don't understand.
6. ☐ Can you say that again?

B Practice these conversations with a partner. Student B uses an expression from the Speaking Skill box. Then switch roles and practice the conversation again using different expressions.

1. A: You need special training to be a computer programmer.
   B: . . .
   A: Well, you need to learn math and technology skills. That's important.

2. A: A job in tourism is an adventure.
   B: . . .
   A: Every day you meet people from different places and cultures.

3. A: Some people are digital nomads, and they work in different countries.
   B: . . .
   A: With an online job, you can work from anywhere with an Internet connection.

GRAMMAR FOR SPEAKING Simple Present *Yes/No* and *Wh-* Questions

Simple present *yes/no* questions	Short answers
Is he/she good at languages?	Yes, he **is**./No, she **isn't**./No, she**'s not**.
Are they creative?	Yes, they **are**./No, they **aren't**./No, they**'re not**.
Do they **have** fun?	Yes, they **do**./No, they **don't**.
Does the photographer **like** to travel?	Yes, she **does**./No, he **doesn't**.

Simple present *wh-* questions	Answers
Where's Thandiwe from?	She's from Zambia.
What's your favorite subject?	Geography.
What do you **love** to do?	I love to travel.
When do you usually **get up**?	At seven during the week and at nine on weekends.
How often are you late for school?	I'm never late! I'm always on time.

C Write questions with the words. Use the correct verb form. Then practice with a partner.

1. A: _____ (your / favorite / be / what / food)
   B: I love sushi!

2. A: _____ (from / your best friend / be / where)
   B: She's from a small town near this city.

3. A: _____ (for work / travel / anyone in your family)
   B: My mother does. She's a pilot.

4. A: _____ (how / go shopping / often / do / your family)
   B: About once a week. We always go on the weekend.

5. A: _____ (how / relax / on weekends / you)
   B: My friends often visit, and we play video games or watch a movie.

D Ask and answer the questions from exercise C with your partner. Give your own answers.

E Complete the questions in this questionnaire with the correct form of *be* or *do* or a *wh-* word. Then ask and answer the questions with a partner. Ask follow-up questions and take notes.

Career Questionnaire

Interview questions	My partner's answers
1. What _____ you study at school or in college?	
2. _____ you interested in a particular career?	
3. What _____ you like to do in your free time?	
4. _____ often do you spend time outdoors?	
5. _____ you have good communication skills?	
6. _____ you a creative person?	
7. _____ is more important to you in a job: adventure or money?	
8. Think of a good friend. How _____ this person describe you? (e.g., helpful, fun, etc.)	

F **ARGUE** Think about your partner's answers in exercise E. Decide on a good job for your partner. Then form a group with another pair of students and follow these steps. | Critical Thinking

1. Tell the group which job is best for your partner. Explain your reasons.
2. Tell the group your opinion of your partner's choice of job for you. Is it a good job for you?

EXPLORING WORK 17

Review

SELF-ASSESS

How well can you . . . ?	Very well.	OK.	I need improvement.
use the key vocabulary	☐	☐	☐
pronounce final -s / -es sounds	☐	☐	☐
use the simple present and adverbs of frequency	☐	☐	☐
say you don't understand something	☐	☐	☐

A   VOCABULARY Complete the tasks.

1. Say answers to the questions. Use complete sentences.
   a. What are your best **skills**?
   b. How well do you **communicate** with your parents or teachers?
   c. What are you **responsible for** at home?

2. Cross out the word that does NOT belong in each group (verb, adjective, or noun). Explain.

   a. positive   adventure   creative   dangerous
   b. experience   candidate   explore   equipment
   c. manage   apply   communicate   ordinary

B   PRONUNCIATION Say these words, adding a final -s ending. Check (✓) the words that add a syllable.

   candidate   experience   manage   photographer   relax   travel   watch

C   GRAMMAR Ask questions for these answers.

1. Yes, I do.
2. No, he doesn't.
3. Usually at noon.
4. She lives in Boston.
5. It's important to be good at English.
6. Twice a week.

D   SPEAKING SKILL Complete the conversations. Say sentences to show that you don't understand.

1. A: Do you have the right skills for the job?
   B: . . .
   A: I mean, what are you good at? For example, do you have good communication skills?

2. A: You have to add -s with *he* or *she*.
   B: . . .
   A: With the simple present in English, you add -s to the verb after *he* or *she*.

RE-ASSESS What skills or language do you still need help with?

Final Tasks

OPTION 1 Role-play a conversation about dream jobs

A Imagine it is the future and you have your dream job. Write notes about the job using these questions.

1. What's your job title?
2. Where do you work?
3. Which special skills do you need?
4. Do you work with other people or on your own?
5. Why is this job important?
6. What are some pros and cons of the job?

B Interview a partner using the questions in exercise A. Take notes about your partner's answers.

C Work with a new partner. Tell them about your partner's answers in exercise B.

> *In the future, Cal is a filmmaker, and he makes animated films . . . .*

▼ A filmmaker prepares to film in his home studio.

See Unit 1 Rubric in the Appendix.

OPTION 2 Discuss what makes a good job

A MODEL A group of students is discussing what is important in a job. Listen. Which of these things do they discuss? Check (✓) Yes or No. 🔊

Do the students discuss . . . ?	Yes	No
1. training and learning new skills	☐	☐
2. coworkers (people you work with)	☐	☐
3. their manager	☐	☐
4. good work hours	☐	☐
5. good pay	☐	☐
6. place of work (shop, office, etc.)	☐	☐
7. vacation	☐	☐

B ANALYZE THE MODEL Listen again and check (✓) the FIVE phrases you hear. How do these phrases make the discussion better? 🔊

1. ☐ We need to discuss . . .
2. ☐ Can I start?
3. ☐ Can I go next?
4. ☐ I think that . . .
5. ☐ What do you think?
6. ☐ Do you want to go next?
7. ☐ Can I say something?

COLLABORATION SKILL   Take Turns

In a group discussion, take turns when you speak and remember to let other people speak.

Start: We need to discuss . . .   Can I start . . . ?
Take your turn: Can I go next?   Can I say something?
Ask someone to speak: Do you want to go next?   What do you think?

📶 **ONLINE** When you communicate online, it's more difficult to know when to speak. Make sure everyone gets a turn. It can help to use people's names.
Ahmed, what do you think?

See Speaking Phrases in the Appendix.

C PLAN Look at the list of items in exercise A and think about what makes a good job. Rank the items in order of importance for a job from 1 to 7. (1 = most important, 7 = least important)

D DISCUSS Work in a group of three or four and follow these steps:

1. Take turns. Present your list of items from exercise C. Explain your reasons.
2. Discuss the lists and try to agree on the final order as a group.

E REPORT As a group, report back to the class.
- If you agreed at the end of your discussion, present your final order.
- If you still disagree, explain why.

The Battle of the Blues is a yearly cricket game between Royal College and S. Thomas' College in Sri Lanka.

GOOD TIMES, GOOD FEELINGS 2

IN THIS UNIT, YOU WILL:
- Watch or listen to a lecture about nostalgia
- Watch a video about a reunion
- Listen to a talk about a memory experiment
- Play two truths and a lie
  OR Present a special object or photo

THINK AND DISCUSS:
1. What is happening in the photo? Why do you think all these people are excited?
2. Read the unit title. What do you do to feel good?

EXPLORE THE THEME

Read the information. Then discuss the questions.

1. Do you agree that taking pictures makes it harder to remember things? Why or why not?
2. Look at the photo and follow the steps for taking a mental photo. Then close your book. What can you remember? Describe the picture.
3. How does the photo make you feel?

Get the PICTURE?

When you see something special, what do you do? You probably take a picture. But in fact, taking a picture can make it harder to remember a special moment. Why? Scientists think there are two reasons. First, sometimes we stop paying attention because we are trying to take a good picture. And second, we don't try to remember the moment—because we have a picture! Next time you want to remember a moment, put away your camera and try taking a mental photo.

Steps for taking a mental photo:

1. Stop and breathe.
2. Look around and really pay attention to what you see and what's happening.
3. Close your eyes and see the picture in your mind.
4. Open your eyes and look carefully at everything again.

A girl feeds a giraffe at Giraffe Manor in Nairobi, Kenya.

A Vocabulary

A Listen and repeat. Check (✓) any words you already know. 🔊

| bring back (v phr) | define (v) | happiness (n) | memory (n) | sadness (n) |
| childhood (n) | emotion (n) | lonely (adj) | remind . . . of (v phr) | situation (n) |

B **MEANING FROM CONTEXT** Read and listen to the article. Think about the meaning of the words in blue. Write each word next to its definition. TWO words have the same definition. 🔊

HAPPY FEELINGS ABOUT THE PAST

Nostalgia can be both a good and a bad **emotion**. In some countries, nostalgia describes a feeling of **sadness** when you think about the past. For example, maybe you feel sad when you walk past your old home. Or you feel **lonely** when you look at photos of old friends. However, in Japan, the word for nostalgia is more positive. You can **define** nostalgia or "*natsukashii*" as something that **brings back** good **memories** of your past. An object like an old train ticket can **remind** you **of** a wonderful holiday. Or a **situation**—like hearing a song from your **childhood**—can bring back feelings of **happiness**.

1. _____ (n) the way something is at a specific time and place
2. _____ (adj) unhappy because you have no friends or people to talk to
3. _____ (v) to explain the meaning of a word or phrase
4. _____ (n) the feeling of being happy
5. _____ (v phr) to make someone remember something from the past
6. _____ (n) the period of life when you are a child
7. _____ (n) a feeling such as love or anger
8. _____ (n) something you remember from the past
9. _____ (n) the feeling of being unhappy

C Complete the sentences with the correct form of the words from exercise A.

1. I have good _____ of my childhood in Tokyo.
2. I like looking at old photos because they _____ me _____ happy times.
3. Some people feel _____ when they finish a really good book.
4. My grandfather likes to listen to music from his _____.
5. Sadness and fear are two very strong _____.
6. How do you manage difficult _____ at school?

7. I always smile when I walk past my old house. It brings me a lot of _____.
8. When there's no one home, I sometimes start to feel _____, so I turn on the TV.
9. Excuse me. Can you _____ this word in my book?
10. This music always _____ memories of my childhood.

VOCABULARY SKILL   Abstract Nouns

We sometimes think of nouns as objects or things you can see, hear, smell, or touch. But abstract nouns are different because you can't see or hear them. Abstract nouns often describe ideas or emotions.

Creativity is an important quality for a photographer.
You have a lot of **experience** as a doctor.

D Complete the following tasks.

1. Underline FIVE abstract nouns in this list.

   brain   childhood   happiness   love   photo   sadness   skill   ticket

2. Choose TWO of the abstract nouns and write questions with them. Then, in pairs, ask and answer your questions.

E **PERSONALIZE** Discuss these questions with a group.

1. Do you have a word for nostalgia in your language? Does the word in your language have a more positive or negative meaning?
2. Think of an object or **situation** that **reminds** you **of** your **childhood**. What experience does it remind you of?

▼ Photographs can remind us of the past.

GOOD TIMES, GOOD FEELINGS   25

A Listening Remembering the Past

Critical Thinking

A PREDICT You are going to hear a lecture about nostalgia. What questions do you think the lecture will answer?

1. ☐ What does *nostalgia* mean?
2. ☐ How can nostalgia make us happy?
3. ☐ Why is nostalgia bad for us?
4. ☐ How does nostalgia help your memory?

B MAIN IDEAS Watch or listen to the lecture. Choose the correct word. 🔊 ▶

1. Nostalgia includes a memory from the past and an (emotion / object).
2. In the past, the meaning of nostalgia was about (happiness / sadness).
3. These days, many doctors think nostalgia can be (helpful / dangerous).
4. We can use nostalgia in (difficult / boring) situations.
5. Some doctors think music can help older people with their (emotions / memories).

C Which answers in exercise A are correct? Were your answers correct?

A man enjoys a childhood experience.

LISTENING SKILL   Understand a Speaker's Purpose

Sometimes speakers introduce their purpose at the beginning of a talk. Then they explain their goals and the main points of the talk.

Today, I'm here to / My goal today is to present my research on the brain.
                                              purpose
First, I plan to talk about . . .
Second/Then, I want to look at . . .

Sometimes speakers don't introduce the purpose right away. Instead, they might tell a story or ask the audience a question. Then they introduce the purpose.

D Listen to the first part of the lecture again. Answer these questions. 🔊

1. When does the speaker state her purpose?
   a. At the beginning   b. After a story
2. What is the speaker's main purpose?
   a. To make us feel happy   b. To give information
3. How many parts are there in the lecture?
   a. Two parts   b. Three parts

E **DETAILS** Listen to the next part of the lecture. Complete each sentence with ONE or TWO words. 🔊

1. The smell of coffee brings the speaker _____.
2. _____ created the word *nostalgia*.
3. Nostalgia can help with _____ in our lives.
4. The speaker says more people _____ nowadays.
5. Many people lose their memories when they _____.
6. When we listen to an _____, the brain becomes more active.

F **FOCUSED LISTENING** Listen and complete each sentence with TWO words. What kind of expressions are these? 🔊

1. When I got up _____, I smelled fresh coffee from the kitchen.
2. Unfortunately, my father died five _____.
3. A doctor created the word *nostalgia* _____.
4. The word *nostalgia* can have different meanings. In _____, it was often about sadness.

G **RANK** Which of these things makes you feel happiest? Rank them in order from 1 to 4. (1 = happiest, 4 = least happy). Then explain your ranking to a partner. | Critical Thinking

____ old pictures of your family   ____ the smell of a holiday food

____ a song from your childhood   ____ visiting your first school

A Speaking

For spelling of verbs ending in -d/-ed and irregular verbs, see the Appendix.

GRAMMAR FOR SPEAKING   Simple Past and Time Clauses

We use the simple past to talk about completed actions or states in the past.

Affirmative
I **was** born in 2002.
We **lived** in an apartment.
I **grew up** in this city.

Negative
My parents **weren't** rich.
We **didn't go** on vacation.

Yes/No Questions
Was your childhood happy?
Were your parents born here?
Did your family **live** here?

Short answers
Yes, it **was**. / No, it **wasn't**.
Yes, they **were**. / No, they **weren't**.
Yes, they **did**. / No, they **didn't**.

Wh- questions
Where were you born?
When did you **move** here?
Why did you **leave** home?

Short answers
In Brazil.
In 2010.
Because I went to college in another city.

We often use the simple past with **time clauses** starting with *when, before,* and *after*.
   When/After I got up this morning, **I smelled** coffee.
   My father **made** coffee **before** he **went** to work.

A Complete these stories with the simple past of the verbs in parentheses. Use contractions. Then practice reading the stories aloud with a partner.

   a. JUAN: "When I was a child, I ¹_____ (play) outside. We ²_____ (not have) video games and computers, so we often ³_____ (go) to the park. Today, when I smell grass, it always reminds me of my childhood."

   b. OMAR: "My grandparents ⁴_____ (move) to a smaller house last year, so they put lots of boxes in our garage. The boxes ⁵_____ (have) black and white photographs from their childhood."

   c. BEN: "When my uncle ⁶_____ (give) me all his old records, I ⁷_____ (not know) how to listen to them. But then, he ⁸_____ (show) me his record player. All those songs from the sixties and seventies are fantastic!"

   d. RABEYA: "We watched an old movie last night. I saw it five years ago and ⁹_____ (love) it then. But last night it was terrible! We ¹⁰_____ (not watch) it to the end."

PRONUNCIATION Simple Past -ed Endings

🔊 There are three ways to pronounce simple past endings. If a verb ends in:
- the sounds /t/ or /d/, the -ed ending adds a syllable. It sounds like /əd/.
  need → need**ed**   start → start**ed**
- the sounds /f/, /k/, /p/, /s/, /ʃ/, or /tʃ/, the -ed ending sounds like /t/.
  look → look**ed**   watch → watch**ed**
- any other consonant sound or a vowel sound, the -ed ending sounds like /d/.
  play → play**ed**   show → show**ed**

B Listen to these sentences. Check (✓) the sound you hear at the end of each verb. Then practice the sentences. 🔊

	/t/ or /d/	/əd/
1. We **worked** in a café.	☐	☐
2. I **learned** English at school.	☐	☐
3. My family **lived** here.	☐	☐
4. He **started** college last week.	☐	☐
5. They **looked** at old photos.	☐	☐
6. Magda **wanted** a new hat.	☐	☐
7. We **played** video games.	☐	☐
8. She **downloaded** a movie.	☐	☐

▼ Things from the past, like record albums, can make people feel nostalgia.

GOOD TIMES, GOOD FEELINGS

C **PERSONALIZE** Complete these sentences about your past. Then take turns reading your sentences to a partner. Pronounce any *-ed* endings correctly.

1. When I was a child, I _____.
2. On my first day at school, I _____.
3. I first watched my favorite film in _____ (year). It was _____ (name).
4. I started to _____ (activity or skill) in _____ (year).
5. Last week in my English class, we studied _____.

D Add the correct verb to complete these questions about the people in exercise A. With a partner, take turns asking about the people. Answer with the correct information.

1. Juan / video games / when he / a child? *Did Juan play video games when he was child?*
2. Juan / often / to the park? _____
3. Why / Omar's grandparents / boxes / in his garage? _____
4. What / the boxes / in them? _____
5. What / Ben's uncle / him? _____
6. Ben / how to listen to them? _____
7. What / Rabeya / last night? _____
8. she / the movie / to the end? _____

   A: Did Juan have video games when he was a child?
   B: No, he didn't.

E Choose a year in your life that was important to you; for example, the year that you finished high school. Complete the chart with your answers. Then ask a partner the questions and write their answers.

	My answers	My partner's answers
1. Which year did you choose?		
2. Why did you choose it?		
3. How old were you?		
4. Where did you live?		
5. Where did you study or work?		
6. Who were some of your best friends?		
7. What was your favorite movie?		
8. What was your favorite song?		

Critical Thinking

F **DESCRIBE** Form a group with another pair of students. Report what you learned about your partner in exercise E.

> *My partner chose 2020 because she started college. She was 18 and lived in São Paulo. . . .*

Video

A Shared Memory

bunch (n) a large amount; e.g., a bunch of people
Outward Bound (n) an organization that has outdoor educational programs for young people
relive (v) to experience something again
cabin (n) a small house made of wood
expect (v) to think something will happen
courage (n) the ability to do something dangerous

▲ Women from the first Women's Outward Bound program in 1965, Minnesota, USA

A Watch the video. Number these actions in the order you see them. ▶

a. _____ They sit around a campfire.
b. _____ They meet each other again.
c. _____ They arrive at the cabins.
d. _____ They swim and climb on ropes.
e. _____ They go canoeing.
f. _____ They meet the new members of Outward Bound.

B Watch again. Choose T for *True* or F for *False*. ▶

1. The women in the video met almost 50 years ago.   T   F
2. In 1965, young women in the U.S. often did a lot of difficult outdoor activities.   T   F
3. One woman heard about Outward Bound on the radio.   T   F
4. The women had to spend three days in the woods with no tent or food.   T   F
5. When the women do some of the activities again, it makes them sad.   T   F
6. As young women, they found courage and new friends at Outward Bound.   T   F

C **PERSONALIZE** Discuss these questions with a partner.

1. Do you want to do a program like Outward Bound? Why? Why not?
2. When did you need courage to do something dangerous? What did you do?
3. Why do you think people remember some events in their lives more than others? What event from your life will you remember when you are older?

GOOD TIMES, GOOD FEELINGS   **31**

B Vocabulary

A Listen and repeat. Check (✓) any words you already know.

brain (n)　　experiment (n)　　human (n)　　reason (n)　　recognize (v)
discover (v)　　forget (v)　　memorable (adj)　　recall (v)　　researcher (n)

See Vocabulary Skill: Abstract Nouns in this unit.

B **MEANING FROM CONTEXT** Listen and read. Think about the meaning of the words in blue. Which blue words are abstract nouns?

HOW MANY FACES CAN YOU REMEMBER?

How many faces do you **recognize** every day of your life? Think about the faces of family members, best friends, friends of friends, and coworkers, and photos of world leaders and celebrities. Your **brain** has to keep all those faces in its memory. **Researchers** at the University of York in the U.K. recently did an **experiment** with memory. They **discovered** that **humans** can remember about 5,000 faces.

Of course, we can recognize a face, but that doesn't mean we can **recall** the person's name. The **reason** is that faces are more **memorable** than names. When we meet someone, we look at their face for a long time. But we might only hear their name once, so it's easy to **forget** a name. That's why some people use your name a few times in a conversation when they meet you. It helps them to remember your name as well as your face.

C Cross out the **bold** words in each sentence and write a word from exercise A.

1. There are about eight billion **people** _____ on Earth.
2. I work with **people who study things** _____ .
3. I **know** _____ your face, but I can't remember your name.
4. Some words in English are **easy to remember** _____ .
5. Doctors **found** _____ a new type of medicine.
6. How many school friends can you **remember** _____ from your childhood?
7. I often **don't remember** _____ phone numbers.
8. Scientists did **a test** _____ on 300 people.
9. You didn't do your homework. Can you give **an explanation** _____ ?
10. Sometimes my **mind** _____ is so tired that I can't think anymore!

D Choose the correct word in these sentences.

1. Ten (researchers / humans) work at our university.
2. It's easy to (recall / forget) a new word, so I write it down and say it in a sentence.
3. I didn't (recognize / discover) your voice on the phone! It sounded different.
4. We remember our vacation last year for the wrong (reason / experiment). It rained all the time!
5. My childhood was (forget / memorable) because my family lived in different countries.
6. An explorer (discovered / recognized) a new river in the jungle.
7. My grandfather is old, but he can still (recall / recognize) a lot of his childhood.
8. (Humans / Brains) are always active, even when we are asleep.

E Work in pairs and play a memory game. Follow these steps:

1. On your own, write a list of ten English words on a piece of paper. Choose different word forms, such as verbs, adjectives, and nouns.
2. Switch papers with your partner. Keep both papers face down.
   - Student A: Take one minute to look at and memorize your partner's ten words. Then give the paper back to your partner. Try to remember and say the ten words.
   - Student B: Check your partner's answers.
3. Switch roles and repeat the activity.

F **EVALUATE** Think about the game in exercise E and answer these questions with your partner.

1. How many of the ten words did you **recall**? How many did you **forget**?
2. Did you **recognize** all the words? Were any of them new to you?
3. Which words were more **memorable**? What was the **reason**?

B Listening   What Do We Remember?

Critical Thinking

A   ANALYZE You are going to listen to a talk about an experiment using the four pairs of photos below. Before you listen, try the experiment:

1. Look at the photos of two men, two women, two rooms, and two beaches. For each pair, which picture do you think is more memorable? Check (✓) the boxes.
2. Did you choose more photos on the top row or on the bottom row?
3. Tell a partner your answers and give reasons for your choices.

> *I think the photo of the man on the bottom row is more memorable because . . .*
> *I chose the room on the top row because . . .*

B   MAIN IDEAS Listen to the talk. Number these questions from 1 to 3 in the order the speaker talks about them. 🔊

a. _____ What happened when scientists did the memory experiment?
b. _____ Which photos are more memorable?
c. _____ Who was Wilma Bainbridge, and what did she research?

C   DETAILS Listen again. Choose T for *True* or F for *False*. 🔊

1. According to the speaker, we know more about the human memory than we did 50 years ago.   T   F
2. The speaker asks listeners to remember the eight pictures.   T   F
3. He thinks dark colors might be more memorable.   T   F

4. He thinks the office is more interesting than the room with a tree.   T   F
5. People often think the bottom photos are easier to remember.   T   F
6. More people remember the top photos.   T   F
7. Bainbridge understands all the reasons people remember the photos.   T   F

NOTE-TAKING SKILL   Use a Split Page to Take Notes

Draw a line down the middle of the page. On the right, take notes about the main ideas and important details as you listen. When you review your notes, use the left side to write questions that the notes answer. This will help you to recall the key information.

Questions	Notes
How well can humans recognize photos?	Humans recognize photos but are not perfect.

D Listen to part of the talk again. Complete the notes on the right side of the chart. Then write questions for your notes. 🔊

Questions	Notes
a.	Wilma Bainbridge created [1] _____.
b.	• We remember about [2] _____% because of [3] _____ and appearance. • We also remember photos with [4] _____. • We don't know why we remember [5] _____% of photos.

CRITICAL THINKING   Recognize Assumptions

An assumption is a belief that something is true, but there are no facts to support it. For example, someone might think, "Photos with happy people are more memorable than photos with sad people." However, they have no facts to support this. It's important to recognize that assumptions can be wrong.

E In the test, people thought the photos on the bottom were more memorable. But the experiment shows this isn't true: Thirty percent more people remembered the photos on the top. Discuss these questions with a group. | Critical Thinking

1. When you did the experiment in exercise A, which photos did you choose?
2. Did you make assumptions?

GOOD TIMES, GOOD FEELINGS   35

B Speaking

SPEAKING SKILL Give Reasons

When you talk about things you like or things you did, you can give reasons.
> I like this photo. **It reminds me of my old friends from school**.
> I learned to play the guitar **because both of my parents play the guitar, too**.

You can also ask the other person to give a reason.

> A: I love the summer.
> B: **Why's that?**
> A: Because we have a long holiday.

> A: We lived in Mexico City when I was a child.
> B: **Why was that?**
> A: My parents had jobs there.

A Complete the conversations. Then practice with a partner.

because   Why was that?   Why's that?

1. A: Which is your favorite photo?

    B: I love this one _____ it shows my great-grandfather when he was 16.

2. A: My favorite month is March.

    B: _____

    A: Because, in my country, it's the end of winter and the beginning of spring.

3. A: When I was a child, we moved a lot.

    B: _____

    A: My father worked for an international company in different countries.

B Complete the chart with your answers and reasons.

> *Favorite season: autumn*   *Reason: I prefer cooler weather. I like the color of the leaves.*

	Your answer	Your reason(s)
1. Favorite month or season		
2. Favorite smell		
3. Favorite old object or photo		
4. Favorite song or piece of music		
5. An old film you like or don't like		
6. Best or worst holiday		

C Work with a partner. Take turns sharing your information from exercise B.

Say an answer: A: *My favorite month is January.*
Ask for the reason: B: *Why's that?*
Give the reason: A: *In my country, it's the middle of summer!*

D **EVALUATE** Read and listen to this article. Discuss the questions with a partner. 🔊 | Critical Thinking

1. Which of the three ways do you use to make more memories?
2. Which do you want to try?
3. Which do not work, in your opinion?

THREE WAYS TO MAKE MORE MEMORIES

1. The Ten-Year Test

When you choose between different activities or experiences, ask yourself, "Which adventure am I more likely to remember in ten years?" Choose that one.

2. "Firsts"

We don't remember our everyday activities, but new experiences or "firsts" stay in our memories forever. So try something for the first time: visit a new place, learn a new language, or try a new sport.

3. Don't always go the easiest way.

A lot of memories are about travel and difficulties along the way. So don't always take the quickest or shortest route. Try walking or cycling, or take a different road.

◀ A mountain road in Fuji-Hakone-Izu National Park, Japan

E **PERSONALIZE** Think about three past events in your life and take notes. Then work in groups and describe each one. Also, explain why you remember each event.

1. An adventure you went on
2. A "first" you did and still remember
3. A difficult journey you took

> *My favorite adventure was a hiking trip. I remember it because of the mountains and the terrible weather....*

Review

SELF-ASSESS

How well can you . . . ?	Very well.	OK.	I need improvement.
use the key vocabulary	☐	☐	☐
pronounce -ed endings	☐	☐	☐
use the simple past	☐	☐	☐
give reasons	☐	☐	☐

A VOCABULARY Complete the tasks with words from this unit.

1. Make a noun from each of these words: *discover, memorable, research*
2. Write the opposite word for each of these words: *happiness, remember*
3. Write a verb with the same meaning as each phrase: *explain the meaning; find something new*
4. Write THREE verbs that begin with the letters *re-*.

B PRONUNCIATION Add *-(e)d* to make the past form of these verbs. Then practice saying each pair. Write the number of syllables for the present verb form and the past verb form.

Present verb	Past verb	Present verb	Past verb
_2_ decide	_3_ decide _d_	___ remind	___ remind ___
___ look	___ look ___	___ start	___ start ___

C GRAMMAR Complete these tasks.

1. Think of a famous person you like and say THREE sentences about the person.
   > . . . was born in . . .
   > When he / she was a child, he / she . . .
   > Nowadays, he's / she's famous because . . .

2. Think of five years that were important to you. Say ONE sentence about each year.
   > I was born in 2004.

D SPEAKING SKILL Complete the sentence and conversation. Say sentences with reasons.

1. We like looking at old photos because . . .
2. A: Most people love the summer.
   B: Why's that?
   A: . . .

RE-ASSESS What skills or language do you still need help with?

Final Tasks

OPTION 1 Play two truths and a lie

A Think of two memories from your childhood. Write 2–3 sentences for each memory. Then make up one false story about your childhood. Write 2–3 sentences.

B Work in groups of three or four and take turns. Read your three memories. Other group members try to guess which memory is false.

A: When I was a child, I spent the summers with my grandparents. They lived by the sea. I remember it well because I learned to surf during the summers. I still love surfing.
B: I think that memory is true.
C: Me, too.
A: Actually, it's false! My grandparents live in a big city. And I'm very bad at surfing!

OPTION 2 Present a special object or photo

See Unit 2 Rubric in the Appendix.

A MODEL Listen to a student giving a presentation. Answer the questions. 🔊

1. What object does the student present?
   a. A book
   b. A dish
   c. A photo

2. Who received the object for her birthday?
   a. Her great-grandmother
   b. Her mother
   c. The student

3. How well does the speaker remember her great-grandmother?
   a. Very well
   b. Well
   c. Not very well

4. Why is the book special?
   a. It has photos of her great-grandmother.
   b. It has her great-grandmother's handwriting.
   c. It has a letter from her great-grandmother.

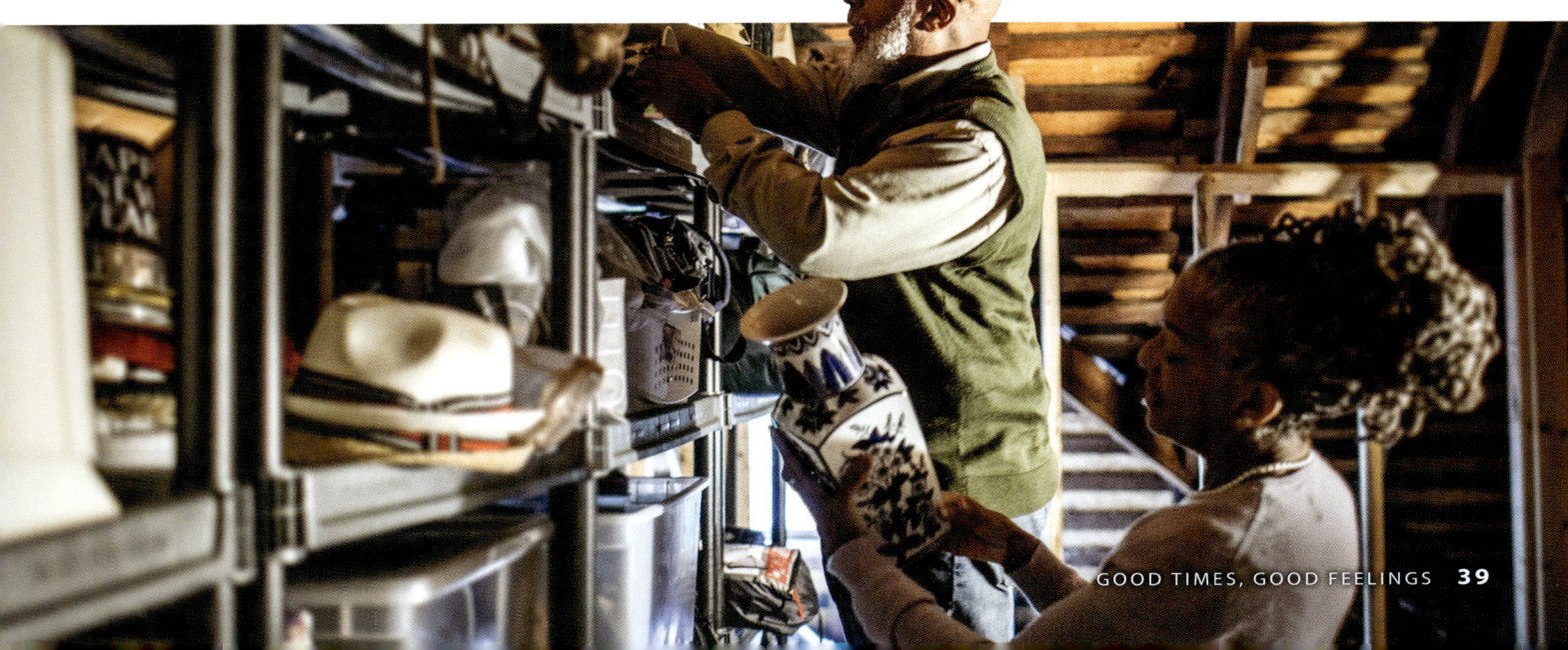

▼ Almost 50% of Americans say a special family object is their most important possession, according to research from OnePoll.

B ANALYZE THE MODEL Listen again. Complete the sentences with the words you hear.

1. Good morning, everyone. I'm _____ to talk about a family object.
2. It _____ my great-grandmother.
3. . . . , but the book _____ me _____ her.
4. The book is _____ to me because of those memories.
5. But it's also _____ she wrote notes next to the recipes.

PRESENTATION SKILL   Structure a Presentation

When you plan a presentation, a three-part structure often works well. First, introduce the presentation. Next, tell a story to get your audience's interest. And finally, explain why the topic is important to you and/or to your audience. Answer these questions:

What is the topic? (object/photo)
I'm here today to talk about . . .
Today, I'd like to present this photo / object.

What is its story?
It's about . . . years old.
It came from . . . / It shows . . . / It belonged to . . .

Why is it important to you?
It's important to me because . . .
It's also special because . . . / It also reminds me of . . .

C PLAN Prepare a presentation for your class about a special object or photo. It can remind you of family, friends, or maybe a place you visited. Take write notes to answer these questions.

1. What is the topic? (object/photo)	
2. What is the story of your object or photo?	
3. Why is it important to you?	

D PRACTICE AND PRESENT Bring your object or photo to class. (If you can't bring the object in, bring a photo of it.) Give your presentation in groups or to the whole class. When you listen to other students, think of a question to ask at the end.

E REPORT With a partner, give each other feedback on your presentations.
- How clear was the topic?
- Did the presenter use the simple past?
- Did the presenter give reason(s) for the importance of the object?
- What was one thing you really liked about the presentation?

THE MARKETING MACHINE 3

A giant cat appears on a 3D billboard in Tokyo, Japan.

IN THIS UNIT, YOU WILL:

- Listen to an interview about mascots
- Watch a video about marketing and advertising
- Watch or listen to an interview with a graphic designer
- Design a mascot
  OR Present an advertisement

THINK AND DISCUSS:

1. Look at the photo. What do you think the cat on the billboard is advertising?
2. Do you think this is a good way to sell something?
3. Read the unit title. What does it mean? What do you think you will learn about in this unit?

EXPLORE THE THEME

Read the information. Then discuss the questions.

1. What do you buy online?
2. Which of these things do you do when you are shopping online?
3. Does any of the information surprise you?

Facts about Digital Marketing

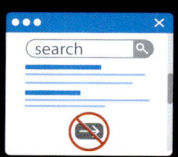 **75%** of people don't go past the first page of a search.

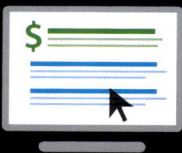 **80%** of people don't click on paid search results. They click on the other results.

 **81%** of customers leave a website because of the pop-up ads.

 **28%** of searches result in a purchase.

 Almost **50%** of users look for videos about a product or service before visiting a store.

Source: SerpWatch

Digital content creators often advertise products.

A Vocabulary

A MEANING FROM CONTEXT Read and listen to the information. Think about the meaning of the words in blue. Write each word next to its definition.

WHAT'S FOR BREAKFAST?

A **popular** breakfast food in the United States is cereal. You can find different kinds of cereal in any supermarket. Cereal boxes are easy to recognize. They often use colorful **characters**, like a tiger or bird, to **advertise**. The fun cartoon characters **represent** the **product** and make **customers**, especially young customers, want the product.

Many cereals for children have the same **quality**—they are very sweet. Some people worry that companies **aim** too many **commercials** at children. These people feel we should **encourage** better eating habits.

1. _____ (v) to make more likely to do something
2. _____ (n) something that is made and sold
3. _____ (n) people who buy something from a shop, company, etc.
4. _____ (n) the way someone or something is
5. _____ (v) to direct or point at
6. _____ (adj) liked by many people
7. _____ (v) to tell people about a product and get them to buy it
8. _____ (n) imaginary animals or people
9. _____ (n) advertisements on the radio, on television, etc.
10. _____ (v) to be a sign for something or speak for something

B Listen and repeat the words from exercise A. Then choose THREE words and write your own sentences with them. Read your sentences to a partner.

VOCABULARY SKILL   Noun Suffixes -ment and -tion

A suffix is a word ending. It changes the form of a word. Common noun suffixes include -ment and -tion. When you see or hear a word with one of these endings, it is usually a noun.

Verb
The company <u>advertises</u> online.
I don't <u>recognize</u> that product.

Noun
The company's **advertisement** is online.
She wanted some **recognition** for her work.

When you add a suffix to a verb, you sometimes need to make other spelling changes. You can use a dictionary to check.

C Write the noun form of each verb. Use a dictionary to help choose the correct suffix and make any spelling changes.

	Verb	Noun		Verb	Noun
1.	advertise	_____	5.	act	_____
2.	excite	_____	6.	entertain	_____
3.	inform	_____	7.	encourage	_____
4.	produce	_____	8.	organize	_____

D Complete each sentence with the correct form of a word in **blue** from exercise A. Then practice the conversations with a partner.

1. A: What are some different ways companies _____ their products?
   B: Well, some companies put advertisements in apps on your phone.

2. A: How do ads _____ people to buy things?
   B: Hmm. Ads sometimes make the product look exciting and fun.

3. A: What's the most _____ type of advertising?
   B: I see a lot of funny ads on social media. My friends like to share them.

4. A: Do you think it's OK to _____ ads at children?
   B: Um, I think it's OK. Kids see ads all the time.

5. A: What was the last _____ you bought online?
   B: I think I bought some jeans.

6. A: What _____ are important in a good friend?
   B: Well, my best friend and I like the same things. That's important.

E **PERSONALIZE** Discuss the questions from exercise D with a group. Give your own answers.

A Listening Mascots and Marketing

Critical Thinking | **A ACTIVATE** You are going to hear an interview about mascots. Look at the characters and discuss the questions with a partner.

1. What do you think the four characters in the photos represent? Match them to a–d.

   a. candy   b. insurance   c. stopping forest fires   d. an instant message app

2. How do you think these characters, called mascots, help sell products or share information?

1. _____

2. _____

3. _____

4. _____

B **MAIN IDEAS** Listen to the interview. Complete each sentence with TWO or THREE words. 🔊

1. Companies use mascots to help customers remember _____.
2. A mascot is better than a spokesperson because a mascot can't do _____.
3. Mascots are successful on social media because users share _____.
4. Some companies pay to use QQ Penguin on toys, clothing, and _____.
5. Mascots can help public service and encourage _____.

LISTENING SKILL   Listen for Examples

Speakers often give examples to explain their ideas. They sometimes use words and expressions to signal examples. Listen for these words and take notes when you hear them.

- for example
- such as …
- Think about …
- for instance
- like …

Companies often use colorful characters, **like a tiger or bird**, to advertise their products. **Think about** the characters on breakfast cereal boxes, **for example**.

C Listen again and match each example to the idea it supports. You will use ONE example twice. 🔊

Idea

1. _____ Mascots help people remember the qualities of a product.
2. _____ Mascots help people recognize a company's name.
3. _____ It's easy to change a mascot.
4. _____ People share information about products with mascots.
5. _____ Mascots can help the environment.

Example

a. Tony the Tiger
b. M&M's candies
c. Smokey the Bear
d. QQ Penguin
e. Geico lizard

D **DETAILS** Read the statements. Then listen again and choose T for *True* or F for *False*. Correct the false statements. 🔊

1. The M&M's mascots use a lot of words to explain the product.   T   F
2. The name of the Geico mascot and name of the company look the same.   T   F
3. The company changed the M&M's mascots to get younger customers.   T   F
4. QQ Penguin started as a mascot for a shopping app.   T   F
5. When a mascot dislikes something, people often dislike the same thing.   T   F

E **PERSONALIZE** Discuss these questions with a group.

1. Can you think of a famous mascot in your country?
2. What does the mascot represent? Does it sell a product or help a public service?
3. Do you think it is successful? Why? Why not?

A Speaking

SPEAKING SKILL Ask for and Give Clarification

Here are some expressions you can use to ask for and give clarification.

A: What do you mean?
B: I mean (that) . . .

A: Could you explain (that)?
B: Sure. In other words, . . .

A: Do you mean (that) . . . ?
B: Exactly. / Not exactly. I mean (that). . .

A: Are you saying (that) . . .?
B: No, I said (that) . . .

ONLINE Online discussions can be more difficult to understand. You might need to ask for and give clarification more often than in a face-to-face discussion. Don't be afraid to ask for clarification.

A Match each question to the correct response. Listen and check. Then practice with a partner.

1. Are you saying a spokesperson is better than a mascot? _____
2. I don't really understand. Is a mascot always a cartoon animal? _____
3. You said that commercials are one kind of ad. What do you mean? _____
4. Do you mean that social media can help sell products? _____

a. Yes. When people share a post online, that's a kind of advertising.
b. Not exactly. A mascot is actually better than a spokesperson in several ways.
c. In other words, a commercial is an ad on TV or radio with audio or video.
d. No, I'm saying that it often is. Sometimes a mascot can be a person or thing.

B Complete the conversations with expressions for clarification. Then practice with a partner.

1. A: I'm doing a presentation on logos in class.
   B: Logos? What are those?
   A: A logo is a design symbol for a business or product.
   B: ¹_____ it's like a sign?
   A: Sort of. ²_____ it's like a sign, but a simple one. It's like a shape.

2. A: I'm reading about micro-advertising.
   B: ³_____? Really small advertisements?
   A: No, I mean advertising for a very small group of people.
   B: ⁴_____ a little more?
   A: Sure. ⁵_____, companies find a group of people with one thing in common. Then the advertiser aims their advertising at that group.

GRAMMAR FOR SPEAKING Simple Present and Present Continuous

We use the simple present to express:
- actions or states that are always true: He **doesn't like** shopping.
- habits or routines: **Do** prices **go up** every year?

We use the simple present with adverbs of frequency (*usually, always,* etc.) and frequency expressions (*every day/month* and *once/twice a day*).

We use the present continuous to express:
- actions happening now/around this time: **I'm buying** my clothes online these days.
- changing situations: Why **are** prices **going down** this year?

We use the present continuous with expressions like now, *at the moment, these days,* and *this week/month.*

For spelling of verbs ending in *-s/-es* and *-ing*, see the Appendix.

C Complete the statements with the simple present or the present continuous. Use contractions.

1. My classmates _____ usually _____ a lot in class. (not talk)
2. My English _____ a lot in this class. (improve)
3. Our teacher _____ only English in class. (speak)
4. I often _____ in the evening, but this week I _____ to study in the morning. (study / try)
5. Everyone in my class _____ more than one language. (know)
6. We _____ about jobs this month. (learn)
7. Sometimes our class _____ every day. (meet)
8. We usually _____ much homework, but we _____ a lot this semester. (not have/get)
9. I _____ a lot of classes at the moment. (not take)

D **PERSONALIZE** Rewrite FOUR of the sentences in exercise C so that they are true for you or your class. Then read your sentences to a partner.

◀ A graphic designer creates a logo.

THE MARKETING MACHINE **49**

E Use the words and phrases to write *yes/no* and *wh-* questions with the simple present and present continuous. Then ask and answer the questions with a partner.

1. usually / enjoy / shopping _____
2. buy / a lot of stuff / this month _____
3. how often / shop / online _____
4. save / money / to buy something _____
   _____
5. what / want / to buy / with your money _____
   _____
6. what / you / learn / about marketing / this semester _____
   _____

A: Do you enjoy shopping?
B: Sometimes. I like shopping for clothes, but I don't like shopping for groceries.

Critical Thinking

F **EVALUATE** Work with a partner. Answer the questions to discuss the advertisement.

1. Describe the advertisement. What do you see?
2. Where do you think the ad appears? Who is the ad for?
3. What is the ad trying to do? What is its goal?
4. Do you think the advertisement works well? Why?

G Work with a group. Find another advertisement online. Discuss the questions from exercise F. Ask for and give clarification as needed.

Advertising Just for You

▲ New digital advertising can recognize a customer's face and personalize ads.

brand (n) a product made by a specific company
ingredient (n) an item used to make something
chap (n) a man (British English)
identical (adj) the same or very similar

A Watch the video. Check (✓) the THREE main ideas. ▶

1. ☐ Most people like to go shopping and buy colorful products.
2. ☐ Companies have different ways to make products look exciting.
3. ☐ Companies often advertise the same type of product in different ways.
4. ☐ The words on products are more important than the colors.
5. ☐ The colors on a product are important for customers of all ages.

B Watch again and complete these sentences with ONE or TWO words. ▶

1. Advertisers make products look exciting to _____.
2. Two different face products have several of the same _____.
3. Advertisers use packaging to advertise to a certain _____.
4. Advertisers sometimes use grey or blue packaging for men. For women, they use _____ or _____.
5. Studies show that children like _____.

C **RANK** What makes you look at a product in a shop? Rank these things in order of importance (1=most important, 5 = least important). Then compare with a group. | Critical Thinking

____ colors   ____ price   ____ label   ____ location in the shop   ____ brand name

B Vocabulary

A Listen and repeat. Check (✓) any words you already know. 🔊

achieve (v)	audience (n)	design (n)	image (n)	result (n)
attract (v)	complicated (adj)	figure out (v phr)	message (n)	stand out (v phr)

B **MEANING FROM CONTEXT** Listen and write the words you hear. Then think about each word's meaning. 🔊

CREATING A MARKETING MESSAGE

What does a company want to ^{1} _____ when they advertise a product? Usually, they want to get more sales and more customers. To do this, they need a good marketing plan. First, they need to ^{2} _____ who their customers are. Then they can decide the best way to advertise for that ^{3} _____. Next, a company needs to consider the ^{4} _____. What should the ad look like? What kind of ^{5} _____ will get people's attention quickly? What will ^{6} _____ new customers? They also need to think about the ^{7} _____: A simple one is often more successful than a ^{8} _____ one. Good advertising needs to ^{9} _____ from other ads. If the marketing plan reuses old ideas and pictures, the company won't get a good ^{10} _____. They won't get more customers and won't make more money.

C Write each word from exercise B next to its definition.

1. _____ (v phr) to be very easy to see or notice
2. _____ (v) to get or reach something, such as a goal
3. _____ (n) people who watch, read, or listen to the same thing
4. _____ (v phr) to understand or to find an answer
5. _____ (n) the situation at the end of a process
6. _____ (n) the way something is made or planned
7. _____ (adj) difficult to understand or explain
8. _____ (n) the main or most important idea in a book, film, etc.
9. _____ (v) to make someone interested in something
10. _____ (n) a photo or picture

D PERSONALIZE Discuss these questions with a partner.

1. What **stands out** in your room at home?
2. What are you trying to **achieve** in this class?
3. How can you **attract** new friends?
4. What's the best way to explain a **complicated** idea?
5. What video games or websites have good **designs**?

E INTERPRET Read and listen to the information in the diagram. Underline the vocabulary words from exercise A. Then answer the questions with a partner. Use the information in the diagram and your own ideas. | Critical Thinking

1. What do you need to know when you are planning a marketing campaign?
2. What or who is an audience?
3. What are different ways you can use to attract your customers?
4. How will you know when you have achieved your goal?

Source: The Organic Agency

B Listening Graphic Design

Critical Thinking | **A EVALUATE** You are going to hear an interview with a graphic designer. Look at the photo and discuss the questions.

1. Describe the photo. What do you see?
2. What do you think it is advertising?
3. Is the image interesting? Does it stand out?

B MAIN IDEAS Watch or listen and choose the correct answers.

1. What is Kate's job?
   a. She's an artist.
   b. She works in marketing.
   c. She's a community organizer.

2. How does Kate know when she did her job well?
   a. Her boss tells her that she did a good job.
   b. Many people share the advertising online with friends.
   c. Customers buy the product or come to the event.

3. What is the most important skill Kate learned in college?
   a. how to think
   b. how to use software
   c. how to work with clients

4. According to Kate, which is the best kind of image for marketing?
   a. a picture with a lot of details
   b. an inexpensive picture
   c. a simple picture

5. According to Kate, how does social media help with marketing?
   a. It's easier to create a design on social media sites.
   b. Companies can see the things that interest people.
   c. Companies can ask the customers questions.

C DETAILS Watch or listen again and complete the sentences. Each answer is TWO or THREE words.

1. Kate got a degree in _____.
2. Other companies hire her company to do marketing and _____.
3. Kate tries to think of _____ ways to make something stand out.
4. In the example Kate gives, a rowing organization wanted to attract _____.
5. Social media is important in marketing because people want to _____.
6. Kate says the most important thing is to _____.

D FOCUSED LISTENING Listen and read part of the interview. Underline FOUR errors. Then listen again and correct the errors.

I'm pretty much the to-go person for my job. Other companies, our clients, hire us to do targeting and advertise products for them. I have to think about the audience for the product and then figure out a way to share our client's message. If I'm successful, the audience, or consumers, will buy the produce.

E EVALUATE Work with a group. Think of an advertisement that stood out for you. Describe the ad. What made you remember it? Think about the information from the interview.

| Critical Thinking

B Speaking

PRONUNCIATION   Aspirated /k/, /p/, and /t/

🔊 When the sounds /k/, /p/, or /t/ come at the beginning of a word or a stressed syllable, they are pronounced with an extra puff of air. We say they are aspirated.

/kʰ/	/pʰ/	/tʰ/
en•**c**our•age	**p**ur•pose	pre•sen•**t**a•tion
qual•ity	re•**p**eat	**t**i•ger

When these sounds are not correctly aspirated, they can be confused with the sounds /b/, /d/, and /g/. The word will be harder to understand or confused with another word.

/kʰ/ /g/	/pʰ/ /b/	/tʰ/ /d/
cap – gap	pig – big	ton – done

When an /s/ sound comes before the /p/, /t/, or /k/ sound, we do not aspirate the sound.

/k/	/p/	/t/
s**k**ill	ex•**p**er•i•en•ces	s**t**ore

A Practice these words. Hold your hand in front of your mouth. Feel the extra puff of air on your hand when you say the second word in each pair. 🔊

1. advertise—adver**t**isement
2. open—o**p**inion
3. gold—**c**old

B Listen and practice. Which /k/, /p/, and /t/ sounds are aspirated? Mark the letters. 🔊

1. Mascots are colorful cartoon characters.
2. Information graphics are popular in advertisements.
3. The company shared an important post online.
4. Let's talk about the problem with the marketing presentation.
5. We want to encourage customers to buy the product.

C **PERSONALIZE** Choose THREE words from exercise B with aspirated letters. Write your own sentences. Then practice reading them to a partner.

CRITICAL THINKING   Analyze Graphics

It is often useful to summarize important information with a graphic, such as an infographic or chart. To understand a graphic, ask these questions:
- **What is the main point?** What is the graphic trying to say? Where does the information come from? Look for a title, headings, and footnotes to find this information.
- **How is the information organized?** Is it organized by time? By country? By categories? With data or percentages?
- **How is the infographic designed?** Headings, bold words, and different colors show important or related information. Pictures and icons usually help show key points.

D Read and listen to the information. Discuss these questions with a partner. 🔊 | Critical Thinking

1. What is the main point of the infographic?
2. How is the information organized?
3. How does the design help you understand the information?

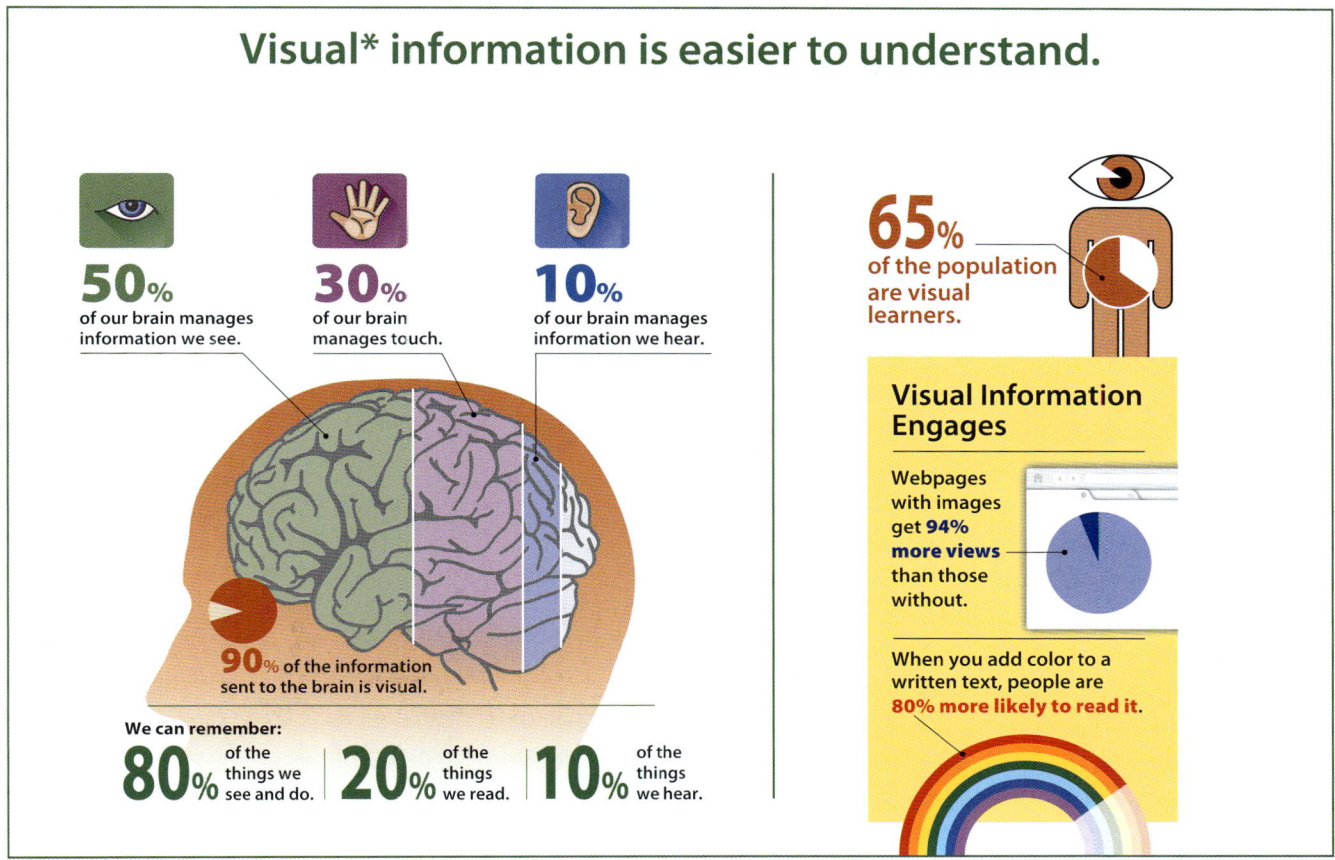

*visual: connected to seeing

Source: NeoMam Studios

E Complete the sentences with information from the infographic.

1. Our brain manages information we _____ , _____ , and _____ .
2. Only _____ percent of our brain manages information we hear.
3. _____ percent of the information sent to the brain is _____ .
4. We can remember 80 percent of the things we _____ .
5. _____ percent of people are not visual learners.
6. A written text with _____ is more interesting than one without color.

F **APPLY** Discuss these questions with a group. | Critical Thinking

1. Where do you see infographics? What is their purpose?
2. What features make an infographic good for marketing?

THE MARKETING MACHINE 57

Review

SELF-ASSESS

How well can you . . . ?	Very well.	OK.	I need improvement.
use the key vocabulary	☐	☐	☐
pronounce aspirated /k/, /p/, and /t/	☐	☐	☐
use the simple present and present continuous	☐	☐	☐
ask for and give clarification	☐	☐	☐

A PRONUNCIATION Say the words. Which sounds are aspirated in these words? Mark the letters.

attract (v)   commercial (n)   customer (n)   popular (adj)   quality (n)
character (n)   complicated (adj) encourage (v)   product (n)   represent (v)

B VOCABULARY Use the words from exercise A to complete the tasks.

1. Complete each sentence. Write the correct form of a word.
   a. I enjoy TV shows with _____ stories. I really like mysteries.
   b. My best _____ is my sense of humor.
   c. I like to _____ a lot of attention. I like when people notice me.
   d. I don't buy a lot of _____ online. I usually go to stores.

2. Write sentences with THREE more words.

C GRAMMAR Choose the correct verb form.

1. The company (advertises / is advertising) a new product at the moment.
2. I (don't like / 'm not liking) the music they play in stores.
3. Why (do you spend / are you spending) more on social media advertising this year?
4. Prices (always increase / are always increasing) around this time of year.

D SPEAKING SKILL Complete the conversations. Say sentences to ask for and give clarification.

1. A: I think we usually buy a product when we remember the design of the package.
   B: I don't think I understand. . . .
   A: Sure. In other words, we buy products when we recognize them.
2. A: I think the information in our presentation is hard to understand.
   B: Are you saying that it's confusing?
   A: . . . it's complicated. Maybe we need an infographic.

RE-ASSESS What skills or language do you still need help with?

Final Tasks

OPTION 1 Design a mascot

COLLABORATION SKILL   Brainstorm with a Group

Brainstorming in groups is a good way to come up with ideas quickly. Encourage everyone to make suggestions, and don't criticize anyone's ideas. After you brainstorm a list of ideas, discuss each idea. Try to choose one that everyone likes.

ONLINE Pay close attention to others when you're online. While you are speaking, watch for signs that other group members want to say something, such as unmuting, leaning forward, gesturing, or the hands up icon.

A Work with a group. Follow these steps to choose a new product or service and a mascot for it.

1. Brainstorm ten different products or services, e.g., bicycles or banking.
2. Choose your favorite idea from the ten products and services.
3. Design a mascot for the new product or service. Consider these questions:
   - Is it an animal? Something else?
   - What color(s) is it?
   - What is it called?
   - How will you use the mascot in your marketing? For example, will it be on TV? On social media?

B Tell the class about your mascot and the product or service.

▼ The Yuru-Kyara Mascot Summit in Hanyu, Saitama, Japan

THE MARKETING MACHINE   59

OPTION 2 Present an advertisement

A MODEL Listen to a group of students present a product or service. Answer the questions.

1. What is the product or service?
   a. An app.
   b. A phone.
   c. A travel website.
2. Where does the advertising appear?
   a. In a magazine.
   b. Online.
   c. On a building.
3. What visuals do they use?
   a. A cartoon character.
   b. An infographic.
   c. A large photo.
4. What is the design like?
   a. Complicated.
   b. Exciting.
   c. Simple.
5. Why does the ad stand out?
   a. It's big.
   b. It's funny.
   c. It's unusual.
6. Who is the audience?
   a. Anyone.
   b. Older people.
   c. Young adults.
7. What is the story or message?
   _____

8. Does the advertising work well?
   a. Yes.
   b. No.

B ANALYZE THE MODEL Listen again and write what you hear.

1. QIAN: Today we are _____ an advertisement for . . .
2. SARA: The _____ is very simple.
3. SARA: The only words are under the _____.
4. HASAN: It _____ a lot of attention because . . .

C PLAN Work with a group. Apply what you learned about marketing. Discuss the questions in exercise A about a product or service you know well. Take notes. Then follow these steps.

- Use your notes to organize your presentation.
- Decide who will present each part.
- Create any visuals you will include in your presentation.
- Take turns practicing your part of the presentation.

D PRACTICE AND PRESENT Practice your presentation as a group. Make helpful suggestions for improvement to your group members. Then give your presentation to the class.

> Today we are presenting an advertisement for . . .
> This advertisement appears . . .

See Unit 3 Rubric in the Appendix.

WILD WEATHER 4

A forest area in Großer Feldberg, Germany

IN THIS UNIT, YOU WILL:
- Watch or listen to a report about strange weather
- Watch a video about tornadoes
- Listen to a documentary about sports and climate change
- Present tips for doing an activity
  OR Present a process

THINK AND DISCUSS:
Großer Feldberg ("Great Field Mountain") is part of the Taunus mountains in Germany. The forests in this area are popular with tourists all year round.
1. Describe the photo. What do you see?
2. Read the unit title. What do you think you will learn about in this unit?

EXPLORE THE THEME

Read the information. Then discuss the questions.

1. What kind of weather do you see in this photo? How does it make you feel?
2. Did you know about any of the examples of extreme weather? Do any surprise you?
3. What type of weather do you think is the most dangerous?
4. What is the most extreme weather where you live?

A storm cloud in Colorado, USA

Extreme Weather around the World

The world is becoming warmer, and this is causing more extreme weather. Here are some examples from recent years.

Rain
Zhengzhou, China, had over 64 cm of rain in one day in July of 2021.

Droughts
Between 2014 and 2016, Brazil had its worst drought in 80 years. This caused water shortages in the city of São Paulo.

Floods
In 2022, Pakistan had some of the worst floods in its history. The floods affected 33 million people and destroyed almost 900,000 homes.

Hurricanes
In 2005, Hurricane Katrina hit New Orleans and caused enormous damage. That year, there were 15 hurricanes in the USA—the most active hurricane season ever recorded[1]. The year 2022 is second with 14 hurricanes.

Snowstorms
Some parts of New York, USA, received over 180 cm of snow from November 16–20, 2022. In December, the area received another 125 cm.

High temperatures
In Isesaki, Japan, temperatures reached 40.2 degrees Celsius (104.5 degrees Fahrenheit) on June 25, 2022. That is the hottest temperature ever recorded during June in Japan.

Tornadoes
The widest tornado ever recorded was in El Reno, Oklahoma, USA, on May 31, 2013. It was 4.18 km wide.

[1] **recorded** (adj) written down

A Vocabulary

A Listen and repeat. Check (✓) any words you already know. 🔊

amount (n)	drought (n)	forecast (n)	predict (v)	storm (n)
destroy (v)	**flood** (n)	**measure** (v)	**rainfall** (n)	**temperature** (n)

B **MEANING FROM CONTEXT** Read the article. Choose the correct words. Then listen and check your answers. 🔊

WATER FROM THE SKY: TOO MUCH OR NOT ENOUGH?

"How much rain did we get?" It's an important question because all life on Earth depends on [1] (storms / rainfall). When we get the usual [2] (forecast / amount) of rain, we're happy. The problems come when we get too much rain or not enough. In southwest and northwest China, for example, there were many [3] (storms / temperatures) in July 2022. They brought too much rain, and there were [4] (droughts / floods) in the area. Many people lost their homes, and some people died.

In the same month, India's capital city, Delhi, had no rain. The [5] (temperature / amount) was 50°C (122°F) with [6] (droughts / floods) in many regions. The terrible weather [7] (destroyed / measured) food crops.

Because rainfall is so important, scientists try to [8] (destroy / predict) the amount of rainfall different parts of the world will receive. To do this, they [9] (measure / flood) air and ocean temperatures and study how the air is moving around the world. They can then make weather [10] (storms / forecasts). The scientists are not always right, but they usually know when we'll probably have large amounts of rain or not enough.

C Write each word in the boxes next to a statement about the weather.

drought   flood   forecast   measure   storm

1. _____ It will be sunny on Wednesday.
2. _____ It rained for five days. There was water everywhere!
3. _____ How many inches of rain did we have last night?
4. _____ I'm not going outside! I'm afraid of lightning.
5. _____ After three years of almost no rain, it's too dry for plants or animals.

amount   destroy   predict   rainfall   temperature

6. _____ Two of the school's walls and the roof fell down during the storm.
7. _____ We had three inches of snow last night.
8. _____ It's cold—only 2.2°C.
9. _____ I think it'll be sunny tomorrow.
10. _____ There was a lot over the weekend, and there were floods everywhere.

D Complete the conversations with words from exercise A. Then practice with a partner.

1. A: What's the weather _____ for tomorrow?
   B: I think it's going to rain, but let me check on my phone.

2. A: What was the worst _____ in your hometown? Were you scared?
   B: One year, we had thunder and lightning, and a tree fell on our house! That was scary!

3. A: In my country, 28°C is hot. What _____ is hot in your country?
   B: I'm from Oman, so in the summer, it's usually over 35°C in the summer.

E **PERSONALIZE** Discuss the three questions in exercise D with a group. Give your own answers.

F **EXPLAIN** This photograph by Abdul Momin is called *A Thirsty Earth*. Describe the photo. Why did the photographer give the photo this name?

Critical Thinking

▼ Chittagong, Bangladesh

WILD WEATHER 65

A Listening Strange Weather

CRITICAL THINKING Remember and Apply What You Know

Before you listen to a talk or lecture, think about what you already know about the topic. You can also write down any words that you expect to hear. This will help you to remember and apply what you already know. For example, you can think about words connected with weather: *rain, sun, temperature,* etc.

Critical Thinking | **A** You are going to watch or listen to a report about strange weather. Look at the photos. What words do they make you think of? Write down your words.

a. _____ dust devil

b. _____ Catatumbo lightning

c. _____ waterspout

d. _____ ball lightning

B MAIN IDEAS Watch or listen to the report and complete the following.

1. Number the photos in exercise A from 1 to 4 in the order the speaker describes them.
2. What is the main purpose of this report? _____

LISTENING SKILL   Listen for Definitions

When speakers introduce new words or ideas, they often define them. When you hear a new word or idea, listen for information after the verb *be*. A definition may be followed by a short description or explanation.

*A storm **is** bad weather with strong wind and rain.*
*A flood **is** when water covers land that is usually dry.*

C Match the types of wild weather to the definitions. Then listen to parts of the report again and check your answers.

1. _____ Catatumbo lightning
2. _____ ball lightning
3. _____ dust devil
4. _____ waterspout

a. It's a round light in the sky. It can be red, orange, or even blue.
b. It's when strong wind moves in a circle over warm water, and a long, thin cloud moves down to the water.
c. It's a lightning storm, and it happens over a river in Venezuela.
d. It's a small tornado. It happens when there is wind and hot weather.

D DETAILS Watch or listen again and answer each question. Choose T for *True* or F for *False*.

1. We usually hear about strange weather in a daily weather forecast.   T   F
2. There are a lot of places in Venezuela with Catatumbo lightning.   T   F
3. Catatumbo lightning happens around 150 nights a year.   T   F
4. Ball lightning can make a noise.   T   F
5. A filmmaker in China recently saw ball lightning.   T   F
6. Kenya has a wet season and a dry season.   T   F
7. Dust devils travel faster than 50 miles per hour.   T   F
8. A waterspout in Texas dropped fish onto a town.   T   F

E PERSONALIZE Discuss these questions with a group.

1. Does strange weather ever happen in your country? What happens?
2. Is the average temperature rising, falling, or staying the same in your country? Why?
3. Imagine you are visiting these places on Earth. What weather do you think you will see?
   - The Sahara Desert
   - Islands in the South Pacific Ocean
   - The Himalayan Mountains

A Speaking

GRAMMAR FOR SPEAKING   Count and Noncount Nouns

Count nouns are nouns that we can count. They can be singular or plural.
- Singular: *a **person**, one **mountain**, an **umbrella**, a terrible **storm***
- Plural: ***people**, two **mountains**, **umbrellas**, terrible **storms**, many **snacks***

Noncount nouns are nouns that we cannot count. They do not usually have plural forms.
temperature**, bright **sunshine**, some **ice**, a lot of **rain

Some nouns can be both count and noncount, but the meanings may be different.
- Count: *It rained three **times** last night.*
- Noncount: *I don't have any **time**.*

Subject–verb agreement

When count and noncount nouns are the subject of a sentence, use the correct verb form. Noncount nouns use singular verbs forms.
- Count: *An **umbrella is** useful in the rain.*   ***Umbrellas are** useful in the rain.*
- Noncount: ***Rain is** important for farming.*   (NOT ~~Rain are important for farming.~~)

A Two friends are packing for a camping trip in the mountains. Complete their conversation with the words from the box. Then practice the conversation with a partner.

| are | bottles | is | is | raincoats | time | times | umbrella |

A: We don't have a lot of ¹_____. The bus leaves in half an hour. Did you pack your bag?

B: I'm almost done.

A: Why are you taking an ²_____?

B: Because umbrellas ³_____ useful when it rains—obviously! Last time I went to the mountains, it rained three ⁴_____!

A: But that umbrella ⁵_____ huge! Leave it. I have two plastic ⁶_____. They're great because they're small and easy to carry. You can take one of them.

B: OK. And can you bring two water ⁷_____?

A: Sure! Water ⁸_____ important. We may go on a long hike.

B For each noun, write *C* for count or *N* for noncount.

__N__ water ____ gloves ____ battery ____ pen ____ food
____ sunscreen ____ umbrella ____ medicine ____ chocolate ____ matches

PRONUNCIATION Syllable Stress

🔊 A syllable is a word or part of a word that has one vowel sound. In words with two or more syllables, we usually stress one syllable. We say it more loudly and clearly.

One syllable	Two syllables	Three syllables
flood	**mea**•sure	pre•**dic**•tion
storm	a•**mount**	**tem**•pera•ture*

*With some words, there are silent letters. For example, the second *e* in *temperature* is silent, so the word has three syllables, not four.

C Listen to the words from exercise B. Mark the main stress and write the number of syllables. 🔊

__2__ **wa**ter ____ gloves ____ battery ____ pen ____ food

____ sunscreen ____ umbrella ____ medicine ____ chocolate ____ matches

D ARGUE Imagine you are planning a camping trip to the mountains. In pairs, discuss which items to take in exercise B. Decide which are very useful to take and which are not useful. | Critical Thinking

> *Why are you taking . . . ?*
> *You (don't) need . . .*
> *. . . is / are (not) useful (because) . . .*

GRAMMAR FOR SPEAKING A, an, some, any, a lot of

We can use *some*, *any*, and *a lot of* with count and noncount nouns. We use *a* and *an* with count nouns only. We use *some* in affirmative statements and *any* in negative statements.

	Count nouns	**Noncount nouns**
Affirmative statements	You should bring **an umbrella**. There are **some mountains**. He has **a lot of** warm **clothes**.	There's **some snow**. We need **some help**. There's **a lot of grass**.
Negative statements	You don't need **an umbrella**. We don't need **any** new **clothes**. It doesn't get **a lot of rain**.	We don't need **water**. There isn't **any ice**. We don't have **a lot of time**.
Questions	Do I need **an umbrella**? Do we need **some** warm **clothes**? Does the area have **a lot of trees**?	Do we need **water**? Do we need **any help**? Do we have **some time**? Do we have **a lot of time**?

E Choose the correct word or phrase in this description of the first photo.

In the first photo, there are ¹ (a / some) beautiful mountains. And in the sky, there are ² (a lot of / any) clouds. There's also ³ (a / some) lake. It looks very cold because there's ⁴ (some / a lot of) snow and ice. There aren't ⁵ (some / any) houses, so I don't think people live here. Visitors would need ⁶ (any / a lot of) warm clothes.

Kenai Fjords National Park, Alaska, USA

F Work with a partner. Describe the second photo. Talk about:

the mountains   the land and the grass   the weather and temperature   people and visitors

Critical Thinking

G **PLAN** Work with a group. You are going to take a three-day vacation. Read the list of possible vacation activities. Then add three or more ideas to the list.

- go hiking in the mountains
- visit some museums
- _____
- have a picnic at the beach
- go on a boat tour
- _____
- go shopping
- _____
- _____

Now read the three-day weather forecast and discuss your weekend plans. Follow these steps:

- As a group, choose two of the activities for each day and complete the schedule below.
- Discuss what you need to bring on the trip for each activity.

Friday	Saturday	Sunday
A lot of sunshine today; cooler temperatures in the morning; hot by early afternoon	Morning rain showers; thunderstorms possible in the afternoon; clear and cool at night	Partly cloudy and warmer; windy in the afternoon, with winds up to 48 kph

Friday	Saturday	Sunday
a.m.	a.m.	a.m.
p.m.	p.m.	p.m.

A: *Friday afternoon will be hot. Let's go to the beach in the afternoon.*
B: *OK. So, we need to bring sunscreen and ...*

Video

Understanding Tornadoes

extreme (adj) very unusual or serious
fascinated (adj) very interested in a subject
column (n) a tall vertical shape

form (v) to begin to happen
turning (adj) moving in a circle around a point

▲ Anton Seimon is an atmospheric scientist and a National Geographic Explorer.

A Read the statements. Watch the video. Choose T for *True* and F for *False*. ▶

1. Anton Seimon is a scientist and a National Geographic Explorer.   T   F
2. He was interested in things like extreme weather from a young age.   T   F
3. There are three main steps to a tornado forming.   T   F
4. Tornadoes are usually four kilometers wide on the ground.   T   F
5. Anton's work helps to predict storms.   T   F

B Watch again. Answer each question in a few words. ▶

1. What subjects fascinated Anton as a child? _____
2. In step one, warm, wet air goes upwards. What does it meet? _____
3. Wind shear means the wind changes. Does it move up or down? _____
4. In step three, the air gets hotter and rises. What kind of movement happens in step four?
   _____
5. What was important about the El Reno tornado in 2013? _____
   _____
6. What happened to Anton's friend during the El Reno tornado? _____

C **RECALL** Watch the video two more times with the sound off. With a partner, take turns narrating the video. Use the information in exercises A and B and your own words. ▶

| Critical Thinking

WILD WEATHER   71

B Vocabulary

A Listen and repeat. Check (✓) any words you already know.

| average (adj) | effect (n) | increase (v) | prevent (v) | rise (v) |
| decrease (v) | heat (n) | location (n) | reach (v) | season (n) |

B **MEANING FROM CONTEXT** Read and listen to the article. Think about the meaning of the words in blue. Write each word next to its definition. TWO words have the same definition.

TOO HOT TO SLEEP

In warm **seasons**, we often notice the **heat** during the day. However, when the temperature **increases** at night, it has an **effect** on our sleep. A new study shows that as global temperatures **rise**, people go to bed later, sleep badly, and wake up earlier.

Researchers at the University of Copenhagen studied the sleep of 50,000 people. They looked at sleep information from their activity trackers. Then the researchers matched that information to the people's **location** and the local temperature. The study found that people sleep longer when the outside temperature is below 10°C. When the outside temperature **reaches** 25°C, it **prevents** people from sleeping. Sleep **decreases** about 15 minutes a night for the **average** person. This might not sound like a lot, but over a long time, less sleep is bad for our health.

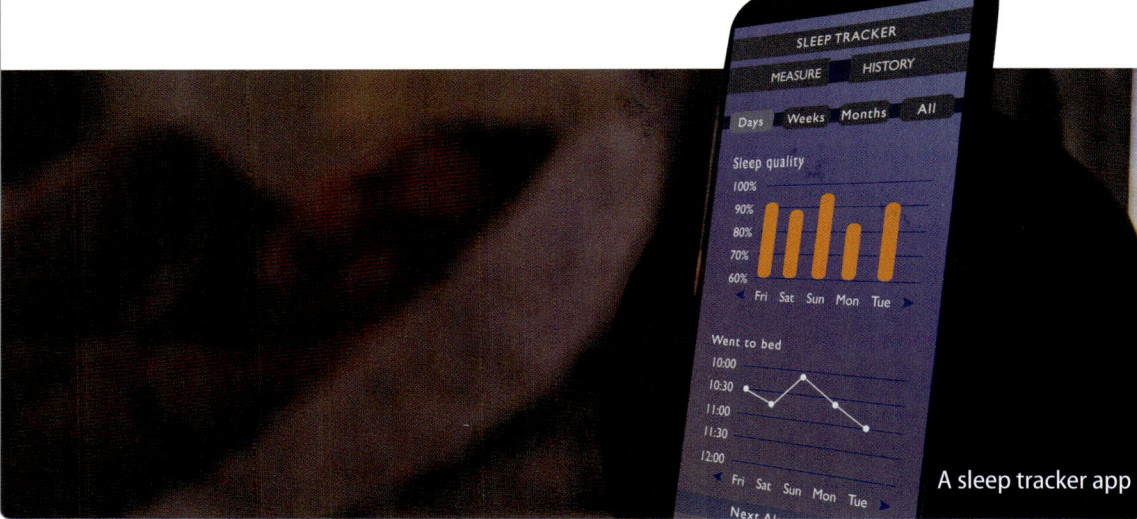

A sleep tracker app

1. _____ (v) to go up in an amount or number

2. _____ (n) the noun form of *hot*

3. _____ (n) a period in the year, such as winter

4. _____ (v) to arrive at something, such as a place, speed, or height

5. _____ (n) a change or result

6. _____ (v) to go down in an amount or number

7. _____ (v) to stop somebody from doing something

8. _____ (n) a place where something happens

9. _____ (adj) typical or normal

VOCABULARY SKILL   Synonyms

Many words have the same or similar meanings.
   *The temperature **increases** during the day. = The temperature **rises** during the day.*

Sometimes one word is better in a particular situation. For example, *tall* and *high* are synonyms, but we use *tall* for people and *high* for places.
   *My brother is very **tall**.*   *The mountain is very **high**.*

Pay attention to how you hear or see words used to learn which word is the best choice.

C Cross out the bold word in each sentence and write the correct form of a synonym from exercise A.

1. The temperature didn't **go down** _____ very much last night.

2. The bed was uncomfortable, but it didn't **stop** _____ me from sleeping.

3. During the summer, the temperature can **get up to** _____ 50°C in Oman.

4. One **result** _____ of climate change is hotter temperatures in some countries, but colder weather in others.

5. The rainy **time** _____ in India is usually from July to mid-September.

6. The seas are **getting higher** _____ as the average temperature increases.

D **PERSONALIZE** Answer the questions in this survey. Then interview your partner and write their answers. Which answers are similar or different?

Sleep Survey		
	You	Your partner
1. What's the **average** amount of sleep you need each night?		
2. How often do you sleep this long?		
3. Does your amount of sleep **increase**, **decrease**, or stay the same during different seasons?		
4. What can **prevent** you from sleeping? (e.g., noise? stress?)		
5. When you sleep badly, what **effect** does this have on you?		

B Listening The Future of Sports

Critical Thinking

A ACTIVATE Describe the photo below. Where are the skiers? Why do you think they are practicing in this way? What problem(s) do you see?

B MAIN IDEAS Listen to a documentary about sports and climate change. Number the ideas in the order you hear them. 🔊

a. _____ Climate change is changing sports schedules.

b. _____ An increase in rainfall and floods will cause problems for some sports.

c. _____ Less snow has a negative effect on money and jobs.

d. _____ Climate change will have an effect on sports in the future.

e. _____ Some countries have to make snow for winter sports.

NOTE-TAKING SKILL Abbreviate Numbers and Measurements

When you take notes, write down important numbers and measurements. You can use abbreviations or symbols for specific measurements.

You hear:
A marathon is forty-two point two kilometers.

You write:
42.2 km. = a marathon

Different speakers might use different types of measurement.

A marathon is twenty-six point two miles.   **26.2 mi.** = a marathon

▼ Skiers practice skiing in Bessans, France.

C Below are some common abbreviations and symbols. Write each one next to the correct word. Then match the word to its definition.

| % | $ | 1/3 | °C | °F | ft. | m. |

Definition

_ft._ 1. foot _b_   a. a kind of money used in the USA, Canada, and Australia

____ 2. percent ____   b. a length equal to 12 inches (in)

____ 3. Celsius ____   c. a scale of temperature; water freezes at 0°

____ 4. a third ____   d. one part in every hundred

____ 5. dollar ____   e. a length equal to 100 centimeters (cm)

____ 6. meter ____   f. a scale of temperature; water freezes at 32°

____ 7. Fahrenheit ____   g. a fraction that means one third

D **DETAILS** Listen again. Write the numbers and figures. Use abbreviations and symbols. 🔊

1. year of the World Cup in Qatar = _____
2. highest summer temperature in Qatar = _____
3. amount U.S. winter sports business is worth = _____
4. number of people U.S. winter sports business employs = _____
5. winter sports decrease in USA = by _____ to _____
6. soccer stadiums in UK to close by 2050 because of floods = ____ in ____
7. golf courses in UK to close by 2050 = _____

E **FOCUSED LISTENING** Listen to these sentences. Write the missing verb or noun and the missing preposition. 🔊

1. Climate change will have an _____ when you play some sports.
2. Usually, the Olympic Games take _____ different countries during the summer months.
3. In 2022, the World Cup _____ Qatar.
4. The winter sports business is worth $60 billion, and it _____ 900,000 workers.
5. The _____ storms and bad weather at sea causes problems for these sports as well.

F **ANALYZE** Discuss these questions with a partner. | Critical Thinking

1. Do you think climate change will have an effect on sports in your country? Which sports?
2. What are some possible solutions to these changes to sports?

B Speaking

> **SPEAKING SKILL** Express Likes and Dislikes
>
> We can use many different verbs to express that we like or don't like something.
> **Likes:**   I (really) like . . .   I enjoy . . .   I prefer . . . (to. . .)   I love . . .
> **Dislikes:** I (really) don't like . . .   I dislike . . .   I hate . . .   I can't stand . . .
>
> Say *I don't mind . . .* when you have no strong preference.
>   I **don't mind** the rain. It doesn't bother me.
>
> When you say you like or dislike something in a conversation, you can give a reason.
>   I **really like** the rain because I can stay inside and read.
>   I **can't stand** the heat. When it's 40°C, I can't walk anywhere.

A Read and listen to the paragraph below. Then answer the question and find the expressions. 🔊

1. What is the definition of a *chionophile*? _____
2. Underline the verbs that express likes.
3. Double-underline one expression that expresses a dislike.

Most people like to live in a warm climate, or they prefer going to hot places for vacation. But I'm a *chionophile*. That means I love cold weather! I enjoy walking through the snow because it's so quiet. That doesn't mean I like to be cold. I can't stand it! But I like to be warm in cold places, so I have a very warm coat.

▶ A man tries to stay warm during a winter storm.

B Work with a partner and take turns. Talk about weather you like and dislike, and give reasons. Use the ideas and expressions below. Do you have the same likes and dislikes?

I like . . .	I dislike . . .	rainy days	sunny weather
I enjoy . . .	I hate. . .	cloudy days	strong wind
I love . . .	I can't stand . . .	storms	thunder and lightning
I prefer . . .	I don't mind . . .	hot / cold weather	snow

A: I enjoy sunny weather. I can go for a run or play tennis.
B: Me, too! I hate storms. I like to spend time outside.

GRAMMAR FOR SPEAKING   Verb + Gerund or Infinitive

After verbs such as *like, love, prefer, don't like, can't stand,* and *hate,* use either the infinitive form or the gerund form. There is little or no important change in meaning.
   I like to live in a warm place.   **I like living** in a warm place.

After other verbs such as *enjoy, dislike,* and *don't mind,* use the gerund form.
   I enjoy walking through snow.   (NOT I enjoy to walk through snow.)

For a list of verbs followed by gerunds and infinitives, see the Appendix.

C Choose the correct answer. In some sentences, both answers are correct. Then practice the conversations with a partner.

A: Do you like ¹ (to go / going) out when it snows?
B: Yes, I do, because I really enjoy ² (to ski / skiing).

A: I can't stand ³ (to watch / watching) old movies. They're so slow! What about you?
B: I don't mind ⁴ (to watch / watching) them. Sometimes they're funny.

A: How do you feel about classical music?
B: I love ⁵ (to listen / listening) to it. It's so relaxing.

A: Do you prefer ⁶ (to drink / drinking) tea or coffee?
B: I don't mind ⁷ (to have / having) either. But I probably drink more coffee in the morning and more tea in the afternoon.

D **PERSONALIZE** Work with a partner. Take turns asking A's questions in exercise C. Give your own answers.

E **CREATE** Work with a group. Ask questions. Talk about some of your likes and dislikes, and give reasons. Add at least three new topics.

go to the movies	play water sports	play tennis	go out in cold weather
listen to classical music	eat fast food	do homework	sit outside in hot weather
watch the Olympic Games	_____	_____	_____

Critical Thinking

Review

SELF-ASSESS

How well can you . . .?	Very well.	OK.	I need improvement.
use the key vocabulary	☐	☐	☐
recognize syllable stress	☐	☐	☐
use count and noncount nouns; *a, an, some, any, a lot of*; gerunds and infinitives	☐	☐	☐
express likes and dislikes	☐	☐	☐

A VOCABULARY Write the missing word from the unit in each sentence.

1. *Stop* is a synonym of *p_____*.
2. *H_____* is the noun form of *hot*.
3. *Drought* is the opposite of *f_____*.
4. *L_____* is a synonym for *place*.
5. Spring is my favorite *s_____*.
6. *Result* is a synonym for *e_____*.

B PRONUNCIATION Match the words to the syllable stress in the chart. Then find ONE more word in this unit for each category and add the words to the chart.

battery	destroy	measure	storm	umbrella
●	●●	●●	●●●	●●●
storm				

C GRAMMAR Write *a, some, any,* and *a lot of* in these sentences. Then look at the nouns in bold. Write C for count and N for noncount next to each word.

1. We should take _____ **camera** with us.
2. Don't worry about bringing lunch. I have _____ **sandwiches** in my bag.
3. There isn't _____ **water** in my bottle. I'll need more by lunchtime.
4. Do we need _____ **money** or is the concert free?

D SPEAKING SKILL Complete each sentence. Say what you like and dislike.

1. When it rains, I don't like . . .
2. During a storm, I hate . . .
3. On a sunny day, I love . . .
4. In the winter, I enjoy . . .

RE-ASSESS What skills or language do you still need help with?

Final Tasks

OPTION 1 Present tips for doing an activity

A Read these tips for playing a sport in the heat.

5 Tips for Doing Sports in the Summer
Don't let hot weather stop you from doing sports.

1. Take regular breaks.
2. Drink water before, during, and after exercise.
3. Wear loose, light-colored clothing.
4. Exercise early or later in the day when it's cooler.
5. Make sure the other players are OK. Be a team player!

◀ Racers run a marathon during a hot summer day.

B In groups, choose one of these topics. Discuss your topic and think of five tips to help others.

1. Five tips for doing sports in the winter
2. Five tips for sleeping better in the summer
3. Five tips for going hiking in the mountains

C Join another group and present your five tips. As you listen to the other group, answer these questions:

- Do you think their tips are useful to others?
- Do you have any questions about their tips?
- Do you have any suggestions to make their tips more useful?

See Unit 4 Rubric in the Appendix.

OPTION 2 Present a process

A **MODEL** A student is presenting a process. He uses these sentences in his presentation. Number them in the order you think is correct. Then listen to check. 🔊

a. _____ This next slide shows the process.
b. _____ As you can see, it looks like a big snowball.
c. _1_ Today, I'd like to talk about a strange type of weather called a snow roller.
d. _____ In stage two, the wind starts to blow.
e. _____ And finally, the snow starts to roll down the mountain.
f. _____ First, I'll give a definition, and then I'll explain the process.
g. _____ Take a look at this photo. It shows a snow roller.
h. _____ In stage one, you have snow on the side of a mountain.

PRESENTATION SKILL   Use Slides

We often use and refer to slides in a presentation. Slides can include:

- The title of your presentation
- A photo or image connected to the topic
- Bullet points with key information; for example, the steps of a process
- A graph or chart showing data or information

When you show a slide and talk about it, use phrases such as these:

Take a look at this photo/chart/slide.
It shows . . .
As you can see, . . . This next slide shows . . .
Look at the . . .

📶 **ONLINE** When you present online, your audience is closer to the screen, so you might need to change your slides. For example, the pictures and text can be smaller.

B **PLAN** Prepare a short presentation with two slides. Choose one idea:

- How something happens in nature (e.g., a type of weather)
- A type of sport and the basic rules (e.g., a sport you like)
- The seasons in your country (e.g., which months and the typical weather for each)

C **PRACTICE AND PRESENT** Practice your one-minute presentation with the slides. Then present it to the class.

FOOD ON THE MOVE 5

A market seller in Indonesia serves sweet and salty snacks.

IN THIS UNIT, YOU WILL:
- Watch or listen to a doctor talk about food and health
- Watch a video about how we taste food
- Listen to a radio show about ugly foods
- Do a food survey
  OR Present an argument about food

THINK AND DISCUSS:
1. Do you know any of the foods in the photo? Which ones look interesting to you?
2. Where and with whom do you eat most of your meals?
3. Read the unit title. What do you think you will learn about in this unit?

EXPLORE THE THEME

Read the information. Then discuss the questions.

1. Which of these foods do you enjoy? How often do you have it?
2. Before you read this information, where did you think these foods came from?
3. Do you know or can you find any other interesting food facts?

Five Foods with Surprising Origins

1 Doughnuts
ORIGIN: The Netherlands

The Dutch brought doughnuts to New York in the early 19th century. These doughnuts looked similar to modern doughnuts, but they were not ring-shaped.

2 Vindaloo
Origin: Portugal

Sailors brought vindaloo from Portugal to Goa in India. Vindaloo is a spicy meat dish. Other types of vindaloo are made with vegetables or tofu.

3 Croissants
Origin: Austria

Surprisingly, croissants do not originally come from France. People first made them in the 13th century in Austria. They did not become popular in France until the 19th century.

4 Churros
Origin: China

There are several stories about the origin of churros. One says that Portuguese sailors first ate them in China. Then they brought the idea to Latin America.

5 Coffee
Origin: Ethiopia

Coffee first went from Africa to Europe and then across the globe. After water, it is the most popular drink in the world. People around the world drink about two billion cups of coffee every day.

FOOD ON THE MOVE

A Vocabulary

A Listen and repeat. Check (✓) any words you already know. Then write each word next to its definition. Use a dictionary to help you. 🔊

| calorie (n) | fast food (n phr) | industry (n) | processed (adj) | throw away (v phr) |
| diet (n) | fresh (adj) | physical (adj) | regular (adj) | weight (n) |

1. _____ (adj) recently grown or made
2. _____ (n) a unit to measure the energy in food
3. _____ (n) a kind of business that makes things
4. _____ (n) how heavy somebody or something is
5. _____ (adj) connected with the body
6. _____ (v phr) to get rid of something you don't want
7. _____ (n) the food you normally eat
8. _____ (adj) (food) changed before selling
9. _____ (n phr) food, such as burgers and french fries, made quickly
10. _____ (adj) doing something often as a routine

B **MEANING FROM CONTEXT** Complete the article with the words from exercise A. Then listen and check your answers. 🔊

WHAT'S NEW IN COOKING?

Around the world, meat is still a ¹_____ part of most people's weekly ²_____. But many doctors and health experts are telling us to eat a smaller amount of meat and to do more ³_____ exercise. And many people *are* trying to eat more fruit and vegetables. This type of food is also better if you are counting ⁴_____ and trying to lose ⁵_____. As a result, the food ⁶_____ is trying to sell us more vegetarian products. Now you can buy vegetarian ⁷_____, like burgers and fried chicken. However, even though this is not meat, it's still ⁸_____ food. It comes in packaging that you ⁹_____, and then you heat the food up in a microwave. So whatever your diet—meat or vegetarian—try to eat food that is ¹⁰_____ rather than out of a package.

▲ A fruit vendor in São Paulo, Brazil

VOCABULARY SKILL Compound Words

Sometimes we put two or more words together to make a new word. You might see these compound words written as one or two words. There are many compound words for food.

Two words: *fast food, french fries, meat eater*
One word: *breadstick, seafood, strawberry*

C Match the words to make compound words connected with food. Use a dictionary to check if they are written as one word or two words.

First word		Second word	
ice	egg	burger	mint
cheese	hot	corn	fruit
pepper	pop	cream	dog
pea	grape	nut	plant

1. _____   5. _____
2. _____   6. _____
3. _____   7. _____
4. _____   8. _____

D **RECALL** Work with a partner and take turns. Play this vocabulary game.

Critical Thinking

- Student A: Read a first word in exercise C aloud.
- Student B: Close your book and try to remember the correct second word.

When you finish, think of two more compound words. Say the first word to your partner. Your partner guesses the second word.

E **PERSONALIZE** Discuss these questions with your partner.

1. How often do you eat each food in exercise C? A lot? Sometimes? Never?
2. When do you eat it? For example, with a meal? At the movies?

A Listening Food Fact or Fiction?

CRITICAL THINKING Recognize a Speaker's Point of View

A point of view is a person's opinion about a topic or idea. A speaker's point of view affects what they say. It's important to recognize a speaker's point of view because it affects the information you hear. Notice how three different speakers can talk about the same topic.

Food advertiser: *Our new healthy chocolate bars are delicious and good for you!*
Doctor: *These chocolate bars have a lot of calories, so don't eat too many.*
Student: *These chocolate bars give me energy to stay awake.*

Critical Thinking | **A** Match the comments about food to each speaker's point of view.

COMMENT

1. _____ You don't need to eat meat if you eat the correct amount of fruit and vegetables.
2. _____ You can eat fruit and vegetables, but you also need meat for good health.
3. _____ You can eat anything, but don't eat more than 2000 calories a day.

SPEAKER

a. Someone who isn't vegan or vegetarian
b. Someone who is advertising a new type of diet
c. Someone who wants you to eat a plant-based diet

There is a lot of different information about food and health. It can be difficult to decide what to believe.

B **ACTIVATE** You are going to hear a doctor talk about food and health. Listen to the first part of his lecture. Choose his point of view. 🔊 | Critical Thinking

The doctor's point of view is:
a. You can find many useful facts about food and health in the news.
b. Everything you learn about food and health is usually wrong.
c. Some facts about food and health are true but not always.

C **MAIN IDEAS** Watch or listen to the lecture. Number the ideas in the order he talks about them. Then discuss which ideas are true with the class. 🔊 ▶

a. _____ Drink eight or more glasses of water a day.
b. _____ When you exercise a lot, you lose weight.
c. _____ There is a right way to eat.
d. _____ Plant-based diets are better than meat-based diets.

LISTENING SKILL Listen for Reasons

Reasons help make ideas clear. They are often important details in a lecture or talk. Listen for words that signal a reason.

- **The reason** is (that) …
- … **because** …
- **That's because** …

Doctors usually tell people to eat a lot of fruit and vegetables every day. **That's because** they help prevent heart problems.

These words come after a reason.

- **That's why** …
- …, **so**

Fruit and vegetables help prevent heart problems and illness. **That's why** doctors tell people to eat five a day.

D **DETAILS** Watch or listen again. Are these statements true or false according to the doctor? 🔊 ▶

1. People are drinking more water because they're buying bottled water. T F
2. Plastic bottles are bad for the environment because we throw them away. T F
3. Drinking a lot of extra water makes you healthier. T F
4. The doctor gives reasons why we should eat less red meat. T F
5. Some vegan products have extra salt or sugar because they are processed. T F
6. Most people can eat more and lose weight because they do more physical exercise. T F
7. The doctor doesn't believe good science supports all the different diets. T F
8. 200 calories of nuts are healthier than 200 calories in a candy bar because nuts are fresh. T F

E **PERSONALIZE** Choose the answers that are true for you. Then compare with a partner.

1. I drink (more than / less than) six glasses of water a day.
2. I prefer to drink water from (a plastic bottle / the tap).
3. (Most of / Some of / Not much of / None of) my diet is meat.
4. I eat (more / less) fresh food than fast food.
5. Overall, I think the doctor in the lecture gave (very / not very) useful advice.

A Speaking

See Critical Thinking: Analyze Graphics in Unit 3.

A ANALYZE Study the infographic at the bottom of the page. Then discuss the questions with your classmates.

1. Which countries is this information about?
2. What percentage of fruit and vegetables do people eat in those countries?
3. What percentage of food do we lose or throw away in these locations?
   - farms
   - storage / transportation
   - processing
   - supermarkets
   - homes
4. When do we lose or throw away the most food in the process? Does this surprise you?

GRAMMAR FOR SPEAKING *A lot of, much, many, few, little, enough*

We use these words to talk about amounts.

Noncount nouns

There's	**a lot of** / **a little** / **not much**	food.
There's	**too much** / **enough** / **not enough** / **too little**	food.

Plural count nouns

There are	**a lot of** / **a few** / **not many**	apples.
There are	**too many** / **enough** / **not enough** / **too few**	apples.

- Use *too much* and *too many* to say you have <u>more than</u> the right quantity.
- Use *(not) enough* to say you have or don't have right quantity.
- Use *too little / too few* to say you have <u>less than</u> the right quantity.

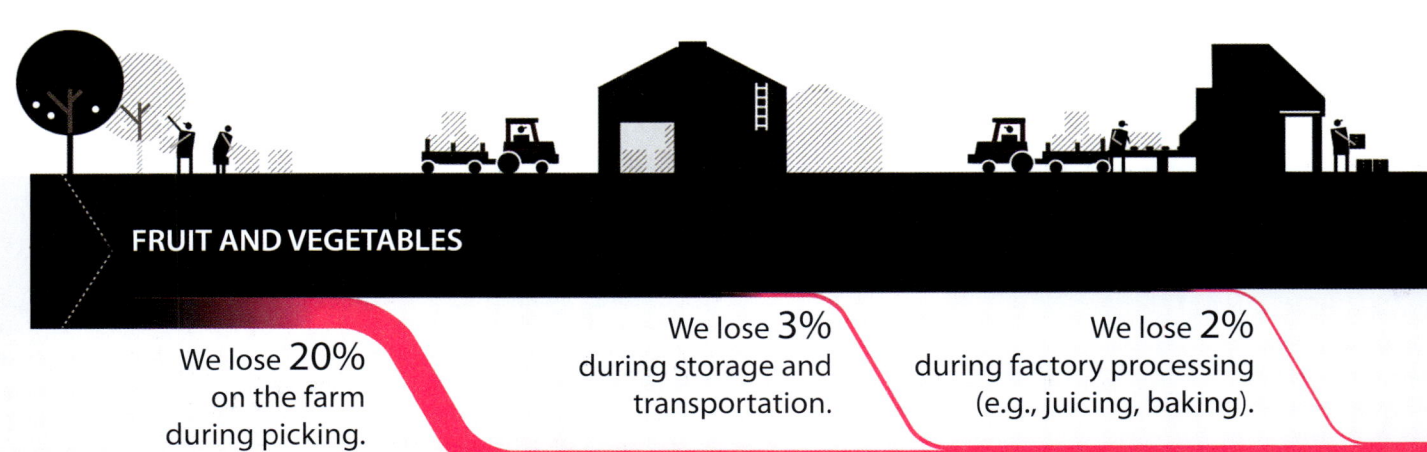

FRUIT AND VEGETABLES

We lose 20% on the farm during picking.

We lose 3% during storage and transportation.

We lose 2% during factory processing (e.g., juicing, baking).

*AUSTRALIA, CANADA, NEW ZEALAND, AND U.S. DATA ONLY

B Choose the correct words to complete this conversation about the infographic at the bottom of the page. Then listen and check.

A: According to this infographic, we all throw away ¹ (**too much** / too many) food.

B: I know! We lose ² (a few / **a lot of**) food at the beginning of the process.

A: Yes, I don't understand the reason they lose 20 percent on the farm. There's not ³ (**much** / many) information about that.

B: Maybe they have ⁴ (**too few** / too little) people to pick all the fruit and vegetables?

A: Maybe. But we also throw away 19 percent of the food in our homes. It doesn't make sense. Why do people throw good food away?

B: I agree. Yesterday, I bought ⁵ (too much / **too many**) oranges by accident. I gave ⁶ (**a few** / a little) to my neighbor, so we both have ⁷ (**enough** / a little) for the week.

A: And overall, we throw away more than we eat! But, at the same time, there are other countries that have ⁸ (**too little** / too few) food. It's crazy!

C What are your food habits? Work with a partner and take turns. Make sentences using the words in the chart and your own ideas.

> *I don't eat many sweets.*

I eat / drink I don't eat / drink	a lot of many / much enough too many / too much too few / too little	apples cheese coffee eggs fast food fruit meat	nuts rice salads soda sweets vegetables yogurt

PRONUNCIATION Long and Short Vowel Sounds

🔊 Vowel sounds can be long or short.
- With **long vowel sounds**, your lips, tongue, and cheeks are more tense.
- With **short vowel sounds**, the lips, tongue, and cheeks are relaxed.

Long	Short
/ iʸ / eat	/ ɪ / it
/ eʸ / paper	/ ɛ / pepper
/ ɑ / not	/ ʌ / nut

D Listen and repeat these word pairs with long and short vowel sounds. Notice how the muscles change in your mouth. 🔊

1. heat–hit
2. cheap–chip
3. taste–test
4. weight–wet
5. cop–cup
6. hot–hut

E You will hear words from exercise D again. Some pairs are the same (heat–heat) and some are different (heat–hit). Write *S* if you hear the same words. Write *D* if you hear different words. 🔊

1. __D__   2. ____   3. ____   4. ____   5. ____   6. ____

F Say these words from this unit with a partner. Categorize them in the chart under the vowel sound. Then listen and check. 🔊

tea   based   lot   eight   hu̱ngry   drink   li̱ttle   fresh   red   cut   pop   meat

/ iʸ /	/ ɪ /	/ eʸ /	/ ɛ /	/ ɑ /	/ ʌ /
tea					

Critical Thinking

G **SOLVE** Take this food quiz with a partner. Give reasons for your answers.

Food Fact or Fiction?

Read these statements about food and decide if they are fact or fiction.

	Fact	Fiction
1. Don't eat any fat. It's bad for you.	☐	☐
2. Eat more carrots because they are good for your eyes.	☐	☐
3. Your body needs a cup of sugar every day.	☐	☐
4. Fast food has too much salt, but a little salt on fresh food is OK.	☐	☐
5. Around 95% of a cucumber is water, so it doesn't have many calories—about 30 in total.	☐	☐

A: I think statement 1 is a fact because there's fat in food like meat and butter.
B: I agree that some fat is bad for you, but not all fat. The human body needs fat.

How We Taste Food

Video

taste buds (n) the small parts on the tongue for tasting
sour (adj) having a sharp taste, like a lemon
bitter (adj) having a strong taste with very little sugar, like coffee

▲ Everyone has a different number of taste buds. The average person has 2,000 to 10,000 taste buds.

A Watch the video. Check (✓) the things that have an effect on taste according to the speaker. Which thing is most important? ▶

☐ color ☐ shape ☐ sound ☐ temperature ☐ packaging ☐ smell ☐ taste buds

B Watch again. Complete each item with ONE word or number. ▶

1. The taste buds on our _____ help us figure out what we're eating.
2. _____ % to _____ % of what we call taste is about the smell of food.
3. If a food is red, the brain guesses it tastes _____.
4. _____ foods can taste more sour.
5. _____ foods can taste more bitter.
6. _____ foods can taste more salty.
7. A dessert on a _____ plate may taste sweeter.
8. A dessert on a _____ plate may taste more bitter.

C **EXPLAIN** Work with a partner. Think of a food you both like to eat. Discuss these questions. | Critical Thinking

1. How important is the smell of this food? Can you describe the smell?
2. When you prepare or eat this food, do you hear any special sounds?
3. What color is this food? Does it taste sweeter, more sour, bitter, or salty?

FOOD ON THE MOVE **91**

B Vocabulary

A MEANING FROM CONTEXT Look at the image. Then read and listen to the information. Think about the meaning of each word in blue. Write each word next to its definition. 🔊

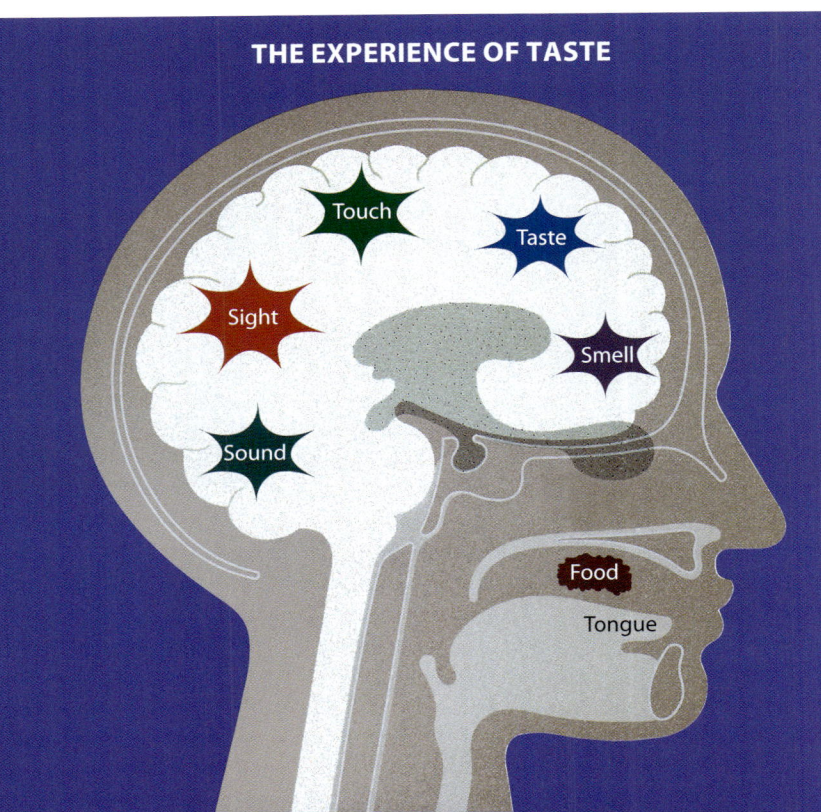

THE EXPERIENCE OF TASTE

When we eat, all the **senses** work together and have an effect on our experience. It begins with the **smell** and **sound** of cooking from the kitchen and the **sight** of food on the table.

Then, when we put the food in our mouth, all this information travels to our brain, and we experience **flavor**. In addition, our memory tells us if we liked this food in the past. Our memory can also **connect** the **taste** with a past experience, like a favorite holiday.

People prefer different types of food as well. Maybe you like a soft banana, but I prefer a harder apple. The way food feels in our mouths or when we **touch** it is also a part of taste.

Finally, the **appearance** of food is important, too. When you see food that is new, strange, or even ugly, do you want to try it? Or are you **nervous** because you might not like the taste? If we understand why we like the foods we do, maybe we will throw less food away.

1. _____ (adj) feeling worried or frightened
2. _____ (n) something you hear
3. _____ (n) sight, hearing, smell, touch, and taste
4. _____ (n) the sense you use your nose for
5. _____ (v) to join together two or more things
6. _____ (n) the feeling of flavor when you put food in your mouth
7. _____ (n) the ability to see
8. _____ (v) to put your hand onto something
9. _____ (n) the way that somebody or something looks on the outside
10. _____ (n) the particular taste of food or drink

B Listen and repeat the words from exercise A. 🔊

C **ANALYZE** The word *touch* can be a verb and a noun: *He touched my hand. / I felt a touch on my hand.* Check (✓) the other words that can be both verbs and nouns. Use a dictionary to help you.

| Critical Thinking

☐ appearance ☐ smell ☐ taste ☐ sight ☐ sound

D Match the two parts of the sentences.

1. I don't like the **appearance** of _____
2. I like the **taste** of _____
3. I'm **nervous** to try _____
4. The **smell** of _____
5. When I hear the **sound** of _____

a. fresh strawberries. They are so sweet.
b. people cooking, it makes me hungry!
c. toast is fantastic when you wake up in the morning.
d. very hot, spicy food. I'm afraid it will hurt my mouth.
e. cauliflower because it looks like a human brain!

E **PERSONALIZE** Work with a partner and take turns. Say FIVE new sentences about the senses using these phrases.

1. I don't like the **appearance** of . . . because . . .
2. I like the **taste** of fruit such as . . .
3. I'm **nervous** to try. . .
4. The **smell** of . . . is . . .
5. When I hear the **sound** of . . . , I think of . . .

F Answer the questions and write notes in the chart. Then tell your partner about your answers.

1. What is your favorite food? Why do you like it?	
2. Do you connect any food with a memory? What is the food? Why?	
3. Think of a food that you ate recently. Describe the senses you used as you ate it.	

B Listening Ugly Food

Critical Thinking | **A ACTIVATE** Look at the photos of food. With a partner, ask and answer these questions about them.

1. Are any of these foods common in your country? Do you like them? Why? Why not?
2. Which of the foods do you want to try? Why?
3. Are there any of them that you don't ever want to try? Why not?

▲ green tomatoes

▲ blue cheese

▲ oysters

▲ passion fruit

NOTE-TAKING SKILL   Use a T-Chart

One way to organize your notes is in a T-chart. For example, you can write main ideas on the left and write any supporting examples and reasons on the right.

Main ideas	**Supporting examples or reasons**
Our senses help us choose food that is good for us.	*Our eyes like bright colors.* *Bright colors mean food is good for us.*

B **MAIN IDEAS** Listen to a radio show about ugly foods. Complete the main ideas (1–5) with ONE or TWO words. 🔊

Main ideas	Supporting examples or reasons
1_____ help us choose food that is good for us.	- eat fruit and vegetables of all 6_____ - smell tells you if something is ready 7_____ - at a market, you can often try 8_____
Sound has an effect on 2_____.	- bells on a truck make ice cream 9_____ - tap melons to 10_____ if ready
The sense of 3_____ is important.	- peach not too soft but not hard - carrot 11_____ rough and bumpy
We taste with our 4_____ first.	- In a study, people liked a meal more because of 12_____. - We are nervous to try food that looks 13_____.
We should eat more 5_____.	- still good to eat - 14_____ food waste - can save 15_____

C **DETAILS** Listen to the radio show again. Complete the supporting examples or reasons (6–15) with ONE or TWO words. Then compare your notes from exercises B and C with a partner. Did you write the same information? 🔊

D **FOCUSED LISTENING** Each phrase from the radio show is missing one adjective. Listen to the sentences and complete the phrases. 🔊

1. _____ red tomatoes
2. smell _____
3. food is fresh and _____ for us
4. makes the ice cream taste _____
5. _____ on the inside and ready to eat
6. appearance is _____
7. doesn't look _____

E **PERSONALIZE** Discuss these questions with a group.
1. What foods from your culture are popular in other parts of the world? Why do you think they are popular?
2. What foods from your culture might seem strange to other people? Why?

B Speaking

SPEAKING SKILL   Tell a Story

When you tell a story and talk about your past, it will be clearer to listeners if you put the events in the order they happened. Use these expressions to tell the order.

Introduction: *In my country, we … / When I was a child, … / Once, a few years ago, …*

Background: *During the holidays, … / Every day, I went to … / We always had …*

Sequence of events: *One day, … / In the morning, … / Then, … / After that, … / Later (on), …*

Ending: *In the end, … / Finally, … / A few years later, … / Even today, …*

You can also make your story more interesting with descriptive adjectives.

The bread was good. (less descriptive) → *The **warm** bread was **delicious**! (more descriptive)*

A Look at the photo of *momos* on the next page. Do you know this food? Do you have any similar type of food in your country?

B Read sentences from a story about momos in the wrong order. Number them in the correct order (1–6). Then listen and check. 🔊

a. _____ In the afternoon, there was usually a delicious smell coming from the kitchen of Pema's house. Her mother made a traditional Nepalese food called momos. First, she made the dough.

b. _____ Pema and I counted them and divided them equally. I loved them because they were warm and spicy!

c. _____ We became good friends, and during the holidays, I played with Pema every day.

d. _____ When I was a child, I remember a new family moved into the house next door. They were from Nepal, and their daughter was called Pema.

e. _____ Then she put meat or vegetables inside the momos and cooked them. Finally, the momos were ready.

f. _____ A few years later, Pema and her family moved away, but even today, I remember the wonderful taste!

C The text in exercise B describes the momos as "warm and spicy." Look at these adjectives to describe food. Check (✓) any you know. Use a dictionary to find the meanings of any you don't know.

bitter	delicious	healthy	salty	sour	sweet	warm
crispy	fresh	homemade	soft	spicy	tasty	wonderful

A man makes momos in Kathmandu, Nepal.

D Work with a partner. Use adjectives in exercise C and your own ideas to describe these types of food.

apples   chocolate cake   french fries   pasta   pizza   rice   your favorite food

> *French fries are crispy and salty. But they aren't very healthy!*

E **CREATE** Think about and plan a food story you can tell. Make notes in the chart.

Critical Thinking

Introduction	
Background	
Sequence of events	
Ending	

F Prepare to tell your food story. Remember to use:
- your notes and ideas from exercise E
- time markers and expressions
- descriptive adjectives from exercise C

When you are ready, work with a partner and take turns to tell your stories.

FOOD ON THE MOVE

Review

SELF-ASSESS

How well can you...?	Very well.	OK.	I need improvement.
use the key vocabulary	☐	☐	☐
pronounce long and short vowels	☐	☐	☐
use *a lot of*, *much*, *many*, *few*, *little*, and *enough*	☐	☐	☐
tell a story	☐	☐	☐

A VOCABULARY Complete these questions with words from the unit. Then say answers to the questions.

1. Which is the most important of the _____ for you? Sight, smell, sound, touch, or taste? Why?
2. What's your favorite _____ of ice cream? Chocolate, strawberry, or something else?
3. Choose a beautiful or ugly vegetable. Can you describe its _____?
4. Which do you prefer: processed food or _____ food?

B PRONUNCIATION Match the words with the same vowel sound. Write the SIX pairs of words. Then practice saying the words.

| cheap | eat | fresh | hit | hungry | little | loss | not | nut | taste | test | weight |

1. _cheap_   _eat_
2. _____
3. _____
4. _____
5. _____
6. _____

C GRAMMAR Complete these sentences about you and your home.

1. In my house, I (have enough / don't have enough) _____
2. In the living room, there (aren't many / isn't much) _____
3. In my bedroom, I always have (too many / too much) _____
4. In the kitchen, there (are / is) (too few / too little) _____

D SPEAKING SKILL Say the first and last sentences from a story about your childhood using these phrases. Your story can be true or imaginary.

- When I was a child, ...
- In the end, ...

RE-ASSESS What skills or language do you still need help with?

Final Tasks

OPTION 1 Do a food survey

A Interview two or three classmates with the questions in this chart. Take notes on the answers.

1. What is one of your favorite meals?			
2. Why do you like it?			
3. What is in it? How do you make it?			

B In groups, tell each other about the answers in your survey.

> *I interviewed Ahmed, and one of his favorite meals is kabsa. It's traditional in his country. He likes it because it has a spicy lemon flavor. You make it with rice, meat, . . .*

▼ Chicken kabsa, the national dish of Saudi Arabia

See Unit 5 Rubric in the Appendix.

OPTION 2 Present an argument about food

A MODEL Listen to someone presenting an argument. What is the main topic of her argument? 🔊

Main topic: _____

B ANALYZE THE MODEL Listen again and check (✓) the techniques she uses in her presentation. 🔊

1. ☐ She asks the audience some questions.
2. ☐ She shows them a photo of food waste.
3. ☐ She gives some interesting facts and figures.
4. ☐ She tells a story about her childhood.
5. ☐ She tells the audience three things to do next.
6. ☐ She asks the audience to do something when they leave.

PRESENTATION SKILL Use an Effective Hook and a Call to Action

When you present an argument, you want to get your listeners' attention. This can help you persuade them to do something.

An **effective hook** is something that gets your audience's attention, such as an interesting image, interesting facts and figures, or a personal story. You can also ask questions for your audience to think about.

Did you know, we lose or throw away over 50 percent of the food we produce?

By the end, you want your audience to do something. This is a **call to action**. For example, perhaps you want your audience to do something differently in their lives after listening to you.

The answer is simple: Cook more fresh food and don't eat too much fast food.

C PLAN Choose one of these arguments about responsible food choices or your own idea.

- We need to eat less meat and have a plant-based diet.
- Schools need to teach children how to cook food.
- We need to drink tap water and not drink water in plastic bottles.

Then prepare a short presentation using this structure:

- Use an effective hook in your introduction.
- Give three reasons for your argument.
- End the presentation with a call to action.

D PRACTICE AND PRESENT Practice presenting your argument to a partner. Then present it to the class or to a group.

HOUSING FOR THE FUTURE 6

L'Arbre Blanc, Montpellier, France

IN THIS UNIT, YOU WILL:
- Watch or listen to a lecture about housing solutions
- Watch a video about steel container buildings
- Listen to an interview about how to build a new city
- Present a house and sell it
  OR Plan a new city

THINK AND DISCUSS:
L'Arbre Blanc is an apartment building in Montpellier, France. The name means *the white tree*. It is called this because the balconies look like leaves on a tree.
1. What do you think is the reason for this design?
2. Do you want to live in a building like this? Explain.

EXPLORE THE THEME

Read the information. Then discuss the questions.

1. What three things do they use to measure sustainable cities? Do these things all have the same importance?
2. Are any of the cities in your country? Do any of the results surprise you?
3. What score do you give your town or city for each category (people, planet, money)?

Sustainable Cities

Sustainable cities are healthy cities. They are comfortable for people to live in. This ranking measures these things:

PEOPLE
Health, education, fair pay, and living costs

PLANET
Energy use, amount of green space, and pollution

MONEY
The business environment, including tourism, employment, and health of the economy

A ranking of 100 of the world's cities

Overall Rank	City	👤	🌐	$
1	Oslo	1	1	39
3	Tokyo	7	7	20
6	London	22	6	23
9	Zürich	2	9	51
10	Amsterdam	10	14	25
15	New York	42	36	14
16	Frankfurt	26	15	24
35	Singapore	5	69	28
41	Toronto	29	57	26
66	Shanghai	49	75	63
71	Kuala Lumpur	62	73	69
74	Istanbul	74	55	79
86	Cairo	79	89	91
96	Nairobi	98	82	95

Source: Arcadis

A Vocabulary

A Listen and repeat. Check (✓) any words you already know.

architect (n) **engineer** (n) **ground** (n) **luxury** (adj) **safe** (adj)
comfortable (adj) **float** (v) **look like** (v phr) **resident** (n) **solution** (n)

B **MEANING FROM CONTEXT** Read and listen to the article. Think about the meaning of the words in blue. Write each word next to its definition.

THE BURJ AL ARAB

The Burj Al Arab is a **luxury** hotel in the city of Dubai. From a distance, it **looks like** the sails on a ship, and the hotel seems to **float** on the water. But, in fact, it sits on a small human-made island.

When they started the project, **engineers** did not know how to create the new island, but they found a **solution**. They used concrete and rocks. It took three years to move enough sand and create **safe ground** above the water. Then an **architect** designed the famous hotel.

Now, the Burj Al Arab has some of the most **comfortable** and expensive rooms in the world. Across from the hotel, local **residents** in Dubai often see helicopters arrive at the top of the building with rich, and sometimes famous, guests.

1. _____ (adj) not dangerous

2. _____ (n) an answer to a problem or difficult situation

3. _____ (n) a person who designs buildings

4. _____ (v phr) to appear similar to something else

5. _____ (n) a person who lives in a particular place
6. _____ (adj) making you feel relaxed
7. _____ (n) the earth; the thing you stand or sit on outside
8. _____ (n) a person who designs and builds machines, roads, etc.
9. _____ (adj) expensive and high-quality
10. _____ (v) to stay on top of the water

VOCABULARY SKILL Adjective Suffixes

You can create adjectives from some nouns and verbs. Common adjective suffixes include -able, -ive, -ful, and -ous. When you add a suffix to a word, use a dictionary to check the spelling.

Noun/Verb	Adjective
comfort	**comfortable**
create	**creative**
care	**careful**
danger	**dangerous**

C Add suffixes to the nouns and verbs to make adjectives. Use a dictionary to help you.

Verb/Noun	Adjective	Verb/Noun	Adjective
1. act	_____	5. fame	_____
2. beauty	_____	6. nerve	_____
3. enjoy	_____	7. use	_____
4. expense	_____	8. value	_____

D **CREATE** Choose THREE adjectives from exercise C and make sentences with them. Then read your sentences to a partner. | Critical Thinking

> *There's a beautiful hotel in the center of my town.*

E **PERSONALIZE** Complete these questions with the adjective form of the word in parentheses. Then ask and answer the questions with a partner.

1. Are there any _____ buildings in your town? What do they **look like**? (beauty)
2. Do you know the names of any _____ **architects**? (fame)
3. Did you ever go up in a very tall building? How far off the **ground** were you? Were you _____? (nerve)
4. Do you have any **luxury** hotels in your town? What makes them look _____? (expense)

HOUSING FOR THE FUTURE

A Listening Housing Solutions

Critical Thinking

A ACTIVATE You are going to hear a lecture about housing solutions. Look at the photo and answer these questions.

1. What is the problem for the people in the photo? What is their housing solution?
2. What are three words you think you will hear in the lecture?

B MAIN IDEAS Watch or listen to the lecture. Match the solutions to the countries.

1. _____ a bamboo house
2. _____ the FLOAT House
3. _____ the LIFT House
4. _____ houseboats

a. Bangladesh
b. the Netherlands
c. Vietnam
d. USA

Flooding can be a problem in southern Cambodia, but these residents are safe in this house.

C **DETAILS** Watch or listen again and check (✓) the features of each type of house in the chart. Some features are true for more than one type of house. 🔊 ▶

Which house . . . ?	Bamboo house	FLOAT House	LIFT House	Houseboat
1. is built above the ground	✓	☐	☐	☐
2. can float	☐	☐	☐	☐
3. can move to different places	☐	☐	☐	☐
4. moves up and down from the ground	☐	☐	☐	☐
5. uses cheap building materials	☐	☐	☐	☐
6. uses plastic water bottles	☐	☐	☐	☐
7. can be very comfortable and modern	☐	☐	☐	☐

D **FOCUSED LISTENING** Each noun phrase is missing THREE words. Listen to these parts of the lecture and complete the phrases. 🔊

1. the middle _____

2. 90% _____

3. the bottom _____

4. about one-quarter _____

5. the basic design _____

LISTENING SKILL Use Context Clues

When you listen to a talk or lecture, you may not understand every word. You can use context clues to help you understand new words. These clues might be before or after the word(s).

> There's always a lot of **congestion** near my house. Every day, <u>there are traffic jams because people are looking for places to park their cars</u>.
> (congestion = the problem of too much traffic)

E Listen to and read parts of the lecture again. Discuss these questions with a partner. 🔊

- What is the meaning of each bold word or phrase?
- Which words before or after the bold word or phrase give context clues?

1. Water can go under the house when there is flooding. But when it's dry, you can use the area under the house as a **storage space** for plants, farm equipment, and animals.
2. Ninety percent of the residents **evacuated** the city by car and drove to safer places further north. Afterwards, when they returned, there weren't enough houses for many of them.
3. About one-quarter of the country is below **sea level**. That's because Dutch engineers removed the sea water and created land to build on.

F **PERSONALIZE** Discuss these questions with a partner.

1. Which type of house from the lecture do you prefer? Why?
2. Do you have any housing problems in your country? What solutions are there?

A Speaking

GRAMMAR FOR SPEAKING Conjunctions *and, but, or, so*

A clause has a subject and a verb. Many sentences have more than one clause.
> *The apartment is clean.* (= one sentence and one clause)
> *The apartment is clean, **and** it's not expensive.* (= one sentence and two clauses)

We can use conjunctions to join two clauses and connect two ideas. Use conjunctions to:

Add information:	*The apartment is clean, **and** it's not expensive.*
Contrast information:	*The kitchen is nice, **but** the living room is too small.*
Offer a choice:	*We can live downtown, **or** we can live near the beach.*
Give a result:	*We want to buy a house, **so** we need to save our money.*

When we speak, we often begin a reply with a conjunction.
> A: *This house has a beautiful kitchen.* A: *This house is amazing!*
> B: ***And** there's a garden in the back!* B: ***But** it's expensive! We can't afford it.*

A Choose the correct conjunction to connect the two clauses. Then say the sentences.

1. We love nature, (so / but) we want to live near a park.
2. It's a beautiful apartment, (and / but) the rent is too high.
3. I can stay here another year, (so / or) I can move to a different apartment.
4. The living room is large, (so / but) the bedrooms are small.
5. We like the house, (or / and) the neighborhood is perfect.
6. My real estate agent never answers his phone, (so / and) I'm looking for a new agent.

B Work with a partner and take turns. Use words from each column to make logical sentences about Ron. More than one answer is possible.

Clause	Conjunction	Clause
Ron loves music,		he goes out with friends.
He works downtown,	and	he takes a train to work.
He's an excellent cook,	but	he goes to concerts in the city.
He often goes hiking,	or	he travels to other countries a lot.
He has a car,	so	he lives in the country.
He works for an international company,		he often eats out at restaurants.
He sometimes stays at home,		he gardens on Saturday mornings.

> *Ron loves music, so he goes to concerts in the city.*

C Use the ideas in exercise B or your own ideas to tell your partner about three people you know.

Shimokitazawa in Tokyo, Japan, is a fun neighborhood with many clothing shops, cafés, and artist studios.

D **CREATE** Your friend is looking for an apartment. Role-play the conversations. Then switch roles. | Critical Thinking

- Student A: Say the first sentence.
- Student B: Reply with the conjunction and add your own ideas.

1. A: This apartment is very modern, and the building is new.
   B: But . . .
2. A: I want to live on this street. It has a lot of good cafés.
   B: And . . .
3. A: I could live in the center of the city.
   B: Or . . .
4. A: The apartment is about a kilometer from our university.
   B: So . . .

PRONUNCIATION Sentence Stress

You often stress one or two words in a clause or sentence. You usually stress content words (words with the most meaning).

Verb:	We **love** nature.
Adjective:	It's a **beautiful** apartment.
Noun:	The house also has a **garden**!
More than one word:	The house has a **garden**, and it has a **swimming pool**!

Sometimes, you can also stress a conjunction to emphasize its meaning.

Emphasize the contrast: It's a beautiful apartment, **but** it's expensive.
Emphasize the addition: It has a beautiful kitchen, **and** there's a garden in the back!

E Listen to these sentences and mark the stressed words. Then listen again and repeat.

1. This pizza is delicious!
2. The apartment is in the city center.
3. He loves music, and he goes to concerts.
4. I like the jacket, but it's expensive.
5. You can live here, or you can live there.
6. A: The bedrooms are comfortable.
   B: And they both have TVs.

F Work with a partner. Repeat a conversation from exercise D, and add stress.

A: I could live in the **center** of the city.
B: **Or** you could live **outside** the city. It's **cheaper**!

CRITICAL THINKING Rank Options

When you rank your options, you think about and compare each choice. You need to decide which option is more important and which is less important. For example, when you choose a place to live, you need to decide what is most important to you: location, size, cost, etc.

Critical Thinking

G You are looking for a new house or apartment. Rank the options in the list from 1 (most important) to 8 (least important).

_____ cost

_____ near green space (parks, etc.)

_____ size

_____ near work

_____ allows pets

_____ facilities (laundry, exercise room, etc.)

_____ near school

_____ has garage or other parking

H Work with a partner. Take turns describing the kind of place you want to live. Use the options from exercise G and your own ideas.

> *Cost is very important for me, so I want a cheap apartment.*

I With your partner, discuss these three houses and apartments. Then list TWO positive features and ONE negative feature about each place to live. Use the information and your own ideas.

Description	Positive	Negative
Option 1: This clean, modern two-bedroom apartment is downtown and close to the university, so it's perfect for students. It's on the third floor, and there is a resident manager.		
Option 2: This beautiful, traditional house is a comfortable place for a family or group of professional people. It's in a quiet area near schools and parks.		
Option 3: This large luxury house has a swimming pool, five bedrooms, and six bathrooms. It's close to the beach and far from the noisy city center.		

J Join another pair and work in groups. Compare your list of positive and negative features from exercise I. Which option is the best for each person in the group?

A: *I'm a student and option 1 is close to a university, so I won't need a car.*
B: *But it has a resident manager. So maybe there are a lot of rules! What about option 2?*

Video

Steel Container Buildings

▲ Container City, Trinity Buoy Wharf, London, UK

spring to mind (v phr) if something springs to mind, you think of it suddenly
pile up (v phr) to increase in amount, in a way that is too much
base (n) lowest part of something
spacious (adj) having a lot of space or room

A Watch the video and number these parts of the video in order (1-3). ▶

a. _____ Ian shows Johnny his steel container house.
b. _____ Different kinds of transportation can move steel containers around.
c. _____ There are houses made from steel containers in London.

B Read the statements. Then watch the video again and choose T for *True* or F for *False*. ▶

1. Johnny says the shipping container is a classic piece of American design from the 1960s.   T   F
2. They made steel containers one size so you could transport them on trucks, trains, or ships.   T   F
3. After about ten years, you can't use steel containers anymore.   T   F
4. It's difficult to build a house using steel containers.   T   F
5. Ian thinks living in a steel container is similar to living in a normal house.   T   F
6. Ian's house is made from two containers.   T   F

C **PERSONALIZE** Discuss these questions with a group.

1. Would you like to live in a shipping container? Why? Why not?
2. Can you think of three more ways to use steel shipping containers?

HOUSING FOR THE FUTURE   111

B Vocabulary

A Listen and repeat. Check (✓) any words you already know. 🔊

| architecture (n) | desert (n) | government (n) | population (n) | private (adj) |
| crowd (n) | energy (n) | nothing (pro) | power (n) | public transportation (n phr) |

B **MEANING FROM CONTEXT** Listen and write the correct form of the words from exercise A. Then think about each word's meaning. 🔊

EGYPT'S NEW CITY

Egypt is famous for its capital city of Cairo. Every year, millions of tourists come to see the ancient ¹_____ in the area. But the city is also famous for its ²_____, busy roads, and slow ³_____. To solve some of Cairo's problems, the ⁴_____ of Egypt has built a completely new city from ⁵_____. The New Administrative Capital is in the middle of the ⁶_____, about 30 miles from Cairo. There are new buildings for the government and office buildings for ⁷_____ businesses. The city can use solar ⁸_____ for its ⁹_____, and there are electric trains for transport. When it is complete, the city will have a ¹⁰_____ of five million residents.

▼ New Administrative Capital, outside Cairo, Egypt

112 UNIT 6 LESSON B

C Match the words in exercise A to their definitions. TWO words have the same definition.

1. _____ (n) all the people in a country or city
2. _____ (n phr) buses and trains that people can use to travel
3. _____ (n) the design and style of buildings
4. _____ (n) a large number of people together in a public place
5. _____ (pro) not anything
6. _____ (n) a place that gets little rainfall; a very dry area of land
7. _____ (n) the people who manage a country or place
8. _____ (adj) not public
9. _____ (n) what comes from electricity, gas, etc.

D Cross out the **bold** words in each sentence and write a word from exercise A.

1. The **style** _____ of these buildings is very old. They're from the last century.
2. There was a **big group** _____ at the stadium last week. I couldn't find a seat!
3. I started English with no knowledge of the language. I knew **zero** _____!
4. In 1900, the **number of people** _____ on Earth was two billion. Now it's eight.
5. All the **energy** _____ in this city comes from those wind turbines out at sea.
6. This parking lot is **not for the public** _____. You can't park here.
7. You can use **a train or a bus** _____ to get to school.
8. This plant needs very little water. It can live in a **very dry area** _____.

E **PERSONALIZE** How much do you know about your town or city? Write your answers.

		You	Your partner
1.	What is the **population**?		
2.	Is the **public transportation** fast or slow? Is it busy?		
3.	Where does most of the **energy** come from? Solar? Gas?		
4.	How old is the **architecture** in the area? What's the oldest building?		
5.	Is there a local **government**? What is it responsible for?		

F **COMPARE** Work with a partner and take turns. Interview your partner with the questions in exercise E. Write your partner's answers in the chart. Then consider the following:

Critical Thinking

- If you live in the same town or city, do you have similar or different answers?
- If you live in different locations, how similar or different are your answers?

B Listening How to Build a New City

Critical Thinking

A PREDICT You are going to listen to an architect describe how to build a new city. In what order do you think you should do these steps?

a. _____ Get money from the government and businesses.

b. _____ Design houses and public transportation.

c. _____ Choose a location.

d. _____ Create places to relax.

e. _____ Figure out the energy and water.

NOTE-TAKING SKILLS Use Diagrams and Flowcharts

When you take notes about different steps in a process, it's often useful to draw a diagram or flowchart with arrows. Here are some notes from a talk about choosing a university.

1. Decide on an area to study. → 2. Research universities. → 3. Visit the locations. → 4. Choose a university.

B MAIN IDEAS Listen to an interview with the architect. What order does she give for the steps from exercise A? Complete the flowchart.

1. c. Choose a location. → 2. → 3. → 4. → 5.

C DETAILS Read the statements. Then listen again and choose T for *True* or F for *False*.

1. Stuart normally talks to architects about one building.   T   F
2. The government hired Zarina to help plan a new city.   T   F
3. Neom in Saudi Arabia will have a population of about 19 million people.   T   F
4. The new city will use water to make its power.   T   F
5. It's not expensive to take the salt out of sea water.   T   F
6. The new city won't allow cars.   T   F
7. Songdo in South Korea has a big park in the middle of the city.   T   F
8. Zarina's new city doesn't have a name yet.   T   F

D **FOCUSED LISTENING** Listen to five of Stuart's questions. Complete each question with TWO words.

1. _____ you tell us about your new project?
2. _____ of location is a good choice for a new city?
3. _____ a problem for a desert city?
4. _____ modern cities move people around?
5. _____ good places to relax in a new city?

E Work with a partner. Try to remember Zarina's answers to the questions in exercise D and make short notes about each one.

F **CREATE** Work with a partner and role-play a conversation between Stuart and Zarina. Then switch roles and practice the conversation again.

Critical Thinking

Student A: You are Stuart. Ask the questions in exercise D.
Student B: You are Zarina. Use your notes from exercise E and answer Stuart's questions.

▼ Model showing Shanghai, China, in the future

HOUSING FOR THE FUTURE 115

B Speaking

SPEAKING SKILL Ask for and Give Opinions

When we discuss ideas, we often:

Ask for others' opinions	Give an opinion	Agree	Disagree
What do you think about . . . ?	I think that . . .	I agree that . . .	I disagree that . . .
What's your opinion?	In my opinion, it . . .	I agree with you.	I don't agree with you.
Do you agree?		Absolutely.	Yes, but . . .
		That's true.	

When we disagree, we can use expressions to be more polite.
- I'm afraid I don't agree.
- I'm sorry, but I disagree because . . .
- I see what you mean, but . . .

A Cover the Speaking Skill box. Correct the common mistakes in each expression. Then practice saying the expressions correctly.

1. How do you think about this idea?
2. What your opinion?
3. Are you agree?
4. In my opinion, is a good idea.
5. I am agree with you.
6. I'm afraid, but I don't agree.
7. I sorry, but I disagree.
8. I see what it means, but I don't agree.

B Match each question or comment to the correct response. Then practice with a partner.

Question or comment

1. What do you think about our city? ____
2. I think that we need a new shopping mall. What's your opinion? ____
3. In my opinion, we should have more bike paths. ____
4. I don't agree that our city needs more houses. The population is too high already. ____
5. We need better public transportation with more buses. ____

Response

a. I agree with you. They're a good way to get around, and riding a bike is good exercise.
b. I think that it's a great place to live. There's so much to do.
c. I see what you mean, but people have to live somewhere.
d. Absolutely! And the price is too high.
e. In my opinion, we don't need more shops because people are shopping online these days.

C **PERSONALIZE** Work with a partner and take turns.

Student A: Read a question or comment from exercise B.
Student B: Answer with a response about your own city or town.

D Work with a new partner. Discuss each of these topics. Use the expressions and structure in the Speaking Skill box.

1. the houses in your neighborhood
2. the location of your town or city (compared to the rest of the country)
3. traffic and public transportation in the area
4. places to relax and have fun

> A: What do you think about the houses in your neighborhood?
> B: In my opinion, they aren't very modern. I don't like the architecture. Do you agree?
> A: Yes. And I also think that . . . / I'm sorry, but I disagree because . . .

E RATE Use the chart to rate the features that are most important in a city. Then work with a group and follow the steps below.

Feature	1 = Very important				5 = Not important
• a very large city	1	2	3	4	5
• interesting architecture	1	2	3	4	5
• a lot of green space	1	2	3	4	5
• good schools and universities	1	2	3	4	5
• cheap cafés and nightlife	1	2	3	4	5
• a lot of shopping malls	1	2	3	4	5
• different museums and galleries	1	2	3	4	5
• not much traffic and noise	1	2	3	4	5

Critical Thinking

1. Ask for and give opinions about the features above. Which features are very important, and which are not important? If you disagree about a feature, discuss it and try to agree on its importance.
2. Decide which are the three most important features and report back to the class.

▼ The Muttrah area in Muscat, Oman

HOUSING FOR THE FUTURE 117

Review

SELF-ASSESS

How well can you...?	Very well.	OK.	I need improvement.
use the key vocabulary	☐	☐	☐
use sentence stress	☐	☐	☐
use conjunctions *and, but, or, so*	☐	☐	☐
ask for and give opinions	☐	☐	☐

A   VOCABULARY   Read the clues and write the words from the unit.

1. What *c* word means a lot of people?
   _____
2. What *p* word is a synonym for *energy*?
   _____
3. What *p* word is the opposite of *public*?
   _____
4. What *a* word designs buildings?
   _____
5. What *r* word lives in a city?
   _____
6. What *t* word often follows *public*?
   _____

B   PRONUNCIATION   Say the sentences on the left and stress the bold word. Think about the information in sentences a-c and match.

1. The **first** apartment was perfect. _____
2. The first apartment was **perfect**. _____
3. The first **apartment** was perfect. _____

a. It was better than the house we saw.
b. The second apartment was not very nice.
c. I don't need to see any more apartments.

C   GRAMMAR   Complete the conversations with conjunctions.

1. A: What do you like to do on weekends?
   B: I like going shopping, _____ I enjoy meeting friends.
2. A: I want to visit the art gallery tomorrow.
   B: _____ it's closed on Mondays.
3. A: Would you like a sandwich, _____ do you want a salad?
   B: A sandwich is fine, thanks.
4. A: Why don't you rent this apartment? It's great.
   B: It's $1000 a month, _____ I can't afford it.

D   SPEAKING SKILL   Unscramble the words and say the sentences.

A: what / you / architecture / think / do / about / modern / ?
B: my / ugly in / it / opinion / 's
A: I / agree / are / that some / but / buildings / not all of them
B: see / I / what / you / but / like them / mean, / I don't

RE-ASSESS   What skills or language do you still need help with?

Final Tasks

OPTION 1 Present a house and sell it

A Choose a house you know well or find one online. (You can search "houses for sale in [place].") You are going to try to sell this house. Make notes about the features of the house, such as:

- architecture and appearance
- location
- size and number of rooms
- near schools and shopping
- garage, yard, or garden
- public transportation
- special rooms (laundry room, exercise room, etc.)
- any other information

B Work with a group and follow these steps.

- Each person has one minute to present and sell their house to the rest of the group.
- You can also answer questions at the end. If possible, show a picture of the house.
- At the end of each presentation, the rest of the group decides if they will buy the house.

> *Today, I'd like to sell you this house. As you can see from this photo, the architecture is beautiful. It's near a lake, and it has four large bedrooms!*

▼ A family looks around a new house with a real estate agent.

HOUSING FOR THE FUTURE 119

See Unit 6 Rubric in the Appendix.

OPTION 2 Plan a new city

A MODEL A group of students are planning a new city. Listen and choose the correct answer or answers. 🔊

1. Which location do they choose?
   a. On the sea.   b. In the desert.   c. Near the sea.   d. In a green space.
2. Why do they choose it?
   a. For the weather.
   b. To protect farmland.
   c. For solar and wind power.
   d. For electric transportation.
3. In the end, how many of the students agree with the choice of location?
   a. One of them.   b. Two of them.   c. All three of them.

B ANALYZE THE MODEL Listen again. Complete these sentences with the word you hear. 🔊

1. That's _____. But what about the temperature?
2. That's a great _____. It also _____ that we can use wind power.
3. _____! It's good to use green energy.
4. Yes, _____ all public transportation can be electric.
5. We can _____ build houses with a view of the sea.
6. I _____ with you.

COLLABORATION SKILL   Encourage Other People in a Discussion

When other people give their opinions, try to encourage them and build on their ideas.

Encouraging each other
Absolutely!   That's a great idea.
That's true.   I agree with you.

Building on ideas
Yes, and . . .   We can also . . .
It also means that . . .   And we need to . . .

📶 **ONLINE** You can encourage other people when they are speaking by using a smile symbol or nodding your head to show you agree. You can also write comments in the chat.

C PLAN Imagine your government has given you money to plan and build an innovative new city. Think about each point below and make notes.

- location (e.g., desert? on the sea?)
- type of energy (e.g., solar? wind?)
- type of transportation
- population and number of houses
- places to relax and have fun
- the name of your city

D PRACTICE AND DISCUSS Work in groups. You have 10 minutes for your meeting. Discuss your ideas from exercise C and plan a new city. Talk about the things you want to include in your city, their benefits, and their challenges. You can draw plans on a large piece of paper.

E PRESENT Prepare and give a short group presentation of your plans to the rest of the class. Use your drawings from exercise D in the presentation.

THE HUMAN BODY 7

You use almost every muscle in your body when you roller-skate, but especially the leg and stomach muscles. Roller-skating normally burns about 500 calories an hour.

IN THIS UNIT, YOU WILL:
- Listen to a conversation about how humans are changing
- Watch a video about what happens when we lose one of our senses
- Watch or listen to a presentation about bacteria
- Survey classmates about the future
  OR Discuss pros and cons of future situations

THINK AND DISCUSS:
1. Read the unit title. What do you want to learn about the human body?
2. Do you think the human body today is different from the human body 100 or 200 years ago? If yes, how?

EXPLORE THE THEME

Read the information. Then discuss the questions.

1. Do any of the facts surprise you?
2. How many parts of the body can you name?
3. Do you know or can you find any other interesting facts about the body?

The Amazing Human Body

 1. You blink around 20 times a minute. That's about ten million times a year.

 2. Scientists believe that the nose can recognize a trillion different scents!

 3. Human teeth are as strong as shark teeth.

 **4.** Earwax is a type of sweat. Your ears make more earwax when you are afraid.

 5. The word *muscle* comes from a Latin word that means "little mouse." The ancient Romans thought a bicep muscle looked like a mouse.

 6. Every year, you lose about 4 kg of dead skin cells.

 7. If you live to age 70, your heart will beat around 2.5 billion times!

 8. Bodies give off a small amount of light. It is too weak for the eye to see.

THE HUMAN BODY

A Vocabulary

A   MEANING FROM CONTEXT   Read and listen to the article. Think about the meaning of the words in blue. 🔊

▶ National Geographic Explorer Christine Lee looks at a skeleton in the Museum of London.

THE MUSEUM OF LONDON

The Museum of London has **possibly** the largest collection of human **bones** in the world. The collection starts from over 5000 years ago and **continues** to the middle of the 19th century.

Most of the bones come from under the city. Every time there is new building work in the city, the museum knows the construction workers will almost **definitely** discover more objects from London's past—especially bones! These bones go to the museum. There, archaeologists use technology from modern **medicine**, such as X-ray machines, to study the bones.

Bioarchaeologists **certainly** learn a lot from the bones. For example, they can study the bones of someone from the 13th century and understand their **lifestyle.** Many people from that **period** worked in the fields. They **probably** spent **double** the amount of time on their feet that we do. As a result, their bones are much larger.

B   Write each word in blue from exercise A next to its definition. TWO words have the same definition. Then listen, check, and repeat. 🔊

1. _____ (n) the hard white parts inside a human or animal
2. _____ (adv) something is true; with no doubt
3. _____ (n) the way a person lives and works
4. _____ (adv) something might be true, but you are not sure
5. _____ (n) the study and science of health care
6. _____ (adv) something is likely to be true
7. _____ (n) a length of time with a beginning and an end
8. _____ (v) to not stop existing or happening
9. _____ (adj) twice as much or many

C Cross out the **bold** words in each sentence and write a word from the box.

a bone	continues	double	medicine	lifestyle	period

1. I fell off my bicycle and broke **my arm** _____.
2. My **routine** _____ is very stressful. I work all the time and never take time off.
3. My aunt is a doctor, and because of her, I'm thinking of a career in **this** _____.
4. Sorry I'm late. The trip took me **twice** _____ the time that I expected.
5. The first 20 years of your life is the **time** _____ when you grow the most.
6. The game **doesn't stop** _____ until one team has 17 points.

VOCABULARY SKILL   Choose the Correct Meaning

When words have more than one meaning, a dictionary can help you choose the correct one for the context. A dictionary also gives you other information about the word.

form /fɔrm/ **(n) 1** the shape of something: *The building is in the form of a T.*
2 a type, kind: *Yoga is a gentle form of exercise.* **3** a printed paper with spaces to be filled in: *When you apply for a visa, you must fill out a form.*

In this sentence, *form* has the first meaning because it refers to the shape of a human body.
Bones and the skeleton create the **form** of the human body.

D Look at these definitions. Write the number of the correct definition next to each sentence below.

period / ˈpɪriəd/ n. **1** any length of time, long or short, that is part of a longer time: *We often have a rainy period in spring.* **2** a particular part of time in history: *The revolutionary period in American history was from 1775 to 1783.* **3** a regular division of time in a school day or a game: *Our lunch period is from 12:15 p.m. to 1 p.m.* **4** a punctuation mark or a dot ending a sentence: *This sentence ends with a period.*

a. _____ I think you need a **period** here, not a question mark.
b. _____ The year I spent in Japan was the happiest **period** in my life.
c. _____ Jana has biology fourth **period** on Tuesdays and Thursdays.
d. _____ The Renaissance was a **period** of growth in culture, art, and science.
e. _____ My team were losing for a short **period** of the game, but they won in the end.
f. _____ In my opinion, the best **period** for music was the 1960s.

E Follow these steps.

1. Choose one of these words and look it up in a dictionary: *book, mean, medicine, object,* or *study*.
2. Choose one of its definitions. Write a sentence with that meaning. Circle the word.
3. Switch sentences with a partner. Look up the word your partner used. Find the correct definition.

A Listening How Humans Are Changing

Critical Thinking

A COMPARE You are going to listen to a conversation about how humans are changing. Look at the photo. With a partner, make a list of differences between ancient humans and modern people. Think about clothing, food, transportation, work, activities, etc.

Ancient humans	Modern humans

B MAIN IDEAS Listen to the conversation between two students. Check (✓) the SIX types of change they discuss. 🔊

☐ 1. height ☐ 3. length of life ☐ 5. bones ☐ 7. brain size
☐ 2. hair   ☐ 4. body temperature ☐ 6. senses ☐ 8. intelligence

---

LISTENING SKILL Understand Time Periods

Listen for time expressions to help you understand the time period a speaker is talking about.

In the past	**In the present**	**In the future**
a hundred years ago	nowadays	in one hundred years
during that period	currently	in years to come
in past centuries	at the moment	in the next few years/century

---

C DETAILS Listen to the conversation again. For each topic, are the speakers referring to a change in the past, present, or future? TWO answers are correct for two of the topics. 🔊

	In the past	In the present	In the future
1. shorter humans	☐	☐	☐
2. better food and medicine	☐	☐	☐
3. longer life	☐	☐	☐
4. higher body temperature	☐	☐	☐
5. lower body temperature	☐	☐	☐
6. weaker humans	☐	☐	☐
7. larger brains	☐	☐	☐
8. double the population	☐	☐	☐

D FOCUSED LISTENING Listen to these sentences from the conversation. Write the exact numbers you hear. 🔊

1. During that period, people only lived to be about _____ years old. Now, the average age is _____.

2. For example, women in many places will probably live to be _____ years old by the year _____.

3. He thinks humans will someday live to around _____ years!

4. In past centuries, the average human temperature was _____ degrees Fahrenheit. But at the moment, the average temperature of a human body is _____ degrees.

5. They think it will continue to fall by about, let me see, _____ degrees Fahrenheit every ten years.

CRITICAL THINKING Question and Check What You Hear

When you hear facts and figures, it's always important to question the information. Sometimes you can be sure the information is 100% true, but sometimes you are less certain. In fact, things you read or hear on the Internet may not be true at all. It's always a good idea to check the information in other sources, such as reliable websites or books in the library, or you could ask an expert.

E With a group, discuss the information from the conversation. For each statement below, decide if you all think it is: | Critical Thinking

a. definitely true   b. possibly true, but you're not sure   c. probably not true

1. _____ The average human was a foot shorter a hundred years ago.
2. _____ People are taller nowadays because of better food and medicine.
3. _____ Someday, humans will live to around 130 years.
4. _____ Human body temperature is lower.
5. _____ People are weaker because we do less physical work.
6. _____ The human brain will continue to get smaller.
7. _____ Technology will make more decisions for us and it will become more intelligent.

F Where could you check the information in exercise E? Discuss different sources with your group such as a website, a book, or an expert.

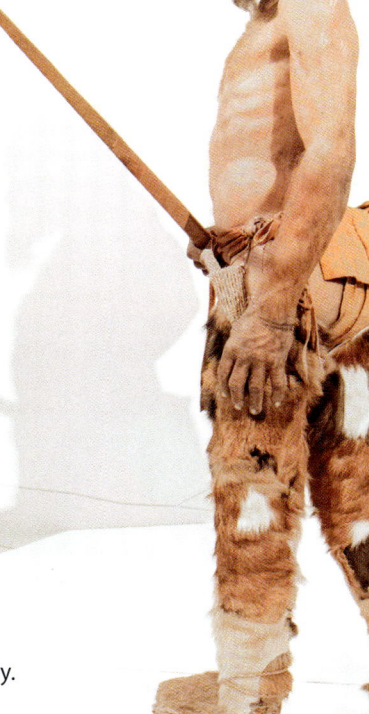

Ötzi, also called the Iceman, lived around 3300 BCE. This model of him is in the South Tyrol Museum of Archaeology in Bolzano, Italy.

A Speaking

Critical Thinking

A IDENTIFY Look at the photos and discuss the questions as a class.

1. What technology does each photo show? How does the technology help people?
2. How do you feel about using technology in this way?

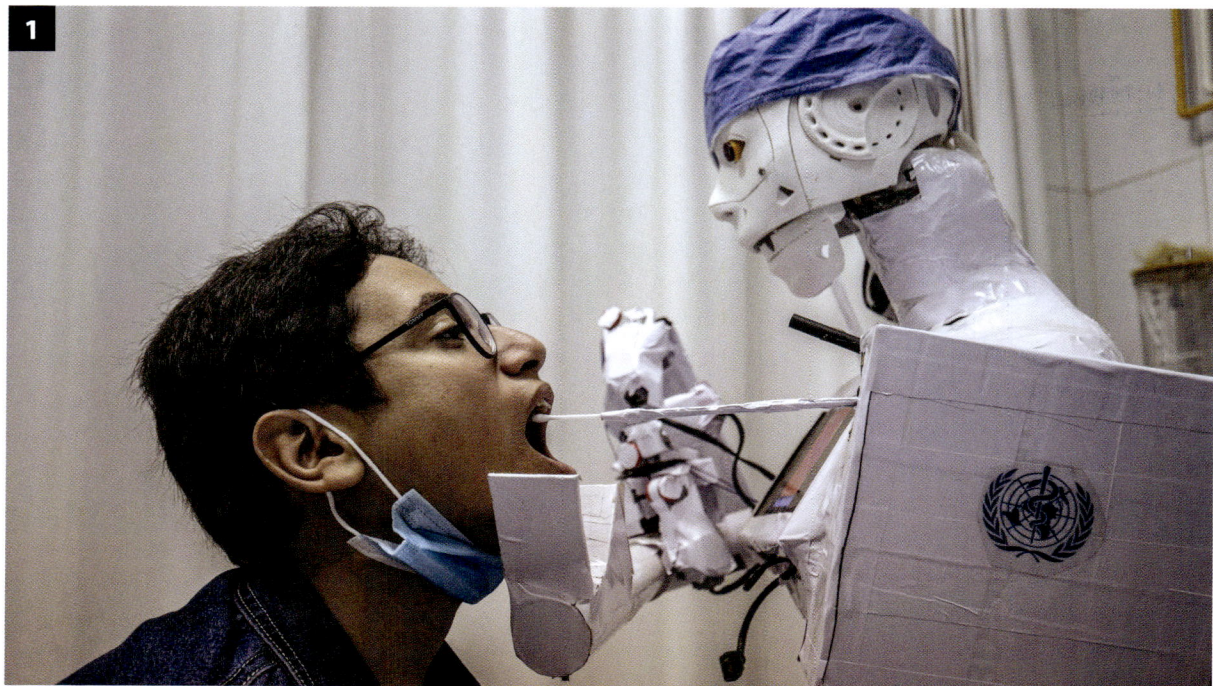

GRAMMAR FOR SPEAKING *Will* for Predictions; Adverbs of Certainty

Will for Predictions

We use *will* or *won't* + base verb to make predictions.

In 20 years, robots **will be** doctors.
In the future, we **won't use** cell phones.

A: **Will** we **live** longer in the future?
B: Yes, we **will**. / No, we **won't**.

A: **Where will** you **live** in 20 years?
B: I don't know!

Adverbs of Certainty: *Possibly, Probably, Definitely,* and *Certainly*

We can use adverbs of certainty after *will* and before *won't*.

Robots **will** <u>probably</u> **(not) be** doctors someday.
I <u>definitely</u> **won't become** a doctor.

We can also use adverbs of certainty to reply in conversations.

A: **Will** you **become** a schoolteacher?
B: <u>Possibly</u>. Or I'll work in a university.

B Work with a partner and take turns. Unscramble the predictions and say the sentences.

1. find / a cure / will / scientists / for cancer
2. live / humans / won't / other planets / on
3. computer technology / will / have / inside / our bodies / we
4. most of / machines and robots / will / do / our work
5. humans / won't / physical exercise / a lot of / do
6. will / there / one / be / world language
7. people / cars / won't / to travel / anymore / use
8. will / teach / all universities / online / not in buildings

C Choose FOUR predictions from exercise B. How much do you agree or disagree with them? Rewrite them *with will/won't* and an adverb of certainty.

1. _____
2. _____
3. _____
4. _____

D **ARGUE** Work with a partner. Share your sentences from exercise C and compare your predictions. Give reasons for your predictions.

| Critical Thinking

A: Scientists will probably find a cure for cancer.
B: I disagree. In my opinion, they probably won't find a cure for cancer. . . .

SPEAKING SKILL   Talk about Possibilities

We can use these adverbs and expressions to talk about possibilities. The language we choose shows how certain we are that something is true.

Ask about possibilities	**Respond**	
How certain are you . . . ?	Definitely. / I'm (very) certain that . . .	100%
Is it possible that you will . . . ?	Probably. / I'm fairly sure that . . .	75%
Do you think that . . . ?	Maybe. / It's possible, (but . . .)	50%
How likely is it that . . . ?	I doubt that . . .	25%

E Match the questions to the responses. Then practice the conversations with a partner.

1. How certain are you about your future career? _____
2. Is it possible that you will become a doctor? _____
3. Do you think you'll live in other countries someday? _____
4. How likely is it that you will do the same job for your whole life? _____

a. Definitely. I love visiting new places and learning new languages.
b. Maybe. I'm interested in medicine, and I like helping people.
c. I'm fairly sure that I want to be a nurse.
d. Oh, I doubt that I'll do that. I like change!

F **PERSONALIZE** Work with the same partner and take turns. Ask the four questions in exercise E. Give your own answers.

Critical Thinking

G **RATE** Read the questions. How possible is each situation? Write a percentage in the chart. For example: 50% (= It's possible, but . . .). Then write one more question of your own.

Future possibilities	You	Your partner
1. In the future, will we have small cell phones inside our brains?	%	%
2. Is it possible that students will stay in school until they are 25?	%	%
3. How likely is it that humans will stop eating meat?	%	%
4. Do you think artificial intelligence will replace artists?	%	%
5. Is it possible that there will be no countries or borders someday?	%	%
6.	%	%

H Work with a partner and take turns. Ask the questions from exercise G. Respond and discuss possibilities. Give reasons for your answers.

A: In the future, will we have small cell phones inside our brains?
B: No, I doubt we will ever have phones in our brains.

How certain is your partner? Write a percentage for them. For example: *Yes, I'm fairly sure.* = 75%

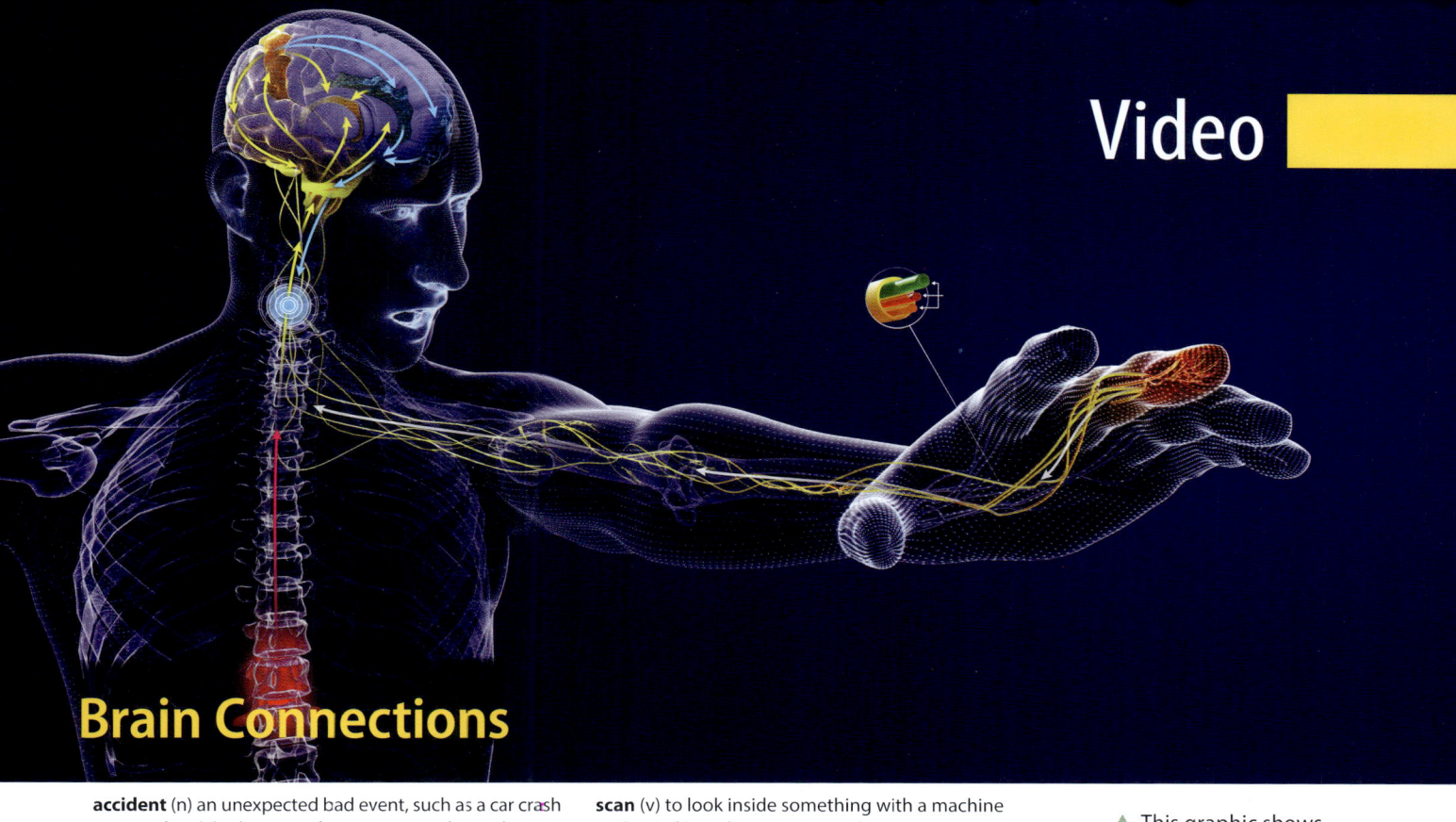

Video

Brain Connections

accident (n) an unexpected bad event, such as a car crash
connection (n) when two things are joined together
scan (v) to look inside something with a machine
active (adj) working in a normal way

▲ This graphic shows how the body sends information about the world to the brain.

A Watch the video and complete these sentences with ONE word. ▶

1. Senses send information to different parts of the _____.
2. When a sense is not very strong, we can use _____ to help us.
3. When we lose a sense, connections in the brain get _____.
4. In addition, _____ connections can grow in the brain.

B Which sentences are true and which are false? Choose T or F. Then watch the video and check your ideas. Correct the false sentences. ▶

1. There are six basic senses.   T   F
2. The brain receives information from the senses.   T   F
3. People can lose a sense over long periods of time or suddenly.   T   F
4. A blind person's hearing can improve.   T   F
5. In deaf people, the part of the brain for hearing is not active.   T   F
6. Scientists now know almost everything about the brain.   T   F

C **PERSONALIZE** Which do you think is your strongest and most important sense? Why? Discuss your ideas with a partner.

THE HUMAN BODY

B Vocabulary

A Listen and repeat. Check (✓) any words you already know. 🔊

| benefit (n) | cause (v) | disease (n) | improve (v) | mental (adj) |
| blood (n) | control (v) | feed (v) | lead to (v phr) | protect (v) |

B **MEANING FROM CONTEXT** Listen and write the correct form of the words from exercise A. Then think about the meaning of each word. 🔊

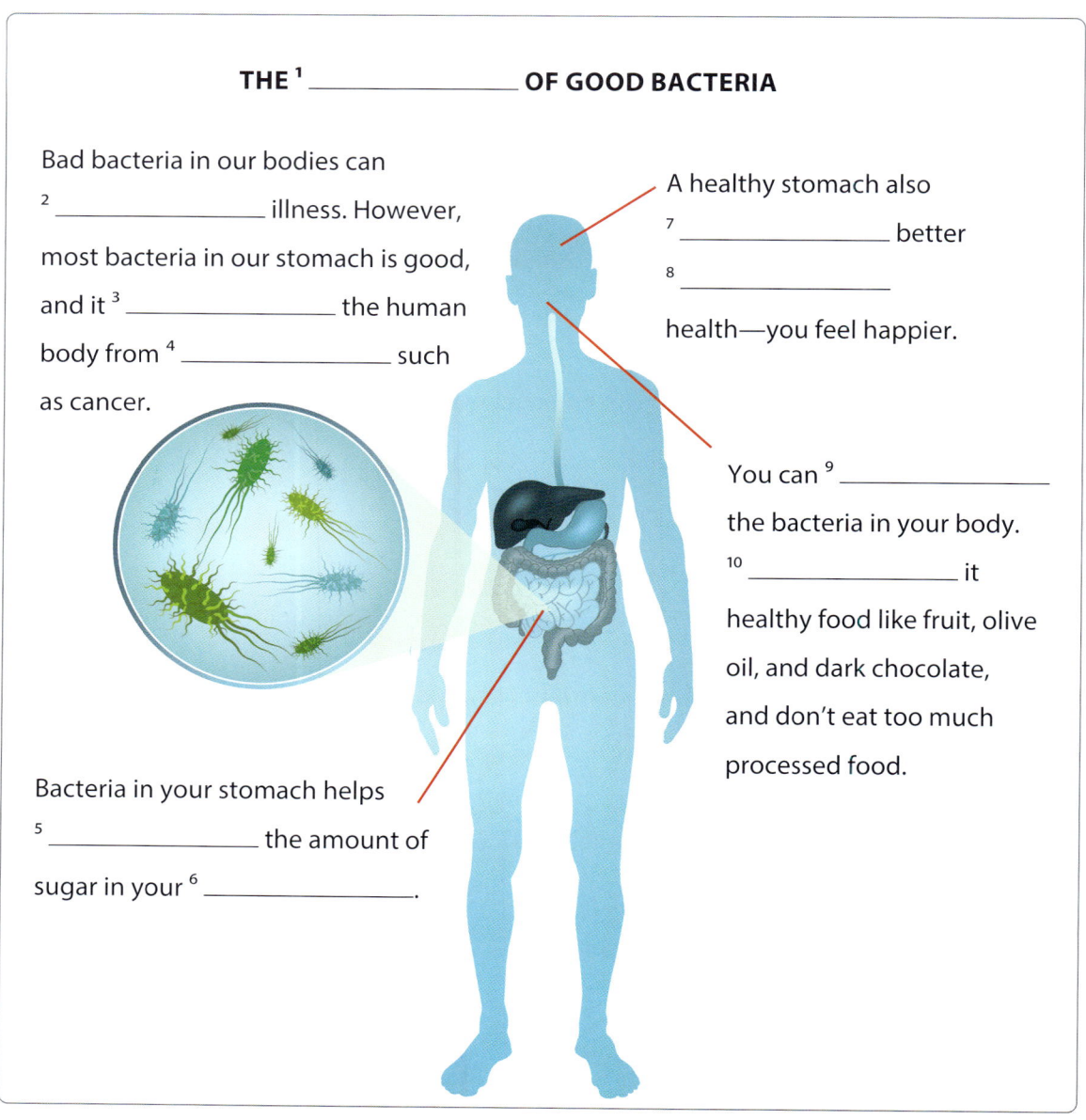

THE ¹_____ OF GOOD BACTERIA

Bad bacteria in our bodies can ²_____ illness. However, most bacteria in our stomach is good, and it ³_____ the human body from ⁴_____ such as cancer.

A healthy stomach also ⁷_____ better ⁸_____ health—you feel happier.

You can ⁹_____ the bacteria in your body. ¹⁰_____ it healthy food like fruit, olive oil, and dark chocolate, and don't eat too much processed food.

Bacteria in your stomach helps ⁵_____ the amount of sugar in your ⁶_____.

132 UNIT 7 LESSON B

C First, choose the correct words to complete this quiz. Then work with a partner and take the quiz. How many questions can you answer correctly?

QUIZ: HEALTH AND THE HUMAN BODY

1. How many liters of **(blood / disease)** are in your body?
   a. about 3
   b. about 5
   c. about 7

2. Which part of the body **(controls / feeds)** the movement of your blood?
   a. stomach
   b. brain
   c. heart

3. Which part of the body controls your **(mental / memorable)** health?
   a. stomach
   b. brain
   c. blood

4. Which activity **(leads to / improves)** your mental health?
   a. any type of physical exercise
   b. looking at social media
   c. eating fast food

5. How many different types of stomach bacteria **(protect / cause)** your body?
   a. more than one hundred
   b. more than a thousand
   c. more than a million

6. To promote good bacteria, which should you do every day?
   a. **(Feed / Control)** the bacteria a lot of fruit.
   b. Buy food with bacteria in it.
   c. Don't exercise too much.

7. What is cancer?
   a. a type of blood
   b. a type of bacteria
   c. a type of disease

D **CREATE** Work with a partner. Write two more quiz questions about the human body (with *a, b, c* answers). Then join another pair and take turns. Ask and answer your questions.

Critical Thinking

B Listening: The Benefits of Bacteria

Critical Thinking

A **PREDICT** You are going to listen to a presentation about the benefits of bacteria. Work with a partner. Look at the three sets of words. Try to predict what the lecturer will say about these words. What is the connection between the words?

```
        bacteria                 bacteria              bacteria
         /    \                     |                     |
       bad   protect              stomach           healthy eating
     disease  good                 sugar                sleep
                                   blood          physical exercise
```

> Bad bacteria can lead to diseases . . .

B **MAIN IDEAS** Listen to the first part of the presentation. Check (✓) the THREE topics the lecturer plans to talk about. 🔊

1. ☐ everything your body needs for good health
2. ☐ benefits of good bacteria
3. ☐ similarities between good and bad bacteria
4. ☐ bacteria in your stomach
5. ☐ how to help the good bacteria in your body
6. ☐ how to make bad bacteria into good bacteria

C Watch or listen to the presentation. Take notes about the words in exercise A. Were your predictions about the words correct? 🔊 ▶

NOTE-TAKING SKILL   Use an Outline

When you listen to a lecture or presentation, you can organize your notes using an outline. A basic outline includes the main ideas and supporting details. You can use letters and numbers to organize the main ideas and supporting details.

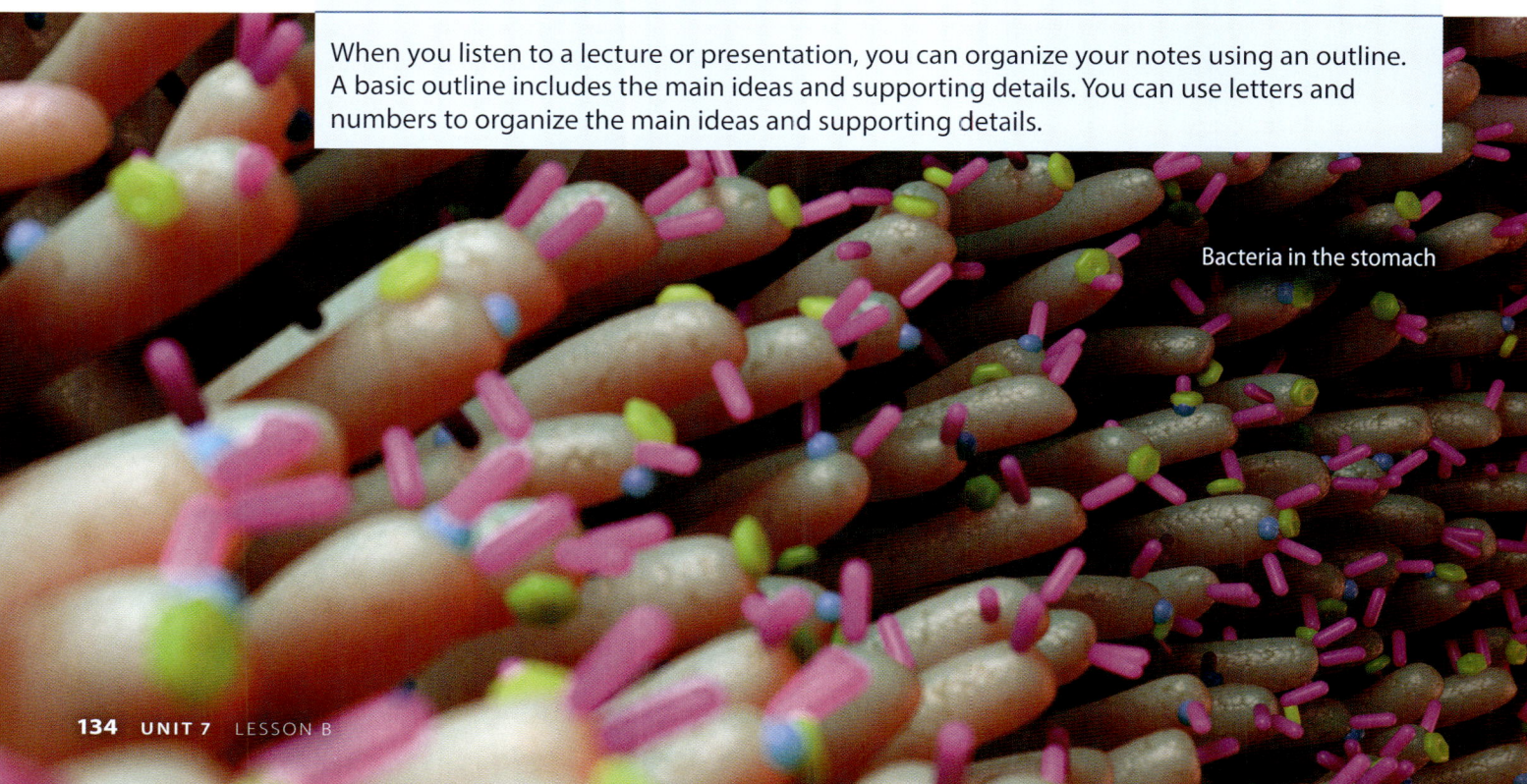

Bacteria in the stomach

D DETAILS Watch or listen again. Complete the notes with ONE or TWO words. 🔊 ▶

The Benefits of Bacteria

1. Difference between good and bad bacteria
   a. Bad bacteria causes different _____ in humans and animals.
   b. Good bacteria is important for the _____ and health

2. Bacteria in stomach
   a. Good stomach bacteria _____ from diseases.
   b. Bacteria in adult stomachs can prevent _____ like _____.
   c. Stomach bacteria helps control _____ in your blood.
   d. Some scientists believe stomach bacteria sends positive _____ to your _____.

3. Help bacteria with a healthy lifestyle.
   a. Don't eat the _____ every day.
   b. Food for good bacteria = fruit, yogurt, olive oil, _____
   c. Sleep 7 to 8 hours a night at _____.
   d. Do 30 minutes of _____ every day.

PRONUNCIATION   Recognize Reduced Forms

🔊 In everyday speech, some speakers reduce certain verb forms, such as *will* and *going to*. It's important to recognize these forms so you can understand a speaker's ideas.

You read or write:	You may hear:
Bad bacteria **will** cause diseases. →	Bad **bacteria'll** cause disease.
But we're **going to** look at the benefits. →	But we're **gonna** look at the benefits.

E Listen to sentences from the presentation that have reduced forms. Write the full forms of the TWO or THREE missing words. Then practice the sentences and try to say the reduced forms. 🔊

1. Today _____ talk about something your body really needs.
2. _____ explore the benefits of bacteria.
3. So, a healthy _____ send positive messages to your brain.
4. And _____ make you happier.
5. Now _____ tell you how to improve your stomach bacteria.

F PERSONALIZE Think about the presentation and discuss these questions with a partner.

1. Before this presentation, did you think all bacteria were bad?
2. Do you think your brain is happier when your stomach is happy?

B Speaking

GRAMMAR FOR SPEAKING   Will and Be Going To

We can use *will* or *be going to* + base verb to **make predictions** about the future.
> I think you**'ll get** a job as a doctor in the future.
> I think you**'re going to be** a doctor when you grow up.

We usually use *be going to* + base verb to **talk about future plans or intentions**.
> I**'m going to study** medicine. Then I**'m going to work** in a hospital.

We usually use *will* + base verb to **make a decision at the time of speaking** (such as a promise to do something).
> A: I don't understand this homework.
> B: Don't worry. I**'ll help** you.

A Choose the correct verb forms in these conversations. Both verb forms are possible in ONE conversation. Listen and check. Then practice the conversations with a partner.

1. A: I have to complete this college application. It's so hard!
   B: Don't worry. I ('ll help / 'm going to help) you.
   A: Really? That'd be great.

2. A: What (will you study / are you going to study) in college?
   B: Biology. I ('ll be / 'm going to be) a doctor.
   A: That's fantastic! Good luck!

3. A: What time do you finish work at the hospital tonight?
   B: At midnight! I ('ll be / 'm going to be) so tired.
   A: Definitely!

4. A: Hi Marek. I'm at the train station. How do I get to your house?
   B: Hi Sarah. Stay there. I ('ll / 'm going to) drive there and meet you.
   A: Oh, thanks!

Critical Thinking

B **ANALYZE** Think about the uses of *will* and be *going to* in exercise A. In which conversation(s) (1-4) does a person:

a. _____ make a prediction?
b. _____ talk about a future plan or intention?
c. _____ make a decision at the time of speaking?

Critical Thinking

C **CREATE** Work with a partner. Write three short conversations with these sentences. Then join another pair and present your conversations.

1. One day I'm going to do it!
2. Don't worry. I'll pay for it.
3. It'll probably arrive tomorrow morning.

Students celebrate their graduation in Costa Mesa, California, USA.

D Look at the timeline that shows John's plans. Complete the sentences below with the correct verb forms. Then share your sentences with a partner.

Past → → → → → → → → → → → Future

- **A week from now:** take his final exams
- **Someday:** get married and have children
- **Present:** taking classes
- **A month from now:** graduate
- **A year from now:** move back to Europe

1. Right now, John _____ at college.
2. In a week, he _____.
3. Then in a month, he _____.
4. In a year, John _____ where his family lives.
5. Someday in the future, perhaps John _____.

E **PERSONALIZE** Complete this timeline for you. Write your plans.

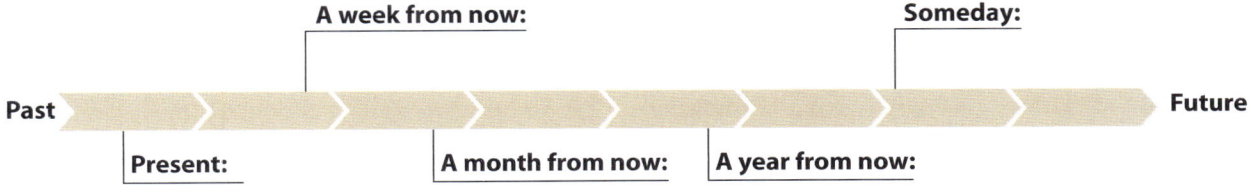

F Work with a group. Take turns. Present and describe your timeline.

> *Right now, I'm at school, but in a week, I'm going to go on vacation!*

THE HUMAN BODY **137**

Review

SELF-ASSESS

How well can you . . . ?	Very well.	OK.	I need improvement.
use the key vocabulary	☐	☐	☐
recognize reduced forms	☐	☐	☐
use *will* and *be going to*	☐	☐	☐
talk about possibilities	☐	☐	☐

A VOCABULARY Choose the correct word in each sentence.

1. I always (feed / cause) my cat at eight o'clock.
2. There's (bone / blood) on your face. Did you cut yourself?
3. You have a very healthy (lifestyle / disease).
4. Regular physical exercise can (improve / lead to) your health.
5. What's the main (period / benefit) of good bacteria?

B PRONUNCIATION Listen to sentences using reduced and full forms. Check (✓) the sentence you hear. 🔊

1. a. ☐ English lessons'll start tomorrow.
   b. ☐ English lessons will start tomorrow.
2. a. ☐ We're gonna pass this exam.
   b. ☐ We're going to pass this exam.
3. a. ☐ What'll you do after school?
   b. ☐ What will you do after school?
4. a. ☐ My daughter's gonna study biology.
   b. ☐ My daughter's going to study biology.

C GRAMMAR Find and correct the mistake in each sentence.

1. I'll to visit the doctor tomorrow.
2. We won't probably go out tonight.
3. She going to be a doctor.
4. I promise I'll calling you back later.
5. What you going to do when you leave college?

D SPEAKING SKILL Say answers to these questions. Use expressions from the box and include reasons.

> I'm very certain that . . .   Probably.   I'm fairly sure that . . .   I doubt that . . .   Maybe.

1. How certain are you that you'll pass all your exams this year?
2. Is it likely that you'll have more than one career in the future?

RE-ASSESS What skills or language do you still need help with?

Final Tasks

OPTION 1 Survey classmates about the future

A Interview your classmates about their futures. Use the words in the survey. If they answer, "Definitely / probably / possibly . . . ," ask for a reason and write your classmate's name.

A: Do you think you'll start a new kind of exercise this year?
B: Probably, because I want to get in better shape.

If they answer, "No, I (definitely / probably / possibly) won't," ask another person. You have ten minutes. Try to write names in every square.

start a new kind of exercise this year	go to college	learn to drive a car	move to a new home in the next five years
pass your exams this year	go camping for a vacation	learn another language someday	do some volunteer work this year
write a book someday	become famous someday	learn to make a new dish this week	travel to another country in the next year
go out with friends this weekend	try a new musical instrument	become a vegetarian someday	run a marathon

▼ Yoga is good physical exercise, and it helps decrease stress.

See Unit 7 Rubric in the Appendix.

OPTION 2 Discuss pros and cons of future situations

A MODEL Listen to a group discussion and answer the questions. Choose one or more answers for each question. 🔊

1. What topic(s) does Yoko introduce?
   a. Robots will do our jobs.
   b. Robots will drive cars.
   c. Robots will work in factories.

2. What pros does Hasan talk about?
   a. Robots are better at everyday jobs.
   b. Humans won't have to do boring jobs.
   c. Humans will have more free time.

3. What cons does Claudia describe?
   a. Humans will get bored.
   b. Humans won't earn money.
   c. Robots will stop working sometimes.

COLLABORATION SKILL   Participate in a Group Discussion

Here are some things you should remember to do in an academic or work discussion.

As an individual, make sure you:
- give your honest opinion
- agree or disagree politely
- listen carefully
- encourage others

As a group, make sure everyone:
- understands the goal
- participates

📶 **ONLINE** If you're having trouble keeping a conversation going, you can agree to pass the conversation. After you finish speaking, name someone else to take a turn.

B PLAN Complete the chart. How likely do you think each statement is? Write *definitely*, *probably*, *maybe*, or *probably not*. Then write one pro and one con for each prediction.

Statement	How likely?	Pros	Cons
Drones will transport everything to people's homes, such as shopping and medicine.			
You'll always meet human doctors online, and there will be robots in hospitals.			
The average human will live to 150 years of age or longer.			

C DISCUSS Work with a group of three. Each group member introduces one of the statements from exercise B and asks the others for ideas. Answer these questions:
- How likely is each future situation?
- What are the pros and cons of each situation for people and communities? Are there more pros or more cons?

D REPORT As a group, report back to the class about one of the topics you discussed. How likely is the prediction? How do you think it could affect the world?

LEARN TO LOVE ART 8

Artist Mike De Butts created this sculpture in Southbank Centre, London, U.K., with a group of other artists. It's made from cloth from around the world, and it's called *Under The Baobab Tree*. The artists say that the sculpture represents the way we live in cities.

IN THIS UNIT, YOU WILL:
- Watch or listen to a class discussion about temporary art
- Watch a video about making art from recycled glass
- Listen to a radio program about a famous musician
- Describe an image or book
  OR Have a class debate about art

THINK AND DISCUSS:
1. Read the caption. Describe the photo.
2. Do you understand the artists' message?
3. Do you enjoy art? What kind of art do you like?

EXPLORE THE THEME

Read the information. Then discuss the questions.

1. When you look at art, do you worry about saying the right thing?
2. Look at the photo and follow the steps below. What are your answers to the questions in steps 2–4?
3. Do you think these steps helped you enjoy the art? Why or why not?

How to Look at and Discuss Art

You don't have to be an artist to appreciate art. Here are a few steps to help you enjoy looking at art.

1. Relax. Don't worry about saying the right thing. Your honest opinion is important. Just remember to be polite!
2. Take a close look. What is the subject of the art? What objects appear in the art? Notice the materials and colors the artist used.
3. How does the art make you feel—happy, sad, nervous, or angry? Do you think the artist has a message?
4. Step back and put it all together. What do you think? Did the art help you think about something in a new way?

Artist Mark Lewis Wagner stands on his chalk drawing in Alameda, California, USA. Wagner's drawing set a Guinness World Record for the largest chalk art by a single artist.

A Vocabulary

A Listen and repeat. Check (✓) any words you already know. 🔊

constantly (adv)	forever (adv)	material (n)	public (adj)	solid (adj)
disappear (v)	last (v)	permanent (adj)	sculpture (n)	temporary (adj)

B **MEANING FROM CONTEXT** Listen and write the correct form of the words from exercise A. Then think about the meaning of each word. 🔊

ARTIST PROFILE: JASON DECAIRES TAYLOR

There's a big difference between Jason deCaires Taylor's art and the art you usually see in museums. Taylor is famous for his ¹_____ in underwater locations and ²_____ spaces around the world. Some of his exhibits are ³_____, but most are ⁴_____. He's interested in making art that won't ⁵_____ and will ⁶_____ ⁷_____. In his project called *The Silent Evolution*, Taylor created sculptures of more than 400 people and put them on the ocean floor near Cancún. The sculptures are made from a heavy and ⁸_____ ⁹_____: cement. However, they are ¹⁰_____ changing as a result of sea animals and plants who make their homes on the sculptures. It isn't easy for people to see the sculptures, but it is a special experience to see them in person.

C Write each word from exercise A next to its definition.

1. _____ (n) something (e.g., stone, glass) you use to make something else
2. _____ (v) to continue for a period of time
3. _____ (adv) for all time
4. _____ (adj) lasting forever or for all time
5. _____ (adj) hard or firm, not soft
6. _____ (v) to stop existing
7. _____ (adj) for everyone's use, not private
8. _____ (adj) lasting only a short time
9. _____ (n) a work of art made from stone, wood, or other materials
10. _____ (adv) always or very often

VOCABULARY SKILL Collocations with Prepositions

Collocations are words that are frequently used together. Certain prepositions often come after certain verbs, adjectives, and nouns.

Verb + preposition	Adjective + preposition	Noun + preposition
think of	good at	reason for
think about	important for	reason to

D Find these verbs, adjectives, and nouns in exercise B. Write the preposition that comes after them.

1. difference _____
2. easy _____
3. famous _____
4. interested _____
5. made _____
6. result _____

E **PERSONALIZE** Complete these questions with prepositions. Then ask and answer the questions with a partner.

1. Are you interested _____ art? Do you think art galleries are important _____ a city? Why? Why not?
2. Do you know the name of an artist? What are they famous _____?
3. Are you good _____ art? What **materials** do you make it _____?
4. What do you think _____ the **sculptures** by Jason deCaires Taylor? Would you like to see them?

The sculpture *The Silent Evolution* by Jason deCaires Taylor is underwater near Cancún, Mexico.

A Listening Temporary Art

Critical Thinking

A PREDICT Look at the photo of the art by Jim Denevan. Discuss these questions.

1. Where is the art? What is it made from?
2. Why is the art temporary?
3. Do you think many people see Jim's art? Explain.

B MAIN IDEAS Watch or listen to a discussion with a professor and some students. Choose the correct answers. 🔊 ▶

1. Which statement about temporary art is true?
   a. It lasts a long time.
   b. It doesn't last long.
   c. You often see it in galleries.

2. Which TWO things make temporary art different from permanent art?
   a. It's cheaper to show.
   b. It brings people together.
   c. You often see it outdoors.

3. Why is temporary art good for the artists?
   a. They can live and work in cities.
   b. It's easier to make than permanent art.
   c. They make money right away.

C DETAILS Listen to part of the discussion again. Complete the notes about each type of temporary art with ONE or TWO words. 🔊

Type of art: _____snow sculpture_____

Reason the art is temporary: It won't [1]_____ in the [2]_____

Location: [3]_____

Location: _____Madrid, Spain_____

Type of art: chalk [4]_____

Reason the art is temporary: [5]_____ and people's feet

Location: _____beach_____

Type of art: [6]_____

Name of artist: _____Jim Denevan_____

How he works: Works in [7]_____ with [8]_____ around him

Reason the art is temporary: [9]_____ and the [10]_____

▲ A sand drawing by artist Jim Denevan in Cannon Beach, Oregon, USA.

LISTENING SKILL Recognize Opinions

When people talk about subjects like art and music, they often give their opinion. Listen for:

Expressions: *Personally, I (don't) think* this music is very good.
Positive adjectives: That's a **beautiful** sculpture. It's so real!
Negative adjectives: I think that painting is **awful**. It looks like a child painted it.

Sometimes the speaker also adds emphasis by stressing certain words or using full word forms.

That's an **incredible** drawing!   I would **not** want to see this in a museum.

D Listen to two parts of the discussion. Decide if the speaker has a positive or negative opinion. Note the words that helped you identify the opinion. 🔊

Part 1
1. The first student has a (positive / negative) opinion of Picasso's art.
2. The second student has a (positive / negative) opinion of Frida Kahlo's art.
3. The second student has a (positive / negative) opinion of Andy Warhol's art.

Part 2
4. The first student has a (positive / negative) opinion of temporary art.
5. The second student has a (positive / negative) opinion of temporary art.

CRITICAL THINKING Synthesize

When you *synthesize* information, you combine ideas from two or more sources. This skill can help you connect ideas and better understand a topic.

E Think about the connection between Jason deCaires Taylor's art in Vocabulary A and the information from the discussion. Discuss these questions with a group.

| Critical Thinking

1. How is Taylor's work similar to and different from the temporary art in the discussion?
2. Do you know any other artists? Is their art permanent or temporary?
3. What kind of temporary art could you find:

- on a beach?
- at the top of a mountain?
- in a city park?
- on a lake or river?

LEARN TO LOVE ART **147**

A Speaking

GRAMMAR FOR SPEAKING   Modals of Present Possibility

Use the modals *might, may,* or *could* + base verb to say that you think something is possible (but you are not certain).

> It **might be** a painting by Picasso.
> The sculpture is strange. It **may be** a human body, but I'm not sure.
> I love this painting, but it **could be** too large for my room.

When you are certain that something is or is not possible, use *must* or *can't* + base verb.

> You **must recognize** this painting. It's very famous.
> It **can't be** a painting by Picasso because it's from this century.

A Look at the photo. Listen and read the conversation. Underline the SIX modals of possibility. How certain is the speaker in each sentence? Check (✓) the correct answer.

Conversation	Very Certain	Possible
A: Is that a real animal?		
B: ¹No, it can't be.	☐	☐
²But it could be a sculpture.	☐	☐
A: ³Wait! It must be someone's hand. There's a thumb and fingers.	☐	☐
B: ⁴You're right. It might be some kind of art.	☐	☐
⁵I think it may be a painting of a snake on a hand.	☐	☐
A: ⁶Could it be for a special occasion?	☐	☐
B: Maybe.		

◀ This image shows a snake painted on a hand. Artist Guido Daniele paints pictures of birds, fish, and other animals on people's hands.

B Practice the conversation in exercise A with a partner. Then switch roles and practice it again.

148   UNIT 8   LESSON A

C **SOLVE** Look at parts of three more pieces of art. Practice the conversation below using your own ideas. Then look at the bottom of the next page to check your ideas.

Critical Thinking

A: What animal do you think this is?
B: Well, it could...
A: Yes, or it might...
B: That's an interesting idea.
A: But it can't... because...
B: You're right. It must...

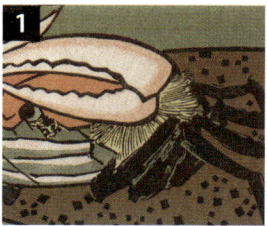  

SPEAKING SKILL   Express Degrees of Uncertainty

When we aren't sure about something, we can say we are not certain with:
- modals of possibility: *could, might, may*
- adverbs: *perhaps, maybe, possibly*
- expressions: *It's a bit / sort of / kind of ..., but I'm not sure/certain.*

   It **could** be a cat, **but I'm not sure. Possibly** it's a bird.
   It **might** be **a sort of** fish, **but I'm not certain**.

D Complete a student's description of the painting below with words from the box.

| bit | certain | maybe | might | must | sort |

This picture ¹_____ be outside at night because there are stars in the sky. The café in the street and the houses look ²_____ of old. ³_____ it's a city like Paris. I also think it ⁴_____ be a painting by Vincent Van Gogh, but I'm not ⁵_____. I've seen other paintings by Van Gogh, and it looks a ⁶_____ like them.

LEARN TO LOVE ART 149

Critical Thinking | **E** **INTERPRET** Work with a partner and look at two more pictures of places. Take turns talking about the places and use language to express uncertainty. Answer these questions.

1. What type of place do you see?
2. Do you think it's temporary or permanent?
3. Who do you think uses this place? Why?

   > *It must be a bed, but I'm not sure about the room.*

   > *It could be a sort of tent.*

F You are going to play a guessing game. Work with a partner and write three sentences:

- Write two sentences that are TRUE about you both. For example:
  We both have a birthday in January.
- Write one sentence that is UNTRUE, but try to make it sound possible. For example:
  We both have a brother with the same middle name.

Critical Thinking | **G** **SOLVE** Now work with another pair and take turns. Read your sentences from exercise F:

1. For each sentence, the other pair discusses if the sentence is true or untrue.
2. When you have listened to and discussed the three sentences, make a final decision about them. Did you guess correctly?

   > *They say their birthdays are in the same month. That might be true because . . .*

   > *They say that they have a brother with the same middle name. That can't be true!*

Answers to exercise C: Were your guesses correct?

Video

Making Art from Recycled Glass

remove (v) to take something away
kiln (n) a large oven with a high temperature, often used for making pots

melt (v) to make something solid become liquid

▲ This stained glass house in Brooklyn, NY, USA, is made from recycled materials. It is part of the ICON series by artist Tom Fruin.

A Watch the video and put the steps in order they are described (1–5). ▶

a. _____ Clean the windows and cut the glass.
b. _____ Melt the bottle glass in a kiln.
c. _____ Create recycled glass objects.
d. _____ Deliver the old window and bottles.
e. _____ Clean the bottles and remove the top and bottom.

B Watch the video again. Choose the correct answers. In TWO sentences, both answers are correct. ▶

1. The artists work in (London / Liverpool) in England.
2. Electric (cars / trucks) bring windows and glass for the artists to use.
3. The artists put the bottles in water and then remove the (labels / top and bottom) from the bottles.
4. The temperature of the kiln can reach seven hundred and (sixty-six / seventy-six) degrees.
5. The glass from the recycled (windows / bottles) gives the color.
6. The artists create glass objects such as (vases / bowls) and stained glass windows.

C **BRAINSTORM** Discuss these questions with a group. | Critical Thinking

1. What are some other ways you could reuse old glass?
2. Think of three other objects you often throw away. Can you think of ways to reuse these objects? For example, could you use them as art?

LEARN TO LOVE ART 151

B Vocabulary

A **MEANING FROM CONTEXT** Read the sentences. Think about the meaning of the words in blue. Choose the correct word or phrase. Then listen and check your answers.

1. We saved our money for a long time, and now we can **afford** to buy a piano. We (have / don't have) enough money.
2. This musician has a special **style**. Her songs are very (similar to / different from) others.
3. The music is **simple**, so it was (easy / hard) for my son to learn.
4. A **typical** dance from the Dominican Republic is the merengue. Merengue music is so (popular / unusual) that people from many other countries also enjoy it.
5. She's going to **perform** at the Tango Club. You'll have to (download a song / buy a ticket) if you want to hear her.
6. It takes more skill to write **original** music than to play songs by (you / other people).
7. The trumpet can be a loud instrument, but its sound **appeals** to me. I really (like / dislike) it.
8. What's the name of this **piece**? I heard it once in a (museum / concert), but I can't remember.
9. They're playing at a classical music competition. There are several **awards** for the (best / worst) musicians.
10. The ukulele is a traditional **instrument** in Hawaii. It's good for playing (songs / sports).

B Listen and repeat the words from exercise A.

▼ Children in Hawaii play ukuleles at the 30th Annual Ukulele Festival, Hawaii, USA.

152 UNIT 8 LESSON B

C Complete the article with SEVEN of the words in blue from exercise A. Use the correct form.

THE UKULELE: THE SOUND OF HAWAII

In the late 1800s, a small musical ¹_____ similar to the guitar arrived in Hawaii with immigrants from Portugal. Hawaiians made a few changes and created the ukulele. The ukulele ²_____ to many people because it isn't expensive and it's fairly ³_____ to play. Many parents can ⁴_____ to buy ukuleles, so schoolchildren in Hawaii learn to play traditional ⁵_____ in their music classes. In addition, more adults are playing the instrument these days and learning to ⁶_____ many different ⁷_____ of music, including rock and pop.

D Complete the conversations with words from the box. Listen and check your answers. Then practice the conversations with a partner. 🔊

| afford | appeal | award | instrument | piece | style | typical |

1. A: I can't remember the name of this song, but I think it's from Ireland.
   B: How do you know?
   A: The ¹_____ of the music sounds Irish. Also, it has a tin whistle. That's a traditional ²_____ with six holes. It's ³_____ in old Irish music.

2. A: I love this ⁴_____ of music!
   B: It doesn't ⁵_____ to me. I prefer calmer music.

3. A: This album won an ⁶_____. Let's buy it.
   B: I can't ⁷_____ it. I don't have enough money.

E Listen to four styles of music and answer the questions for each style in the chart. Then compare your answers with a partner. 🔊

	Which instruments can you hear? (e.g., guitar, drums, piano, saxophone)	What style is the music? (e.g., rock, classical, jazz)	Does the music appeal to you? Why? Why not?
1.			
2.			
3.			
4.			

B Listening — Jake Shimabukuro

Critical Thinking

A DESCRIBE Look at the photo and read the caption. Then discuss the questions.

1. What information do you know about the man in the photo?

   ☐ age   ☐ job   ☐ nationality

2. What does the expression on the man's face tell you?
3. Would you like to hear this man's music? Why? Why not?

B MAIN IDEAS Listen to the radio program. Choose the speaker's main purpose.

The speaker's main purpose is:

a. To entertain the audience with a funny story
b. To tell the audience about a musician
c. To persuade the audience to buy an album
d. To teach the audience about Hawaiian culture

C DETAILS Listen again. Choose the correct words in these sentences. In THREE sentences, both answers are correct.

1. The host (often plays / doesn't often play) ukulele music on her radio program.
2. Jake Shimabukuro's (mother / father) started teaching him the ukulele when he was four.
3. As a teenager, he performed at a (local café / theater) in Honolulu.
4. Jake plays (songs by other musicians / his own songs).
5. Jake also writes music for (other ukulele performers / film and TV).
6. He plays (on his own / with other musicians).
7. He plays (one style / many styles) of music.
8. The host introduces a song that (Jake performed online / made Jake famous).

PRONUNCIATION Recognize Connected Speech

🔊 Sometimes when people speak, two words can sound like one word. If the first word ends with a consonant sound and the next word starts with a vowel sound, they can sound connected. You need to be able to recognize the sounds to understand the meaning.

Separate	**Connected**
Jake is from Hawaii.	*Jake is from Hawaii.*
He lives in Honolulu.	*He lives in Honolulu.*
He was born in 1976.	*He was born in 1976.*

Jake Shimabukuro is a famous ukulele player from Hawaii. He performs his music around the world.

D Look at these sentences and mark the connected words. Then listen and check. 🔊

1. Jake often performs concerts.
2. He plays all over the world.
3. He performed at a local club.
4. Jake also writes his own songs.
5. An ukulele isn't expensive.
6. Jake won an award in 2012.

E **FOCUSED LISTENING** Listen and complete this part of the radio program. Write the TWO connected words you hear. 🔊

Often, Jake plays on ¹_____, but sometimes he plays with other musicians. For example, on the album *Peace Love Ukulele*, Jake ²_____ ukulele with a drummer and a bass guitar player. ³_____ album called *Grand Ukulele*, he played ⁴_____ orchestra. And his latest album is called *Jake and Friends*. He plays with a lot ⁵_____ famous musicians with different styles of music.

F Practice reading the paragraph in exercise E aloud. Try using connected speech. When you are ready, work with a partner and take turns reading the text.

LEARN TO LOVE ART   **155**

B Speaking

GRAMMAR FOR SPEAKING   Modals and Questions for Suggestions

You can use *should, could, might,* and *let's* + base verb to make suggestions.

You **should watch** this TV show. It's great.   You **might like** this book.
We **could go** to a concert tonight.   **Let's watch** a movie this evening.

With *could, should,* and *might,* we sometimes add the words *maybe* and *perhaps.*
Maybe we **should watch** this movie?

You can also use these question forms to make suggestions.
- *How about / What about . . .* + *-ing* verb: **How about going** to a concert?
- *Why don't we* + base verb: **Why don't we watch** a movie?

A Choose the correct words to complete the conversations. Listen and check. Then practice the conversations with a partner. 🔊

1. A: I'm so bored! Why don't we ¹(do / doing) something interesting?
   B: OK. How about ²(play / playing) a game?
   A: No, let's go out somewhere.
   B: We could ³(to go / go) to an art gallery downtown.

2. A: I'm reading a book about the history of my country. You should ⁴(read / reading) it!
   B: Hmm, I prefer fiction. You know, books with good stories and a lot of action.
   A: Maybe you'd ⁵(like / to like) this, then. It's historical, but it has a lot of action.

3. A: Jake Shimabukuro is playing live next week! ⁶(How about / Let's) buy tickets (. / ?)
   B: Sorry, who's playing?
   A: Jake Shimabukuro. He's a musician from Hawaii, and he plays the ukulele.
   B: ⁷(Perhaps / Why don't) you should ask Anna instead (. / ?) I don't think I'd like it.

▼ Two people look at art in a gallery.

B **CREATE** With a partner, choose one of the conversations in exercise A. Write two or three more lines for the discussion and include one more suggestion. Then practice your new conversation.

| Critical Thinking

C Read the first lines from six exchanges. Write the next line with a suggestion. Then work with a partner and take turns saying the sentences. Reply with your suggestions.

1. I don't know the meaning of this word in English.
2. I want to go to see a movie tonight, but it's sold out.
3. I don't have any plans for the weekend.
4. I don't think I have any food in the house.
5. I'm tired of shopping. Can we take a break?
6. I'm bored with this music.

   A: *I don't know the meaning of this word in English.*
   B: *You should look up the word in a dictionary....*

D **PERSONALIZE** Look at the different types of creative arts and entertainment in the chart. Try to think of an example for each one. Write it in the chart and write one reason you liked it.

	Your example / Your reason	Your group's suggestions
Movie		
Book (type of book or author)		
Music (album, song, or musician)		
Artist (painter, a photographer, etc.)		
Online video		
TV series		
Place (e.g., a gallery or museum)		
Other suggestions		

E Work with a group and take turns. Ask for and make suggestions for each type of art or entertainment in exercise D. When you make a suggestion, give your reasons.

A: *Do you have any suggestions for a good movie?*
B: *Yes, you should see... It's great because...*

Write your group's suggestions in the chart. After your class today, why don't you try out one of their suggestions?

LEARN TO LOVE ART

Review

SELF-ASSESS

How well can you . . . ?	Very well.	OK.	I need improvement.
use the key vocabulary	☐	☐	☐
use modals of possibility and questions for suggestions	☐	☐	☐
express degrees of uncertainty	☐	☐	☐

A VOCABULARY Read the questions and write the words from the unit.

1. What *t* word is the opposite of *permanent*? _____
2. A guitar and a piano are types of what *i* word? _____
3. What *a* word can you win? _____
4. What *f* word means for all time? _____
5. What *d* word means you can no longer see something? _____

B GRAMMAR Complete each sentence with the correct form of a verb in the box. Which sentences are about possibility? Which are suggestions? Write *P* or *S* after each sentence.

| be | buy | could | learn | watch | visit |

1. This sculpture might _____ a person or an animal. ____
2. How about _____ this part of the museum? ____
3. Maybe we should _____ tickets for the concert. ____
4. Why don't we _____ the next part of the show? ____
5. It has strings, so it _____ be a type of guitar. ____

C SPEAKING SKILL Complete the description of Jason deCaires Taylor's sculptures (see Vocabulary A). Use words and expressions to soften ideas. Then read the description aloud.

It looks like a ¹k_____ of underwater art gallery, but I'm not ²s_____. ³M_____ the sculptures are made from rocks from the sea, or they ⁴c_____ be rocks that the artist moved to the bottom of the sea. I'm not ⁵c_____.

RE-ASSESS What skills or language do you still need help with?

Final Tasks

OPTION 1 Describe an image or book

A Choose a picture (painting or photograph) or a book you like. Prepare a one-minute description of it. You can use some or all of these expressions:

The picture / book I have chosen today is called . . .
The artist / author is . . .
It shows . . . / It's about . . .
I like it because . . . / I think you should read it because . . .

B Work with a group and take turns. Show your picture or book and give your one-minute description. Afterwards, each person can ask the presenter one question.

> *This is a picture of an artist on the street in Paris, France. He's making a drawing of Paris. There is a painting on the wall behind him. It shows a woman with a camera. She's taking a picture of the city. I like it because . . .*

▼ Paris, France

LEARN TO LOVE ART 159

See Unit 8 Rubric in the Appendix.

OPTION 2 Have a class debate

A MODEL Listen to two different parts of a classroom debate. 🔊

1. What are they debating? Students should study _____ and _____ before subjects like _____ and _____.

2. Do they begin with the arguments for or against? _____

3. What does the second speaker think creativity can solve?
   _____

B ANALYZE THE MODEL Listen again and write the missing words. 🔊

1. OK, today we're going to _____ the following idea . . .
2. We'll begin with the _____ for this statement.
3. In _____, we need scientists to . . .
4. Right. Now we will _____ the arguments against.
5. First, we _____ that creativity is an important skill in the 21st century.
6. Another _____ is that art makes . . .

COLLABORATION SKILL   Debate an Idea

A debate is when an idea has two sides. You have two groups of people: One side is **for** the idea (agrees with it). The other side is **against** the idea (disagrees with it). Each side needs to plan and prepare their arguments. Use these expressions to:

Begin the debate:	Today, we're going to debate the idea . . .
	We will present the arguments for / against the idea.
Present ideas:	We think / believe that . . . / In addition, . . .
Give examples:	For example / For instance, . . .
Give reasons:	One / Another reason is that / because . . .

C PLAN Work in a group of four and divide your group into two pairs. Debate this idea: *Student should study math and science before subjects like art and music.*

- Pair A: Plan two arguments *for* the idea. Think of reasons and examples.
- Pair B: Plan two arguments *against* the idea. Think of reasons and examples.

D DISCUSS Work in groups again and follow these steps:

1. Pair A introduces the idea and presents their arguments for it. (1–2 minutes)
2. Pair B presents their arguments against it. (1–2 minutes)
3. Discuss the arguments. You can also ask each other questions. (2–3 minutes)

E REPORT Each group summarizes their discussion for the rest of the class. List and write the main arguments for and against on the board. Then take a final class vote.

OUR RELATIONSHIP WITH NATURE 9

Kate Hamsikova dives with a wild bottlenose dolphin in Lahinch, Ireland.

IN THIS UNIT, YOU WILL:
- Watch or listen to a report about penguins
- Watch a video about farmers who use falcons
- Listen to a discussion about Kar ba Town, Zimbabwe
- Play a vocabulary game
  OR Give a presentation about the natural world

THINK AND DISCUSS:
1. Look at the photo and read the caption. Did you ever have a special experience in nature? Describe it.
2. Read the unit title. What kind of relationship do you have with nature? Do you spend time outside often? Sometimes? Never?

161

EXPLORE THE THEME

Read the information. Then discuss the questions.

1. Think about each person's actions and good habits. Do you do any of these things?
2. Think about the actions you DON'T do. Why don't you do them?
3. Do you want to change some of your habits or the habits of people you know?

How to Be an Environmental Hero

These five kinds of people make their everyday life environmentally friendly.

1. The Foodie

Elena and her family want to eat healthy and help the environment. They buy organic food. Farmers grow this food without chemicals that hurt pollinators such as bees. Be(e) the change you want!

3/4 of crops depend on pollinators

2. The Fashionista

Making new clothes requires chemicals. These chemicals pollute around 20% of all lakes and rivers. Instead of buying new clothes, Anne loves to go shopping in secondhand stores. Be stylish and thoughtful like Anne.

Source: Adelphi, Research & Consulting for Sustainability & Climate

3. The DIY-Person

Javier wants to build a new garden shed. When he's buying the wood, he looks for labels that say, "From a Sustainable Forest." Sustainable forests have a greater variety of wildlife.

4. The Travelers

Jack and Lisa love to spend their holidays in nature. They prefer ecotourism. They are always careful not to hurt the beautiful places they visit. Respect nature while you enjoy it!

5. The Digital-Native

Tayo uses his digital devices every day. When he has a small problem with them, he doesn't buy new devices right away. He brings them to a repair shop. Be smart and green like Tayo!

A Vocabulary

A Listen and repeat. Check (✓) any words you already know.

| allow (v) | coast (n) | leisure (n) | relationship (n) | tourism (n) |
| behavior (n) | continent (n) | ocean (n) | species (n) | wildlife (n) |

B **MEANING FROM CONTEXT** Listen and write the words from exercise A. Then think about each word's meaning.

HOW TO DO WILDLIFE TOURISM RIGHT

The tourists in this photo are taking pictures of [1]_____ in Tanzania. They want to get close to the lions and learn more about them. But are they doing it right? [2]_____ can have a negative effect on animals. Here are tips to follow:

1. **See animals in the wild.**

   Try to watch animals in their natural environment, such as in a forest or in the jungle, and not in a zoo. Animals are happier in the wild, and you will see more natural animal [3]_____.

2. **Don't get too close.**

   TV shows often show a close [4]_____ between humans and wild animals, but this is not natural. For example, research on elephants on the African [5]_____ shows that they feel stress when tourists are near. So we shouldn't [6]_____ people to stand too near wild animals.

3. **Think about your actions.**

   [7]_____ activities, like surfing along the [8]_____ or diving in the [9]_____, might affect feeding areas of some animal [10]_____. So do your research first and choose areas away from animals such as seals and penguins.

◀ Serengeti National Park, Tanzania

C Complete the sentences with the correct form of the words from exercise A.

1. Europe, Asia, and Africa are names of _____.
2. The Arctic, Atlantic, and Pacific are names of _____.
3. The security officer didn't _____ me to enter the building.
4. I live on an island with a very beautiful _____. It attracts a lot of tourists.
5. Costa Rica is famous for its national parks and _____.
6. Lions, leopards, and tigers are different _____ of big cats.
7. _____ is very important for many countries because visitors spend money.
8. Cooking and reading are popular _____ activities.
9. The teacher was angry with the students for their bad _____.
10. The _____ between a human and their pet can be very close.

VOCABULARY SKILL Collocations

Collocations are words we often use together. For example:

Adjective + noun	**Verb + noun**	**Noun + noun**
international tourism	increase tourism	tourism industry
green tourism	promote tourism	wildlife tourism

For other collocations, see Vocabulary Skill: Collocations in Unit 8.

D Match TWO words from the boxes and write the collocations in the sentences.

| allow | human | save | activity | species | traffic |
| common | leisure | space | behavior | tourism | wildlife |

1. There's less wildlife here because of the growing population and **human behavior**.
2. _____ will become affordable. For now, it's expensive to leave Earth.
3. This part of the city is for people and bikes only. We don't _____ here.
4. My favorite _____ is scuba diving. I try to go every month.
5. Ants are the most _____ of insect. There are trillions of them!
6. Conservationists are people who try to _____.

E **PERSONALIZE** Make notes to answer the questions. Then share ideas with a partner.

1. How big is the **tourism** industry in your country? How important is it?
2. What type of **leisure** activities are there for tourists?
3. Do you have any **wildlife tourism**? Where can tourists see different **species** of animals?
4. What are the names of the **continents**?

A Listening   The Penguins at Simon's Town

Critical Thinking | **A DESCRIBE** Look at the photo and read the caption. Discuss the questions.

1. What is the man taking a photo of? Why?
2. What effect do you think these tourists have on the penguins? Do you think it is positive, negative, or both? Why?

B MAIN IDEAS Watch or listen to a report about the penguins at Simon's Town. Choose Y for *Yes* or N for *No* for each question. 🔊 ▶

1. Do most species of penguin live in Antarctica?   Y   N
2. Are penguins in danger because of human behavior?   Y   N
3. Is the number of penguins at Simon's Town decreasing?   Y   N
4. Can tourists at Simon's Town touch the penguins?   Y   N
5. Do people fish in the sea around the colony at Simon's Town?   Y   N
6. Are people allowed to dive and sail near the colony?   Y   N

Mélanie Wenger is a National Geographic Explorer. ▶
As a photographer, she is interested in the relationship between humans and nature.

Tourists view the penguins at Foxy Beach, Simon's Town, South Africa.

C DETAILS Listen to the first part of the report again and complete the information.

1. Number of penguin species in the world: _____
2. Southern Hemisphere continents: Antarctica, Australia, Africa, and _____
3. Number of penguin colonies in South Africa: _____
4. Pairs of penguins at Simon's Town: _____
5. Decrease of penguins around South Africa in the last 30 years: _____%
6. Distance between people and penguins: _____ meters

LISTENING SKILL Recognize Cause and Effect

Speakers often talk about cause-effect relationships. Listen for words that:

- **Signal causes:** *because (of), as a result of, due to*
  Because there are more tourists, there is less wildlife.
  There is less wildlife **because of** tourists.

- **Signal effects:** *as a result, so, therefore, cause*
  They don't allow tourists here. **As a result**, there is more wildlife.
  Tourism and overfishing **cause** problems for the penguins.

When you take notes, you can show cause and effect relationships with arrows. →

D Listen to three parts of the report. Complete the causes and effects with ONE or TWO words.

1. _____ → decrease in South African penguins
2. careful control of tourists at Simon's Town → _____ number of penguins
3. too much fishing → not enough food for _____
4. fishing _____ → penguins at Simon's Town have enough food
5. don't allow leisure activities → penguins _____

E FOCUSED LISTENING Listen to two parts of the report. Choose the words you hear.

This is one of the six ¹(groups / colonies) of African penguins in South Africa and the only one that ²(remains stable / stays the same). The other ³(groups / colonies) have seen their numbers ⁴(decrease / collapse) in the past five years.

The question is now, what will the future be . . . ? Because we have to understand that human ⁵(actions / behavior) can really ⁶(affect / impact) the future of the species. Penguins are wild animals, so there's still a three-meter ⁷(space / distance) to keep with them.

See Vocabulary Skill: Synonyms in Unit 4.

F CREATE Imagine you are a journalist and you have an interview with Mélanie. Think of three questions to ask her about her work and the penguins. Then work with a partner. Role-play two interviews using your questions.

Critical Thinking

OUR RELATIONSHIP WITH NATURE

A Speaking

Critical Thinking

A **RECALL** Listening A was about penguins. With a partner, try to remember what these items referred to.

18   Southern Hemisphere   decrease   tourism   overfishing   Simon's Town   safe

For more spelling rules, see the Appendix.

GRAMMAR FOR SPEAKING   Comparative Adjectives

We use comparative adjectives to talk about the difference between two people, places, or things.

Adjectives with	Example	Comparative form
one syllable	tall, large	**taller** (than), **larger** (than)
two syllables ending in -y	happy, pretty	**happier** (than), **prettier** (than)
two or more syllables	interesting	**more/less interesting** (than)
irregular adjectives	good, bad	**better, worse**

A giraffe is **taller than** an elephant.
Wildlife documentaries are **more interesting than** other TV shows.

We often use comparative forms when we give our opinion.
  A: Do you prefer English or math?
  B: **I think** English is **more interesting** ~~than math~~ because . . .

We don't always use the *than* phrase when we know what it refers to.

B Look at the photos and read the information about two more species of penguin. With a partner, say sentences to compare the two species. Use the adjectives in the box.

big   heavy   light   colorful   short   small   tall

> *The population of the Adélie Penguin **is bigger than** the population of the Rockhopper Penguin.*

Penguin Fact File		
70 cm (27.5 in)	Average height	56 cm (22 in)
4.5 kg (10 lbs)	Average weight	2.5 kg (5.5 lb)
4,740,000	Estimated population	480,600

Adélie Penguin

Rockhopper Penguin

168   UNIT 9   LESSON A

C Complete the conversations with comparative adjectives. Listen and check. Then practice with a partner. 🔊

1. A: I want to watch a movie, but I can't decide. What's ¹_____ (good)?
   A comedy or a drama?
   B: Comedies are ²_____ (popular), but why not watch an action movie?
   They're ³_____ (exciting).

2. A: Let's visit somewhere new. Do you want to go somewhere ⁴_____ (quiet), like the mountains? Or do you want to go somewhere ⁵_____ (busy), like the city?
   B: Let's go to the city. Shopping is ⁶_____ (enjoyable) than hiking!

3. A: The public transportation in my city gets ⁷_____ (bad) every year. So I need to buy either a car or a bicycle. What do you think?
   B: Well, a car is ⁸_____ (comfortable), but a bicycle is ⁹_____ (expensive). How far do you travel every day?

D **CREATE** Work with a partner and take turns. Then switch roles and repeat the conversations. | Critical Thinking

Student A: Read one of speaker A's parts in exercise C.
Student B: Close your book and answer with your own words. Use comparative adjectives.

SPEAKING SKILL   Compare and Contrast

When we compare and contrast ideas, we often use the following words and phrases.
- **To signal differences**: in contrast, however, on the other hand
  The park in our city is a relaxing place. **In contrast**, *the city center is very noisy and more stressful.*
- **To signal similarities**: similarly, in the same way, likewise
  Natural places can be fun. **Likewise**, *urban areas can be fun—but for different reasons.*

We often use these words and phrases in more formal situations, such as presenting an argument. In informal situations, we often use *but* and *too*.

E Compare and contrast these things with a partner. Use words and phrases from the Speaking Skill box.

1. Cars allow you to travel places quickly / bicycles are slower but less expensive
2. Cycling is excellent exercise / walking is also a good way to exercise.
3. Lions are beautiful to look at / they can be very dangerous.
4. Watching sports is fun / playing sports is fun.
5. Plastic is a useful material / it's very bad for the environment.
6. The tourism business creates jobs / the leisure industry creates jobs.

   > *Cars allow you to travel places quickly. In contrast, bicycles are slower but less expensive.*

Critical Thinking | **F** **COMPARE** You are going to compare natural places (such as parks) with urban places (such as shopping malls). Discuss these questions with a partner.

1. How important is spending time in nature to you: very important, fairly important, or not very important? Explain.
2. Check (✓) the activities that you enjoy in natural places and urban places. Add two more ideas of your own. Explain your choices to your partner.

   ☐ walking in a park or public garden   ☐ going to a movie theater
   ☐ shopping at a mall   ☐ exercising / playing sports outside
   ☐ watching animals outdoors or at a zoo ☐ _____
   ☐ sitting near a river, a lake, or an ocean ☐ _____

G Look at the two photos below and think about how the places are different. Add your ideas to this chart. Your ideas can be facts or your opinions.

Natural places	Urban places
- quieter	- noisier
- less stressful	- more stressful

H With your partner from exercise F, compare and contrast the two kinds of places.

A: I think natural places are quieter. In contrast, urban places are noisier, but I prefer that.
B: Really? I prefer quieter places with wildlife. It's less stressful.

▼ Nahuel Huapi National Park, Argentina   ▼ Asakusa District, Tokyo, Japan

Video

Falcon Farmers

crops (n) plants that farmers grow, such as fruit trees
chase (v) to follow something quickly to catch it
rows (n) people or things in straight lines
scare (v) to cause fear; to frighten

▲ A peregrine falcon

A Watch the video. Check (✓) the things you see.

1. ☐ A falcon is sitting on a trainer's hand.
2. ☐ A falcon is chasing another bird.
3. ☐ A dog is climbing up the fruit trees.
4. ☐ A man is using an electronic device to find the falcon.
5. ☐ A falcon is eating blueberries and cherries.

B Watch again. Complete the sentences with ONE word or number from the video.

1. On fruit farms, birds can damage 5 to 10 percent of the _____.
2. In the wild, falcons hunt other birds for food, but the trainers teach the falcons to _____ away the birds.
3. The falcons are like athletes and eat a special _____.
4. A dog runs up and down the rows of trees to _____ the birds off the ground.
5. The birds work _____ days a week and about _____ hours a day.
6. Their human owners take very good care of them because they are so _____.

C **APPLY** Work with a partner and discuss the questions. Then join another pair and compare your answers. | Critical Thinking

1. Can you think of another animal that helps humans with their work?
2. What jobs does it do? Why is it special?

B Vocabulary

A **MEANING FROM CONTEXT** Read and listen to the article. Think about the meaning of the words in blue. 🔊

THE MOUNTAIN GORILLA

There are about 1000 mountain gorillas in the world. They live in the African countries of Rwanda, Congo, and Uganda. In the past, these gorillas were in danger from **illegal** hunting and the **conflict** of war. The animals also suffered from air **pollution** from forest fires. However, in recent years, the gorilla population has increased because there are new national parks and wildlife **reserves**. The parks **belong to** the governments, but tourists can visit and enjoy the beautiful **scenery**. They **limit** the number of tourists carefully, and tourists only watch the gorillas from a distance. The gorillas could **attack** the tourists if they get too close! Things are improving, but there are still problems. Farmers **require** more land to grow their **crops**, and companies are looking for oil. As more humans move into the area and cut down forests, the mountain gorillas might lose their home in the future.

B Write the words in blue from exercise A next to their definitions. Then write the correct part of speech for each word: v for *verb*, adj for *adjective*, or n for *noun*.

1. __belong to__ (__v__) to be owned by someone
2. _____ (____) the things that make land, air, and water dirty
3. _____ (____) natural features such as mountains, forests, and rivers
4. _____ (____) to need something
5. _____ (____) a situation when people or countries disagree, argue, or fight
6. _____ (____) to try to hurt
7. _____ (____) an area of land protected for wildlife
8. _____ (____) to control
9. _____ (____) plants that farmers grow for food, such as corn or onions
10. _____ (____) against the law

▼ Gorillas usually live in family groups of five to ten.

C Listen and repeat the words in exercise B.

D Read these headlines from different newspapers. Write a word from the box next to each headline.

conflict	crops	illegal	pollution	scenery

1. Amount of Trash and Plastic on the Streets Increases _____
2. Man Stopped by Police for Driving 120 Miles an Hour _____
3. Summer Drought Kills 90% of Corn _____
4. Government Disagrees about Cost of New Public Transportation _____
5. Local Council Builds Ugly Skyscraper in Front of Mountain View _____

E Complete this conversation with words from the box. Listen and check. Then practice with a partner.

attack	belong to	limit	reserve	require

TOURIST: Do the gorillas ever ¹_____ humans?

TOUR GUIDE: No, never, because the nature ²_____ has a fence around it. They ³_____ the gorillas to that part of the national park.

TOURIST: That's good to know!

TOUR GUIDE: But anyway, gorillas leave humans alone if we don't get too close.

TOURIST: So who does the area ⁴_____?

TOUR GUIDE: The government. They ⁵_____ you to get permission to enter.

F **PERSONALIZE** Complete these sentences with your own ideas about nature in your country. If necessary, research your answers online. Then share your sentences with a partner.

In my country, . . .

- the most beautiful **scenery** is in _____
- our national parks **belong to** _____
- there's a nature **reserve** in _____
- you can see fields with **crops** of _____
- people are worried about **pollution** from _____

B Listening Kariba Town, Zimbabwe

Critical Thinking

A PREDICT You are going to hear a conversation about Kariba Town in Zimbabwe, Africa. Look at the photo and read the caption. Then discuss the questions.

1. There is a lake behind Kariba Dam and an animal reserve. What do you think tourists can do there?
2. What effect do you think tourists have on Kariba Town?

B MAIN IDEA Read the statements. Listen to the conversation and check (✓) the main idea.

1. ☐ Tourists visit Kariba Town to see the scenery and wildlife and to go boating and fishing on Lake Kariba.
2. ☐ Most people in Kariba Town stay indoors at night because animals walk down the streets and around houses.
3. ☐ There are benefits to having more people in Kariba Town. However, there are also some conflicts between people and nature.
4. ☐ Many people want to leave Kariba Town and let the animals live there.

C DETAILS Listen again. Complete these sentences with no more than THREE words.

1. The lake is popular for fishing, but now there is a problem with _____.
2. There is pollution in the lake because people throw away _____.
3. Tourism helps Kariba Town because it creates _____.
4. There is conflict because people want to grow—and animals want to eat—_____.
5. At night, elephants might walk outside your house, and leopards could walk down the _____.
6. When the water behind the dam began to rise, people had to save _____.
7. People hunt animals in the wildlife reserve even though it's _____.
8. The wild animals bring tourists into the country and _____.

PRONUNCIATION   Recognize Reduced Words

🔊 In everyday conversation, speakers don't usually stress structure words such as *is* and *than*. These words are usually reduced to the schwa sound: /ə/. Be aware of this so that you can better understand what others are saying.

　　　　　/ə/　　　　　　　/ə/
Wildlife <u>is</u> more important <u>than</u> tourism.

　　　/ə/　　　　　　/ə/　/ə/
There <u>are</u> fewer tourists <u>than</u> in <u>the</u> past.

Kariba Dam was built across the Zambezi River in the late 1950s. It created Lake Kariba, one of the world's largest human-made lakes.

D Listen to these sentences. Which of the bold words are reduced? Mark the reduced words that sound like schwa /ə/.

1. **There are** fewer tourists **than** last year.
2. There's **more** pollution **than** in **the** past.
3. Animal attacks **are less** common.
4. **The** land **for** animals **is** getting smaller.
5. **The** problem **of** overfishing **is** growing.
6. Kariba **has** problems **with** pollution.

CRITICAL THINKING Analyze Arguments

When you think about a problem, it's important to understand and analyze all sides of an argument. It helps you to understand other people's viewpoints.

One side of an argument: *It's important to protect land for the animals in the nature reserve.*
Another side of the argument: *However, people need to grow crops for food and money.*

E Read arguments about some of the problems in Kariba Town. Put them in order from 1 (the strongest argument) to 5 (the weakest argument).

Critical Thinking

a. _____ A farmer: "I need more land to grow crops to feed local people."

b. _____ A local person: "I know hunting is illegal, but I need to feed my family."

c. _____ A tour guide: "We need the leisure activities on the lake, or tourists will stop coming."

d. _____ A fisher: "Tourists throw away their plastic in the lake. We need to stop it because this has a negative effect on fishing."

e. _____ A conservationist: "Wild animals are an important part of nature and of the area. We need to protect them."

F Work with a group. Compare your order in exercise E and discuss the arguments. Try to agree on a final order.

B Speaking

For more spelling rules, see the Appendix

GRAMMAR FOR SPEAKING Superlative Adjectives

We use superlative adjectives to talk about the difference between three or more people, places, or things.

Adjectives with	Example	Superlative form
one syllable	tall, large	**the tallest, the largest**
two syllables ending in -y	happy, pretty	**the happiest, the prettiest**
two or more syllables	interesting	**the most/least interesting**
irregular adjectives	good, bad	**the best, the worst**

We often use the superlative to compare parts of a group or category.
  The blue whale is **the biggest** animal on the planet.
  The Little Penguin in New Zealand and Australia is **the smallest** kind of penguin.

A Tourists often ask questions like the ones below. Complete the questions with superlative adjectives.

1. What's _____ place for tourists? (popular)
2. Which area has _____ scenery? (beautiful)
3. What's _____ building in your city? (old)
4. What's _____ hotel? (less/expensive)
5. What's _____ park in your city? (large)
6. Which restaurant has _____ food? (traditional)
7. Where is _____ place to go shopping? (good)
8. What is _____ place in the city? (high)
9. What's _____ way to travel around town? (quick)
10. Where is _____ place to see nature and wildlife? (interesting)

B Work with a partner and role-play a conversation. Then switch roles and ask different questions.

Student A: You are a tourist visiting Student B's town or city. Ask some of the questions in exercise A.
Student B: Answer student A's questions with your own ideas.

Critical Thinking

C **DISCOVER** If you weren't sure of the answer to any questions in exercise A, try to find the information after class.

A Maasai staffperson prepares for a tour group near Mount Kilimanjaro.

D Read this text from a TV advertisement for eco-tourism. Choose the correct words. Then listen and check your answers.

ENJOY AN ECO VACATION

This year, why not take a ¹(more / most) environmentally friendly holiday? Our eco-hotel in southern Kenya offers you the ²(more / most) comfortable rooms in the area. It has views of Africa's ³(most / least) beautiful scenery, including its ⁴(higher / highest) mountain—Mount Kilimanjaro. Our hotel is next to the famous Kimana wildlife reserve where you can see lions, elephants, cheetahs, and zebras. ⁵(A / The) most important goal of the hotel is to help this wildlife, so part of your money helps the reserve. Our hotel also runs on solar power, and all the food comes from local farmers. So we have ⁶(the best / a better) environmental record than other hotels in the area. What are you waiting for? Book now for ⁷(a more amazing / the most amazing) trip of a lifetime.

E **CREATE** Work with a partner. Write a short script for a TV advertisement for your local area. | Critical Thinking

1. Think about and discuss why tourists would come to visit. Your ad could talk about:
   - local wildlife and parks
   - beautiful scenery
   - hotels and restaurants
   - transportation and shopping
   - other features
2. Write about 80–100 words. Try to use a lot of comparative and superlative adjectives. Then practice reading your ad aloud. Make it sound like a TV ad. Each of you should read one part.

F Join another pair. Take turns reading your ad aloud. When you listen, count the number of comparative and superlative adjectives you hear.

OUR RELATIONSHIP WITH NATURE

Review

SELF-ASSESS

How well can you . . . ?	Very well.	OK.	I need improvement.
use the key vocabulary	☐	☐	☐
recognize reduced words	☐	☐	☐
use comparative and superlative adjectives	☐	☐	☐
compare and contrast	☐	☐	☐

A VOCABULARY Write TWO or THREE words from the box in each category. ONE word does not fit any category.

> attack   coast   continent   conflict   illegal   ocean   reserve   species   wildlife

1. Words about animals: _____
2. Words about water: _____
3. Words with a negative meaning: _____

B PRONUNCIATION Listen and mark the reduced bold words with a schwa /ə/ sound. 🔊

1. **There are** fewer species **of** birds **now**.
2. **The** Indian Ocean **is** smaller **than the** Atlantic.
3. **Our** new park **is** bigger **than the** old **one**.

C GRAMMAR Write sentences with comparative adjectives using the words and phrases in 1–2. Write sentences with superlative adjectives in 3–4.

1. cats / dogs / friendly
2. elephants / giraffes / large
3. snakes / long / species of animal
4. a shopping mall / relaxing / place in a city

1. _____
2. _____
3. _____
4. _____

D SPEAKING SKILL Complete and say these sentences. Use your own ideas.

1. Pollution has a negative effect on the world. Similarly, . . .
2. There are a lot of cars in our city. However, . . .
3. Tourism can be good because it makes money for local people. On the other hand, . . .

RE-ASSESS What skills or language do you still need help with?

Final Tasks

OPTION 1 Play a vocabulary game

A On your own, write down two or three words for each of these categories:

a species of animal	
a country or continent	
a type of transportation	
a fruit or vegetable	
a type of advertising	
a type of weather	
any useful object	

B Now play a vocabulary game using comparative and superlative adjectives. Follow these steps.

1. Work with a partner. You each say one word from a category in exercise A. Then you each make a sentence using a comparative adjective.
   A: cat   A: A cat is smaller than a lion.
   B: lion   B: A lion is more dangerous than a cat.

2. Work in a group of three. You each say one word from a category in exercise A. Then you each make a sentence using a superlative adjective. You can also give an opinion and a reason for your answer.
   A: cat   A: A cat is the smallest animal.
   B: lion   B: A lion is the most dangerous.
   C: elephant   C: I think an elephant is the most beautiful because it's so large but peaceful.

▼ An Arabian tahr mountain goat looks over the Jebel Balcony Walk in the Omani Grand Canyon, Oman.

See Unit 9 Rubric in the Appendix.

OPTION 2 Give a presentation about the natural world

A MODEL Listen to a student's presentation about the natural world. 🔊

1. What is the topic of the student's presentation? _____
2. What does she want the audience to understand at the end of the presentation? _____
3. What does she show the audience? _____
4. What can you see in the photo? _____
5. What can you *not* see in the photo? _____

PRESENTATION SKILL Plan Your Presentation

Plan your presentation by brainstorming and using a spider map:
- Brainstorm different ideas for the topic. Then choose the best idea.
- Write your best idea in the middle of the spider map (see below).
- Add three or four key points to your spider map and add details.

B PLAN You are going to give a presentation about a part of the natural world. Explain why it is important to you and why we should protect it. Follow these instructions and use a spider map like the one below.

1. Brainstorm different ideas about the natural world that are important to you. Then choose the best idea for your presentation. Write the idea in the center of your spider map.
2. Write three or four key points or main ideas on the lines, or "arms."
3. Write details for each key point.
4. Decide which points you will talk about first, second, and so on in your presentation.

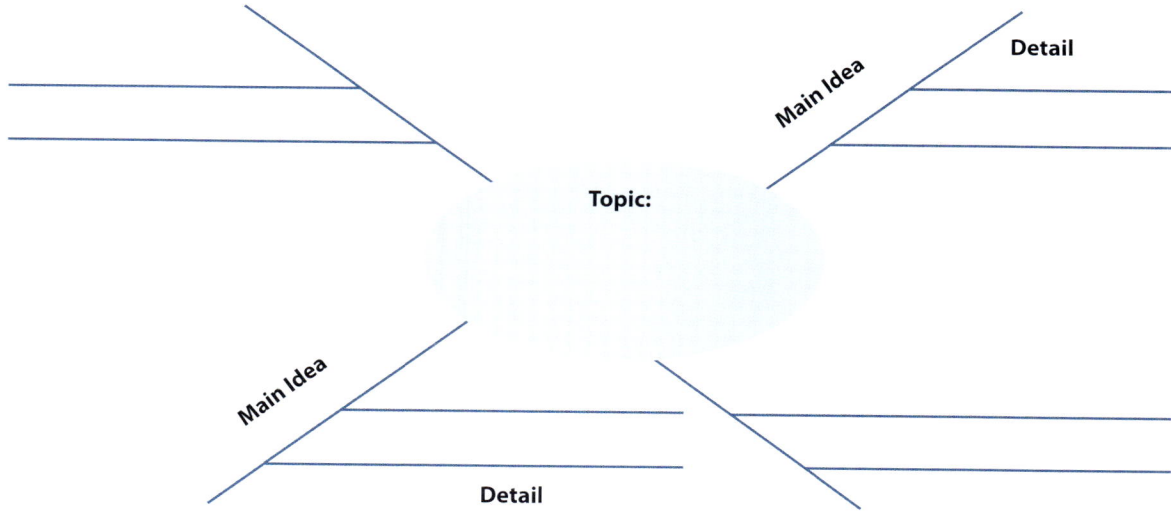

C PRACTICE AND PRESENT Practice your presentation with a partner and give each other feedback. Then give your presentation to the class.

HOW WE COMMUNICATE 10

People by the water near Djibouti City, Djibouti

IN THIS UNIT, YOU WILL:
- Listen to a report about solving communication problems
- Watch a video about a special school
- Watch or listen to a lecture about the importance of gestures
- Explain a piece of technology
  OR Present a form of communication

THINK AND DISCUSS:
1. Look at the photo and read the caption. What do you think these people are doing?
2. How do you use your cell phone to communicate?
3. Read the unit title. What kinds of topics do you think you will discuss in this unit?

EXPLORE THE THEME

Read the information. Then discuss the questions.

1. Compare the information in the two charts. What does the information tell us about how we communicate in real life vs. online?
2. Do you think this is a problem? What kinds of problems could this cause?

The Vasconcelos Library is in the downtown area of Mexico City, Mexico. It is over 38,000 square meters and is called a "megalibrary" for its size. Bookshelves appear to hang from the ceiling, and there is a whale bone sculpture by artist Garbriel Orozco in the main hall. There are 2.8 million libraries in the world; however, only 378,455 libraries have Internet access, according to the International Federation of Library Associations and Institutions (IFLA).

Vasconcelos Library, Mexico City, Mexico

The World of Languages

Languages with the greatest number of first-language speakers (in millions)

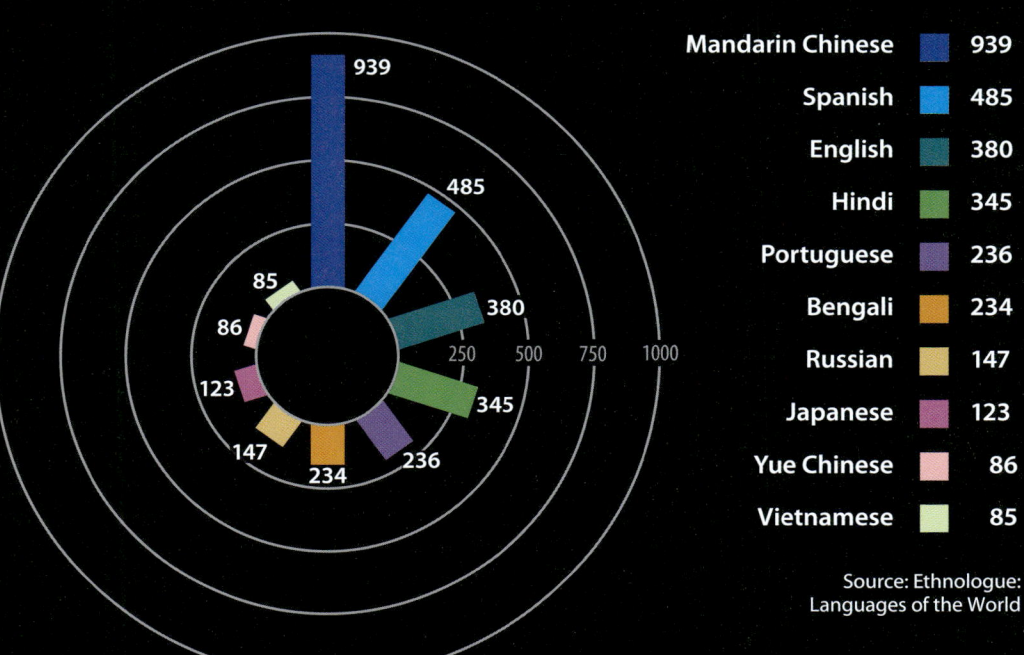

Mandarin Chinese	939
Spanish	485
English	380
Hindi	345
Portuguese	236
Bengali	234
Russian	147
Japanese	123
Yue Chinese	86
Vietnamese	85

Source: Ethnologue: Languages of the World

Languages used on websites worldwide

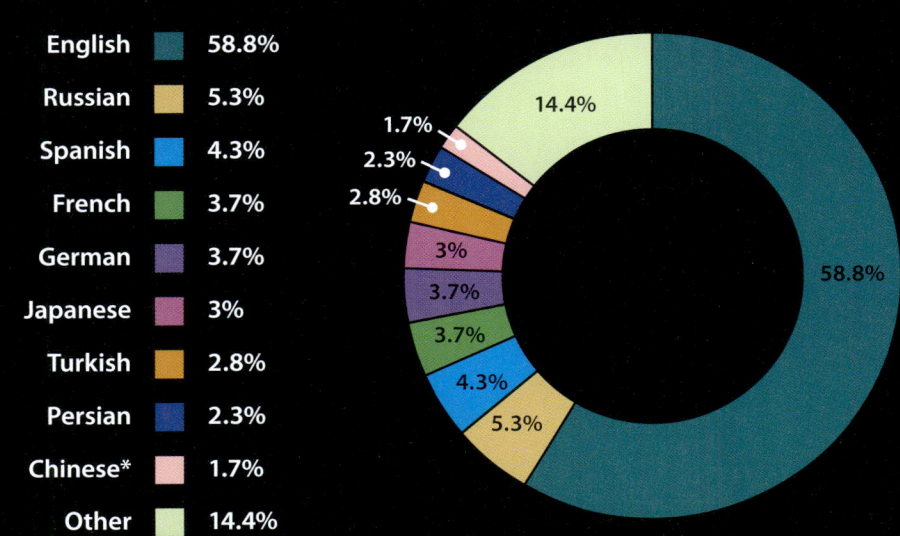

English	58.8%
Russian	5.3%
Spanish	4.3%
French	3.7%
German	3.7%
Japanese	3%
Turkish	2.8%
Persian	2.3%
Chinese*	1.7%
Other	14.4%

* Includes all dialects and forms of the language.
Source: Statistica

HOW WE COMMUNICATE   183

A Vocabulary

A Listen and repeat the words. Then write the words and part of speech next to their definitions. 🔊

| access (v) | give away (v phr) | invent (v) | make sure (v phr) | system (n) |
| according to (adv phr) | inform (v) | look up (v phr) | offer (v) | wide (adj) |

1. _____ (____) a group of things or pieces of equipment that work together
2. _____ (____) to create a new kind of thing
3. _____ (____) to make something available to use
4. _____ (____) to search for or try to find information
5. _____ (____) including many people or things
6. _____ (____) to tell people about something, often in an official way
7. _____ (____) to give something (e.g., money or information) for free
8. _____ (____) as stated or reported by somebody
9. _____ (____) to be able to use or have something
10. _____ (____) to do something to be certain something else happens

B **MEANING FROM CONTEXT** Choose the correct word or phrase to complete each sentence. Then listen and check your answers. 🔊

1. This message is very important. Please (make sure / give away) your teacher receives it.
2. At my school, we study a (wide / system) number of different subjects.
3. It's easy to (inform / access) information on the Internet.
4. You can (invent / look up) a word on your dictionary app if you don't know the meaning.
5. (According to / Looking up) a recent report, more people have cell phones than computers.
6. We have a new computer (access / system), but I don't know how to use it!
7. After you put money in the machine, it (offers / gives away) you a choice of different drinks.
8. The university will (offer / inform) you if you fail a class.
9. He (made sure / gave away) his car to a friend.
10. Who (invented / informed) the first modern computer?

C Complete the paragraph with the correct form of the words from the box. ONE word is extra. Then listen and check. 🔊

| access | according to | give away | inform | invent | offer | wide |

MEET KEN BANKS

National Geographic Explorer Ken Banks knows a lot about mobile technology. He's famous because he [1]_____ FrontlineSMS in

2005. At that time, many people couldn't ² _____ the Internet easily in some parts of the world. But Ken's software ³ _____ them a way to communicate without the Internet. They downloaded his software and connected their cell phones to a computer. Then they could send information from their phones. And users didn't have to pay—Ken ⁴ _____ his software for free! People still use FrontlineSMS today, and Ken has created a ⁵ _____ variety of other computer technology. ⁶ _____ Ken, the most exciting part of his work is "seeing what people are doing with our technology."

Ken Banks

VOCABULARY SKILL   Phrasal Verbs

Phrasal verbs are very common in English. They have two parts: a verb and a particle (a word like *for* or *up*). The meaning of a phrasal verb is usually different from the two separate words.

   I **looked up** the word in the dictionary. (= tried to find)

   We always **get up** at six. (= get out of bed)

   Ken **gave away** his software on the website. (= gave something for free)

When you learn a phrasal verb, you can check this information in your dictionary:
- Does it need an object?

   I **looked up** <u>the word</u>. (verb + object)

   I **get up** at six o'clock. (no object)
- Can the object go in two different places?

   Look up <u>the word</u>. / **Look** <u>it</u> **up.**

D Read these questions about technology and communication. Underline FIVE phrasal verbs and discuss their meaning with a partner. Check your ideas in a dictionary.

1. According to one survey, 71 percent of people check their phones right after they wake up. Do you usually check your phone before you get up?
2. How often do you back up the information and pictures on your phone or computer? Have you ever lost information? What happened?
3. Many websites require a password. What types of websites ask you to log on with a password?
4. When you need information about English, where do you look it up? Which websites do you use?

E **PERSONALIZE** Work in groups. Ask and answer the questions in exercise D.

A Listening Solving Communication Problems

Critical Thinking

A RANK Rank the following ways you use the Internet from most important (1) to least important (6).

_____ chat with friends   _____ look up facts and information

_____ do banking and pay bills   _____ shop for clothes, music, etc.

_____ read or hear the news   _____ use social media

B Work with a group and compare your lists. Give reasons for your answers. Then discuss other ways you use the Internet.

> I use the Internet to chat with friends a lot, so that's the most important to me. But I never do banking online, so that's the least important.
> I also watch movies on the Internet. That's really important to me.

C MAIN IDEAS Listen to a report. Check (✓) the THREE main ideas.

1. ☐ Not everyone in the world has Internet access.
2. ☐ The United Nations uses Ken's software.
3. ☐ Ken Banks creates software to help people communicate.
4. ☐ Ken created software to help a wildlife reserve in South Africa.
5. ☐ People use Ken's software to solve their own problems.

▼ People texting in Uganda

LISTENING SKILL   Listen for Key Words

Speakers usually stress and emphasize **key words**. These are words with the most meaning such as verbs, adjectives, nouns, and numbers. When you listen for specific or important information, listen carefully for the words the speaker stresses.

> In some parts of the world, it's still very **difficult** to **access** the **Internet**. And even when it is working, the **Internet connection** can be very **slow**.

D **DETAILS** Listen again for key words. Choose the correct answers. 🔊

1. What does the United Nations say about the Internet?
   a. All people can communicate with it.
   b. It can be very slow in some places.
   c. All people should have access to it.

2. What percentage of the world's population doesn't have Internet access?
   a. 13.7%   b. 30.7%   c. 37%

3. What type of work did Ken start doing in Africa 20 years ago?
   a. He did conservation work.   b. He introduced the Internet.   c. He fixed cell phones.

4. How did Kruger National Park use Ken's software?
   a. To look for animals.   b. To get opinions.   c. To sell tickets.

5. What type of technology did Ken's new software need?
   a. The Internet.   b. Cell phones.   c. Solar power.

6. How much did Ken charge for his software?
   a. Nothing, because he gave it away.
   b. The same price as a cell phone.
   c. Different prices for different countries.

7. In how many countries have people used Ken's software?
   a. 117   b. More than 170   c. About 1,700

E **FOCUSED LISTENING** Listen to and read part of the report. Underline FOUR errors. Then listen again and correct the errors. 🔊

Reporting to the United Nations, the Internet is a basic human right. The organization believes that all countries should make certain their people can access it. However, the Internet is still not available anywhere. The United Nations estimates that nearly three billion people—that's 37% of the world's people—still can't access the Internet. Some people want to change this.

F **ANALYZE** Discuss these questions with a group. Afterwards, report back to the class and compare your ideas.

| Critical Thinking

1. Do you agree that the Internet is a basic human right? Why? Why not?
2. Why do you think Ken gave his software away for free?
3. Can you think of one more problem that technology solves?

A Speaking

PRONUNCIATION Consonant Clusters

🔊 A consonant cluster is two or more consonant sounds together in a syllable, with no vowel sounds in between. You hear them:
- at the beginning of a syllable: **sp**eed, **pr**int, **scr**een, hi•**sto**•ry
- at the end of a syllable: fa**st**, lear**ns**, wor**ked**, so**ft**•ware

Sometimes, two consonant letters together are not a cluster. They make one sound:
  tele**ph**one   ph = /f/
  ri**ng**   ng = /ŋ/

Sometimes the letter *e* between two consonants is silent, so they become a consonant cluster:
  wor**ked**   ked = /kt/
  ga**mes**   mes = /mz/

A Listen to these words. Check (✓) the NINE words with consonant clusters. Then practice the words. 🔊

☐ blind   ☐ invent   ☐ microphone   ☐ projector   ☐ television
☐ first   ☐ lived   ☐ people   ☐ speech   ☐ world

B The letters in the boxes below are often part of consonant clusters. Write the missing letters in the words. Then listen, check, and repeat. 🔊

1. Write these letters in the consonant clusters at the beginning of the words.

| k | l | m | p | r | t | w |

s____all   s____eak   b____ain   s____i   s____reet   s____im   p____an

2. Write these letters in the consonant clusters at the end of the words.

| c | f | k | l | m | n | s |

par____ed   ju____p   lea____t   ha____d   he____p   gi____t   fa____t

Critical Thinking | **C** **DISCOVER** Look back through the vocabulary pages of previous units in this book. Find FIVE words with consonant clusters and practice them with a partner.

D Work with a partner and take turns. Read the list of important inventions aloud. Pay attention to the pronunciation of consonant clusters. Write each event on the timeline below.

> *1824, Braille system* of *writing for blind people. So that goes between 1800 and 1850.*

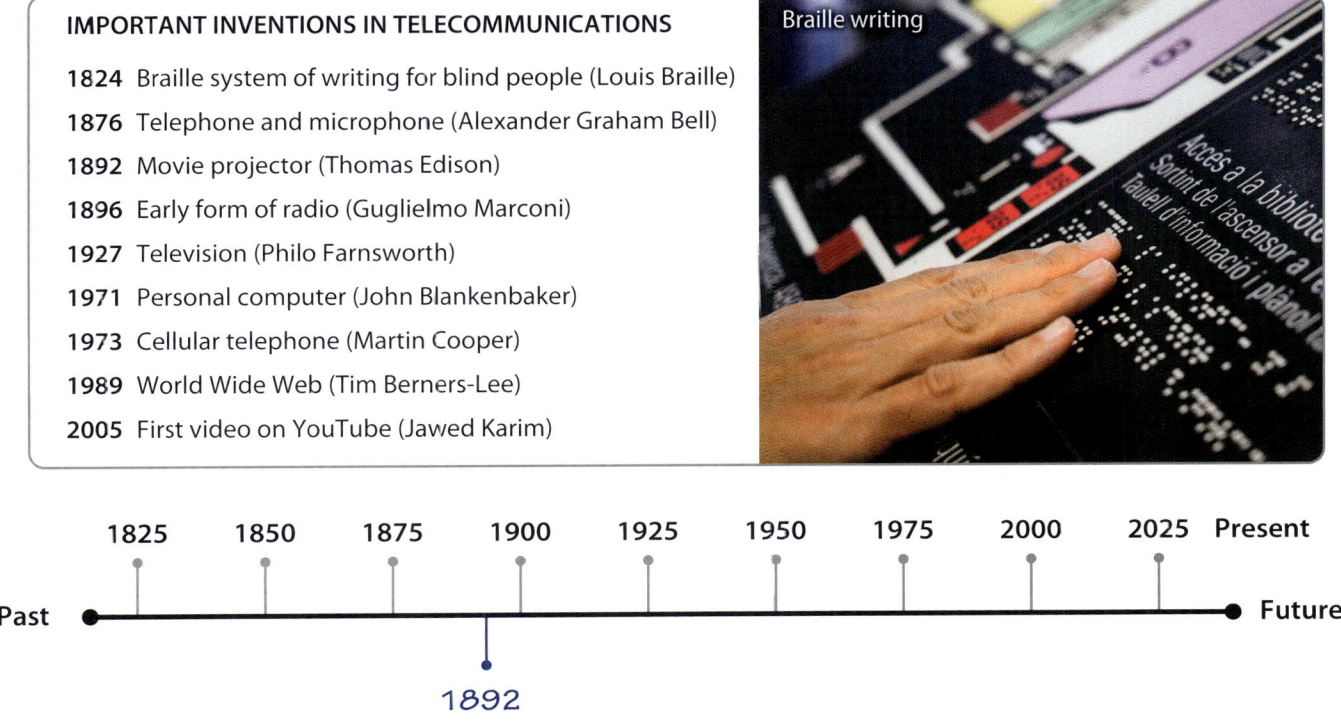

Braille writing

IMPORTANT INVENTIONS IN TELECOMMUNICATIONS

1824 Braille system of writing for blind people (Louis Braille)
1876 Telephone and microphone (Alexander Graham Bell)
1892 Movie projector (Thomas Edison)
1896 Early form of radio (Guglielmo Marconi)
1927 Television (Philo Farnsworth)
1971 Personal computer (John Blankenbaker)
1973 Cellular telephone (Martin Cooper)
1989 World Wide Web (Tim Berners-Lee)
2005 First video on YouTube (Jawed Karim)

1892
movie projector

E Think of one more invention. Where does it belong on the timeline? Tell your partner.

GRAMMAR FOR SPEAKING   Present Perfect

We use the present perfect (*have/has* + past participle of the verb) to talk about:

- Actions that began in the past and continue to the present. We often use *for* or *since*.

    I **have worked** here <u>since 2021</u>. (*since* + start time)
    I**'ve had** this job <u>for seven years</u>. (*for* + amount of time)

- Actions that have happened one or more times in the past. The exact time of the action is not important or stated.

    I **haven't read** that book, so I can't tell you anything about it.
    Tom**'s seen** that movie three times!

Affirmative	Negative
I/You/We/They**'ve started**.	We **haven't seen** the report.
He/She/It**'s finished**.	He **hasn't left** the office yet.

Questions	Answers
Have you **heard** the news?	Yes, I **have**. / No, I **haven't**.
Has the letter **arrived**?	Yes, it **has**. / No, it **hasn't**.
How long **have** you **known**?	For about two weeks.

For spelling of verbs ending in *-d/-ed* and irregular past participles, see the Appendix.

HOW WE COMMUNICATE **189**

F Complete these conversations. Use the present perfect, contractions, and information from the timeline in exercise D. Then practice with a partner.

1. A: How long has Braille printing _____ around?
   B: For a long time! It _____ been around since _____.

2. A: How long _____ the telephone existed?
   B: It's _____ for _____ years.

3. A: How old is television?
   B: It's pretty old! There _____ been TVs _____ 1927.

4. A: How long _____ we had cell phones?
   B: We've _____ cell phones since _____.

5. A: When was the first YouTube video uploaded?
   B: In 2005. Since then, people _____ over 800 million videos.

G Look at the other inventions in exercise D. Ask and answer *how long* questions with a partner.

A: How long have we had . . . / How long has . . . been around?
B: We've had it since . . . / It's been around for . . . years.

GRAMMAR FOR SPEAKING   Present Perfect and Simple Past

We often answer a present perfect question with the simple past because we refer to a specific past time.
A: **Have** you **had** any video chats recently?
B: Yes, I **talked** with my brother online <u>last night</u>.

H Read the list of ways to communicate and add two more ideas. Then ask and answer questions about ways to communicate with a partner. Write your partner's responses in the chart.

	Ways to communicate	Done recently?		With/To whom?
1.	Call on the phone	☐ Yes	☐ No	
2.	Have a video chat	☐ Yes	☐ No	
3.	Send a text message	☐ Yes	☐ No	
4.	Have a face-to-face conversation	☐ Yes	☐ No	
5.	Write a letter	☐ Yes	☐ No	
6.	Send an email	☐ Yes	☐ No	
7.		☐ Yes	☐ No	
8.		☐ Yes	☐ No	

A: Have you called anyone on the phone recently?
B: Yes, I called my grandmother last week.

Video

A School for Communication

stammer (v) to speak with many pauses or repeated sounds   **fiancé/fiancée** (n) the person you are engaged to before you get married

▲ A speech therapist can help people of all ages with speech and language problems.

A Watch the video. Write the missing numbers. ▶

1. The average person speaks 7,000 to _____ words a day.
2. One person in _____ stammers.
3. Jessica couldn't speak until she was _____ years old.
4. Her special class is _____ days long.
5. _____ month later, Jessica can enjoy doing her job without extra help.

B Read the statements. Then watch the video again and choose T for *True* and F for *False*. Correct the false statements. ▶

1. People who stammer have the most trouble when they begin to speak.   T   F
2. Jessica has stammered since she was a teenager.   T   F
3. She needs a friend to help with communication in her job.   T   F
4. The class have to talk about their families on the first day.   T   F
5. The teachers teach students about breathing and parts of their bodies.   T   F
6. On the last day, Jessica gives a speech in front of people.   T   F

C **RECALL** Watch the video two more times with the sound off. With a partner, take turns narrating the video. You can use these sentence starters to help you: | Critical Thinking

- When people stammer, they . . .
- This is Jessica. She . . .
- Jessica works as a . . .
- Today, Jessica begins . . .
- The teachers help the students to . . .
- At the end of the course, Jessica . . .

B Vocabulary

A MEANING FROM CONTEXT Read and listen to the article. Think about the meaning of the words and phrases in blue. Write the words next to their definitions. 🔊

> ### AMERICAN SIGN LANGUAGE
>
> American **Sign** Language, or ASL, is a language that people in deaf communities use instead of **speech**. ASL uses signs **in addition to** body positions and facial expressions to **express** ideas. ASL signs are different from the gestures most people use. For example, we all wave, shrug our shoulders, and make shapes with our hands. We **point** at objects so that other people know what to **pay attention to**. However, our gestures are very limited compared to the system of signs in ASL.
>
> As with speaking, the **importance** of culture is clear in sign language. Different countries have different versions of sign language. ASL is quite different from BSL, or British Sign Language, for example.
>
> In recent years, some **experts** have encouraged parents of hearing children to teach ASL to their babies. It's a way to **support** their language development before they are able to speak. In addition, many schools in the U.S. recognize ASL as a **foreign** language, and students can get credit to study it.

1. _____ (n) people who know a lot of information about a subject
2. _____ (n) an action or way to communicate without speaking
3. _____ (v) to show or communicate a thought or feeling
4. _____ (n) how important or valuable something is
5. _____ (v) to encourage or help

▼ Two friends communicate with American Sign Language.

6. _____ (v) to hold a finger towards something

7. _____ (adj) coming from a different country

8. _____ (n) spoken language

9. _____ (v phr) to watch or listen to carefully

10. _____ (adv phr) along with or together with (another person, thing, etc.)

B Listen and repeat the words in exercise A. 🔊

C Use your dictionary to find other forms of the vocabulary words.

See Vocabulary Skill: Word Families in Unit 1.

	Noun	Verb	Adjective
1.	importance	--------	
2.	expert	--------	
3.	speech		--------
4.		support	
5.		express	
6.	addition		
7.		--------	foreign

D Complete each sentence with the correct form of a word from the chart in exercise C.

1. My French is limited. I can read it, but I can't _____ it.

2. What is the _____ of learning another language?

3. She's a(n) _____ in languages. She speaks 12 of them fluently.

4. The language lab on campus _____ all students. It offers tutoring for people who need _____ help.

5. After the dinner party, he sent flowers as a(n) _____ of thanks.

6. I think my new phone was made in a(n) _____ country because the writing on the back isn't in English.

E **PERSONALIZE** Discuss these questions with a partner.

1. What do you **pay attention to** when you meet someone for the first time?
2. Do you know any **signs** in ASL or another sign language? Share them with your partner and explain what the signs mean.
3. In some cultures, it's considered impolite to **point** at people. Why do you think that is? Is this true for your culture?
4. Do your friends **support** you? In what ways do you support them?
5. When is it important to get advice or information from an **expert**? When is it OK to get it from the Internet or other source?

B Listening   The Importance of Gestures

Critical Thinking

A   INTERPRET Look at the woman in the middle of the photo. Then discuss the questions.

1. Do you think the woman who is standing is a visitor or the host in this house? Why?
2. She is making a gesture with her hands and head. Do you know what it means?
3. How do you greet someone in your culture? What gesture do you make? Is this different from other countries?

B   MAIN IDEAS You are going to listen to a presentation about gestures. Before you listen, read the statements and guess if they are *True* or *False*. Then watch or listen and check.

1. Gestures are only used in some cultures.   T   F
2. Animals use gestures between each other.   T   F
3. Some gestures are the same in different countries.   T   F
4. Gestures can help when you don't speak a language.   T   F
5. Gestures help you remember information.   T   F
6. We can't use gestures with online communication and technology.   T   F

C   DETAILS Watch or listen again. Complete the notes with a number or ONE or TWO words for each sentence.

Topics	Examples
Gestures for greeting people	1. If the speaker meets you for the first time, he will _____ your hand. 2. In a country like _____, people might bow.
Gestures in animals	3. Some members of the ape family point at their mouth when they are _____.
Gestures in different countries	4. Italians know _____ hand gestures.
International gestures	5. Putting your _____ on your lips means "Be quiet." 6. Nodding usually means "yes," but not in _____.
Gestures to help a listener understand	7. In a _____, you can lift your hands to say, "I'm sorry. I don't know."
Gestures to help speakers remember	8. Gestures help to recall memories and the details of a _____.
Gestures and technology	9. Emoticons are basically _____ of gestures. 10. When you talk through a camera, it's helpful to use _____.

194   UNIT 10   LESSON B

Tika Gurung greets her relatives in Burlington, Vermont, USA.

CRITICAL THINKING Recognize Cultural Differences

When you learn about or meet people from other cultures, their behavior might seem different or unusual. However, remember that *your* behavior may also seem different to them. When you think about another culture, also think about your own culture. What are the similarities and differences?

> I shake hands when I meet someone for the first time, but someone else may bow slightly and hold their hands together.

D Work with a partner. Read about behavior in three different cultures. Then reflect on and discuss how people behave in the same situation in your culture. How similar or different is the behavior?

1. In the USA, many people hold a fork in their left hand and a knife in their right hand. They cut up the food and then put the knife down. Then they pass the fork to the right hand and eat the food with it.
2. In Thailand, visitors always remove their shoes before entering someone's house and sometimes before going into a shop.
3. In Brazil, during a conversation in the street or at work, two speakers will often stand very close to each other and touch each other's arms or backs from time to time.

Critical Thinking

E **ANALYZE** Imagine a foreigner is visiting your country for the first time. What cultural differences do you think they would notice? With another student from your country, make a list of three possible differences for the visitor. Then report your ideas to the class.

- greeting for the first time
- visiting someone's house
- eating a meal
- time (being punctual or a bit late)
- the distance between people when they talk

Critical Thinking

HOW WE COMMUNICATE 195

B Speaking

Critical Thinking

A EXPLAIN Look at the photo. It shows people getting help with technology at an Apple Store. Are you good with technology? What do you do when you have a problem with your phone or computer?

Waterloo, Ontario, Canada

SPEAKING SKILL   Explain and Check

When someone asks you for help (for example, with a new piece of technology), explain the steps using clear instructions. You should also check that the listener understands.

If someone says:	Explain	Then check
I don't understand how to . . .	First, you need to . . .	Does that make sense?
Can you help?	Then you . . .	Is that clear?
What do I do next?	If you . . . this, then . . .	Does that help?

B Read and listen to the conversation. Underline any expressions that help explain or check information. Then practice with a partner. 🔊

A: Is that a new phone?
B: Yes, I bought it yesterday.
A: I think mine is a similar model, but yours is the newer version. Do you like it?
B: Yes, but I don't understand how to set up my contacts. Can you help?
A: Sure. First, you need to click on this square. It lets you add the contact information. Does that help?
B: I think so. So I just click on that to add each new person?
A: Exactly. Type in the details there—name, phone number, whatever.
B: What do I do next? To save the details, I mean.
A: Then you press the *save* icon.
B: Oh, I see. The other thing is the apps. It's different from my old phone.
A: If you click on this icon, then you can download a lot of useful apps. Search here for the apps and download them. Does that make sense?
B: Oh, yes. Thanks.

C Complete this conversation with TWO words in each sentence. Then listen and check. 🔊

A: I ¹_____ how to use this chart for American Sign Language.
²_____ help?

B: ³_____ need to know that each sign is a letter of the alphabet. For example, this is how to make an "A." Does that ⁴_____?

A: I think so. So people spell words to talk?

B: Not really. You can spell words with your fingers by using the signs for letters, but it takes too much time. ⁵_____ use this sign, then it means *hello*. ⁶_____ clear?

A: Yes, but how does the grammar work?

B: Now, that's interesting! In ASL, you don't change the verb to show past tense. You need to wave your hand over your shoulder; ⁷_____ make the other signs. That means *past* or *before*. ⁸_____ help?

D CREATE Work with a partner and role-play conversations. | Critical Thinking

Conversation 1
Student A: Ask how to set up a social media profile. Ask follow-up questions.
Student B: Explain how to set up a social media profile. Use these steps and your own ideas:

1. Click on "Account."
2. Fill in personal details and a password.
3. Upload a photo for your profile.
4. Share your first post.
5. Find friends and comment on their posts.

Conversation 2
Student B: Ask how to place a grocery order online. Ask follow-up questions.
Student A: Explain how to place a grocery order online. Use these steps and your own ideas:

1. Log on to the order page.
2. Click "Start order."
3. Click on the food items you want.
4. If you choose the wrong item, click "Cancel."
5. Click "Buy" and give payment details.

E EVALUATE Reflect on your partner's explanation in exercise D and give feedback. | Critical Thinking

- Did your partner explain each part of the process clearly?
- Did your partner check that you understood?

HOW WE COMMUNICATE

Review

SELF-ASSESS

How well can you . . . ?	Very well	OK	I need improvement
use the key vocabulary	☐	☐	☐
say words with consonant clusters	☐	☐	☐
use the present perfect	☐	☐	☐
explain and check	☐	☐	☐

A VOCABULARY Choose the correct word in these sentences.

1. (According / In addition) to using text messages, I communicate with friends on video chat.
2. Please pay (attention / access) to me and look at the board.
3. After I pass my exams, I'm going to (look up / give away) all my schoolbooks.
4. I want to (make sure / support) this charity. Where can I give them some money?
5. I am writing to (inform / invent) you about our new product.

B PRONUNCIATION Underline the TWO words with consonant clusters in each sentence. Then practice saying the sentences.

1. Can you print these documents for me?
2. People spend a lot of money on technology.
3. My presentation is about some new software.

C GRAMMAR Complete this conversation with the present perfect and contractions. Choose *since* or *for*.

A: Hi! Is that a new smartphone?

B: Sort of. I ¹_____ (have) it ² (since / for) March.

A: I've only had mine a year, but it ³_____ (stop) working. I need a new one.

B: By the way, ⁴_____ you _____ (see) Alice recently?

A: No, I ⁵_____ (not / see) her ⁶ (since / for) several weeks.

B: Me neither. I sent her an email, but it came back.

A: She changed her email address. She's had a new one ⁷ (since / for) May.

D SPEAKING SKILL Unscramble the words and say the sentences to explain and check.

1. need to / first / the app / open / you
2. if you / turns on / press this, / then it
3. here / you / open / then / the menu
4. that / make / does / sense ?

RE-ASSESS What skills or language do you still need help with?

Final Tasks

OPTION 1 Explain a piece of technology

A Choose one of the following things to explain to your partner.

- a favorite app
- your smartphone
- a video chat service
- your own choice of technology
- a social media platform
- your favorite online app/website for learning English
- your favorite video game

Make notes about what you need to explain. Answer these questions.

What's the name of the technology? How do you use it?
What do you use it for? Why do you like it?

B Work with a partner. Take turns explaining your piece of technology. Remember to check your partner's understanding.

OPTION 2 Present a form of communication

See Unit 10 Rubric in the Appendix.

A **MODEL** Listen to the end of a presentation and answer these questions. 🔊

1. What was the topic of the student's presentation?

   _____

2. What is the first student's question?

   _____

3. What information does the second student want?

   _____

▼ According to a recent survey, 62% of people get a new phone every 3–4 years.

B ANALYZE THE MODEL Listen again and complete these expressions. 🔊

1. I have _____ for a few questions.
2. Does _____ have a question?
3. Thank you for your _____ talk.
4. Does that make _____?
5. _____ question! I'm not exactly sure of the answer.
6. But I can probably _____ for you.

PRESENTATION SKILL Invite and Answer Questions from the Audience

At the end of a presentation, there is often time to invite questions from your audience. You can finish your presentation like this:

Thank you for listening to my presentation.
Are there any questions?
I have time for a few questions.

When an audience member asks a question, begin your answer like this:
Thank you for your question. / That's a very interesting question.

If you don't know the answer, be honest! You can answer like this:
Great question! I'm not exactly sure of the answer. But I can find out and get back to you.
I'm afraid I don't know the answer to that. Does anyone else in the group/class know?

C PLAN Prepare a short presentation about a form of communication. Choose an idea from the box or your own idea. Complete the chart. Think about the advantages and disadvantages for different people and communities.

| social media | books | video conference tools | text messaging | TV |

Introduce the topic	
Talk about the two advantages	
Talk about the two disadvantages	
Conclude and end	
Invite questions	

D PRACTICE AND PRESENT Work with a group and take turns. Give your presentations and invite questions at the end. Each member asks one question.

Appendix

I. SPEAKING PHRASES

Giving an Opinion *I think...* *I believe...* *In my opinion/view...* *If you ask me,...* *Personally,...*	**Asking for an Opinion** *What do you think?* *What's your opinion?* *What are your thoughts?* *How do you feel about...?* *Do you have anything to add?*
Showing Interest *Really?* *Wow!* *That's funny / interesting / incredible / awful!* *Seriously?* *No kidding!*	**Giving a Tip or Suggestion** *You/We should/could/shouldn't...* *I suggest (that)...* *Let's...* *How about... + (noun/gerund)* *Why don't we/you...*
Agreeing **Disagreeing** *I agree.* *I disagree.* *Right!* *I'm not sure about that.* *Good point.* *I don't agree.* *Exactly.* *That's a good point, but I disagree.* *Absolutely.*	**Asking for Repetition** *I'm sorry?* *Excuse me?* *Could you repeat that?* *Could you say that again?* *Sorry, I didn't catch that.* *Sorry, I missed that.*
Clarifying *What do you mean?* *What does that mean?* *Do you mean...?* *Could you explain that?* *I'm not sure I understand.* *I'm not sure what you mean.*	**Checking Others' Understanding** *Do you understand?* *Is that clear?* *Are you following me?* *Do you have any questions?*
Rephrasing *In other words,...* *To put it another way,...* *What I mean to say...* *The point I'm making is...*	**Interrupting** *Excuse me. / Pardon me.* *I'm sorry to interrupt...* *Can I stop you for a second?* *I'd like to add something.*
Taking Turns *Can/May I say something?* *Could I add something?* *May I continue?* *Let me finish, please.*	**Supporting /Praising Others** *That's a great/excellent idea.* *You make a great point.* *Well done.* *That's fantastic.*
Introducing a Topic *I'm/We're going to talk about...* *My topic is...* *I'm/We're going to present...* *I plan to discuss...* *Let's start with...*	**Listing or Sequencing** *There are many types/kinds of/ways...* *First/First of all/The first point/To start/To begin...* *Second/Secondly/The second point...* *Next/Another/Also/Then/In addition...* *Last/Finally/The last point...*

Giving an Example The first example is . . . For instance, . . . For example, ... such as . . . . . . like . . .	**Repeating and Rephrasing** What you need to know is . . . I'll say this again . . . So again, let me repeat . . . The most important point is . . .
Defining . . . , which means . . . What that means is . . . In other words, . . . Another way to say that is . . . That is . . .	**Talking about a Visual** This graph/infographic/diagram shows/explains . . . The line/box/image represents . . . The main point of this visual is . . . From this we can see . . .
Concluding To sum up, . . . In conclusion, . . . In summary, . . .	**Participating in a Meeting** Welcome, everyone. The purpose of today's meeting is . . . Today's meeting is to discuss . . . Let's move on to the next item. Let me share my screen. Can I share my screen? Can you see my screen? You can post your questions in the chat box.

II. PRONUNCIATION GUIDE

Vowel and Consonant Symbols

Vowel Sounds

Key Word	Symbol
1. **e**at, d**ee**p	/i^y/
2. **i**t, d**i**p	/ɪ/
3. l**a**te, p**ai**n	/e^y/
4. l**e**t, p**e**n	/ɛ/
5. c**a**t, f**a**n	/æ/
6. b**ir**d, t**ur**n	/ɜr/
7. c**u**p, s**u**ffer* **a**bout, symb**o**l	/ʌ/ /ə/
8. h**o**t, st**o**p	/ɑ/
9. t**oo**, n**ew**	/u^w/
10. g**oo**d, c**ou**ld	/ʊ/
11. r**oa**d, n**o**te	/o^w/
12. l**aw**, w**a**lk	/ɔ/
13. f**i**ne, r**i**ce	/a^y/
14. **ou**t, n**ow**	/a^w/
15. b**oy**, j**oi**n	/ɔ^y/

Consonant Sounds

Key Word	Symbol	Key Word	Symbol
1. **p**ie	/p/	13. **sh**oe	/ʃ/
2. **b**oy	/b/	14. mea**s**ure	/ʒ/
3. **t**en	/t/	15. **ch**oose	/tʃ/
4. **d**ay	/d/	16. **j**ob	/dʒ/
5. **k**ey	/k/	17. **m**y	/m/
6. **g**o	/g/	18. **n**o	/n/
7. **f**ine	/f/	19. si**ng**	/ŋ/
8. **v**an	/v/	20. **l**et	/l/
9. **th**ink	/θ/	21. **r**ed	/r/
10. **th**ey	/ð/	22. **w**e	/w/
11. **s**ee	/s/	23. **y**es	/y/
12. **z**oo	/z/	24. **h**ome	/h/

*The vowel sound/symbol in *cup* and *suffer* is used in stressed words and syllables; the vowel sound/symbol in *about* and *symbol* is used in unstressed syllables.

Source: *Well Said: Pronunciation for Clear Communication*, Fourth Edition,
National Geographic Learning/Cengage Learning, 2017.

III. GRAMMAR/VOCABULARY REFERENCES

Spelling Rules for Verbs Ending in -s/-es

1. Add -s to most verbs.	enjoy	enjoys	see	sees
	like	likes	speak	speaks
2. For verbs that end with -ch, -sh, -ss, -x, or -z, add -es.	fix	fixes	wash	washes
	miss	misses	watch	watches
3. For verbs that end in a consonant + y, change the -y to -i and add -es.	study	studies	worry	worries
4. These verbs have special spelling.	do	does	have	has
	go	goes		

Spelling Rules for Verbs Ending in -ing

1. Add -ing to most verbs. This includes any verb ending in -w, -x, or -y.	eat	eating	mix	mixing
	go	going	show	showing
	help	helping	study	studying
2. For verbs that end in a consonant + e, drop the -e and add -ing.	become	becoming	write	writing
3. For verbs that end in -ie, change the -ie to -y and add -ing.	lie	lying	tie	tying
4. For one-syllable verbs that end in a consonant + vowel + consonant (CVC), double the final consonant and add -ing.	plan	planning	stop	stopping
	put	putting	win	winning
5. For two-syllable verbs that end in CVC, double the final consonant only if the last syllable is stressed.	be•gin	beginning	for•get	forgetting

Spelling Rules for Verbs Ending in -d/-ed (Regular Verbs)

1. Add -(e)d to most regular verbs. This includes any regular verbs ending in -w or -x.	call	called	laugh	laughed
	open	opened	start	started
2. For regular verbs that end in a consonant + y, change the -y to -i and add -ed.	carry	carried	study	studied
	identify	identified	worry	worried
3. For regular verbs that end in a vowel + y, just add -ed.	enjoy	enjoyed	stay	stayed
4. For one-syllable regular verbs that end in a consonant + vowel + consonant (CVC), double the final consonant and add -ed.	jog	jogging	stop	stopping
	plan	planning	win	winning
5. For two-syllable verbs that end in CVC, double the final consonant only if the last syllable is stressed.	per•mit	permitted	re•fer	referred

Spelling Rules for Comparative and Superlative Adjective

1. For one-syllable adjectives and adverbs, add -(e)r / -(e)st.	large fast	larg**er** fast**er**	larg**est** fast**est**
2. For one-syllable adjectives that end in a consonant + vowel + consonant (CVC), double the final consonant and add -er /-est.	big hot	big**ger** hot**ter**	big**gest** hot**test**
3. For two-syllable adjectives that end in -y, change the -y to -i and add -er/-est.	ea·sy hap·py	eas**ier** happ**ier**	eas**iest** happ**iest**
4. For most other adjectives with two or more syllables, use *more* and *most*.	care·ful im·portant	**more** careful **more** important	**most** careful **most** important

Verbs Followed by Gerunds or Infinitives

Verbs Followed by Gerunds		Verbs Followed by Gerunds or Infinitives		Verbs Followed by Infinitives	
appreciate	mention	begin	prefer	agree	offer
avoid	mind	continue	remember*	appear	plan
consider	miss	forget*	(can/can't) stand	ask	pretend
discuss	practice	hate	start	choose	promise
dislike	quit	like	stop*	claim	refuse
enjoy	recommend	love	try (in past form tried)*	decide	seem
finish	regret	need*		demand	tend
imagine	suggest			expect	try
keep	understand	*The meaning changes between use of gerund and infinitive.		hope	want
				learn	

Vocabulary Notebook Template

A vocabulary notebook is a way to keep track of the words you are learning.
There are many ways to organize a vocabulary notebook. Here is one way:

Word & part of speech	Definition or synonyms	Antonyms	Example sentence
unique (adj)	unlike anything else; special	common, ordinary	My name is unique; I don't know anyone else who has it.

You many also want to include a translation, other word forms, collocations, etc.
Note what's helpful for you to remember the words.

Irregular Verbs

Base Verb	Simple Past Verb	Past Participle	Base Verb	Simple Past Verb	Past Participle
become	became	become	know	knew	known
begin	began	begun	lead	led	led
bet	bet	bet	leave	left	left
bite	bit	bitten	lend	lent	lent
break	broke	broken	let	let	let
bring	brought	brought	lose	lost	lost
build	built	built	make	made	made
buy	bought	bought	mean	meant	meant
choose	chose	chosen	meet	met	met
come	came	come	pay	paid	paid
cost	cost	cost	put	put	put
cut	cut	cut	quit	quit	quit
dig	dug	dug	read	read	read
draw	drew	drawn	ride	rode	ridden
drink	drank	drunk	run	ran	run
drive	drove	driven	say	said	said
eat	ate	eaten	see	saw	seen
fall	fell	fallen	sell	sold	sold
feed	fed	fed	send	sent	sent
feel	felt	felt	set	set	set
fight	fought	fought	sing	sang	sung
find	found	found	sit	sat	sat
fly	flew	flown	sleep	slept	slept
forget	forgot	forgotten	speak	spoke	spoken
forgive	forgave	forgiven	spend	spent	spent
freeze	froze	frozen	stand	stood	stood
get	got	gotten	swim	swam	swum
give	gave	given	take	took	taken
go	went	gone	teach	taught	taught
grow	grew	grown	tell	told	told
hear	heard	heard	think	thought	thought
hide	hid	hidden	understand	understood	understood
hit	hit	hit	wake	woke	woken
hold	held	held	wear	wore	worn
hurt	hurt	hurt	win	won	won
keep	kept	kept	write	wrote	written

IV. VOCABULARY INDEX

AW = Academic word

Unit 1	Page	CEFR Level
adventure	6	A2
apply	14	B1
candidate **AW**	14	B1
communicate **AW**	6	B1
creative **AW**	6	B1
dangerous	6	A2
enthusiastic	14	B2
equipment **AW**	14	B1
experience	6	B1
explore	6	B1
interview	14	B1
manage	14	B1
opportunity	6	B1
ordinary	6	B1
perfect	14	A2
positive **AW**	14	B1
responsible for	14	B1
skills	6	B1
training	14	B1
view	6	B1

Unit 2	Page	CEFR Level
brain	34	A2
bring back	26	A2
childhood	26	B1
define **AW**	26	B1
discover	34	B1
emotion	26	B2
experiment	34	B1
forget	34	A2
happiness	26	B1
human	34	B1
lonely	26	B1
memorable	34	B2
memory	26	A2
reason	34	A2
recall	34	B2
recognize	34	B1
remind … of	26	B1
researcher **AW**	34	B2
sadness	26	B2
situation	26	B1

Unit 3	Page	CEFR Level
achieve **AW**	54	B1
advertise	46	B1
aim	46	B1
attract	54	B1
audience	54	B1
character	46	B1
commercial	46	B2
complicated	54	B1
customer	46	A2
design **AW**	54	B1
encourage	46	B1
figure out	54	B2
image **AW**	54	B2
message	54	A1
popular	46	A2
product	46	B1
quality	46	B2
represent	46	B2
result	54	B1
stand out	54	B2

Unit 4	Page	CEFR Level
amount	66	B1
average	74	B1
decrease	74	B1
destroy	66	B1
drought	66	C1
effect	74	B1
flood	66	B1
forecast	66	B1
heat	74	B1
increase	74	B1
location **AW**	74	B2
measure	66	B2
predict **AW**	66	B1
prevent	74	B1
rainfall **AW**	66	B1
reach	74	B1
rise	74	B1
season	74	B1
storm	66	A2
temperature	66	A2

Unit 5	Page	CEFR Level
appearance	94	B1
calorie	86	OF
connect	94	B1
diet	86	B1
fast food	86	A2
flavor	94	B1
fresh	86	A2
industry	86	B1
nervous	94	B1
physical **AW**	86	B2
processed **AW**	86	B2
regular	86	B1
sense	94	B1
sight	94	B1
smell	94	B1
sound	94	A2
taste	94	B1
throw away	86	B1
touch	94	B1
weight	86	B1

Unit 6	Page	CEFR Level
architect AW	106	B1
architecture	114	B1
comfortable	106	A2
crowd	114	A2
desert	114	A2
energy AW	114	B1
engineer	106	A2
float	106	B1
government	114	B1
ground	106	B1
look like	106	B1
luxury	106	B1
nothing	114	A2
population	114	B1
power	114	B1
private	114	B1
public transportation	114	B1
resident AW	106	B2
safe	106	A2
solution	106	B1

Unit 7	Page	CEFR Level
benefit AW	134	B1
blood	134	A2
bone	126	B1
cause	134	B2
certainly	126	A2
continue	126	B1
control	134	B1
definitely AW	126	B1
disease	134	B1
double	126	A2
feed	134	B1
improve	134	A2
lead to	134	B2
lifestyle AW	126	B2
medicine	126	B1
mental AW	134	B2
period AW	126	B1
possibly	126	A2
probably	126	A2
protect	134	B1

Unit 8	Page	CEFR Level
afford	154	B1
appeal	154	B2
award	154	B2
constantly AW	146	B2
disappear	146	B1
forever	146	B1
instrument	154	A2
last	146	B1
material	146	B2
original	154	B1
perform	154	B1
permanent	146	B1
piece	154	B2
public	146	B1
sculpture	146	B1
simple	154	A2
solid	146	B2
style	154	B1
temporary AW	146	B1
typical	154	B1

Unit 9	Page	CEFR Level
allow	166	B1
attack	174	B1
behavior	166	B1
belong to	174	A2
coast	166	B1
conflict AW	174	B2
continent AW	166	B1
crop	174	B1
illegal AW	174	B2
leisure AW	166	B1
limit	174	B2
ocean	166	B1
pollution	174	B1
relationship	166	B1
require AW	174	B1
reserve	174	B2
scenery	174	B1
species	166	B2
tourism	166	B1
wildlife	166	B1

Unit 10	Page	CEFR Level
access AW	186	B1
according to	186	B1
expert AW	194	B1
express	194	B2
foreign	194	A2
give away	186	B1
importance	194	B1
in addition to	194	B1
inform	186	B1
invent	186	B1
look up	186	B1
make sure	186	A2
offer	186	A2
pay attention to	194	B1
point	194	A2
sign	194	B1
speech	194	B1
support	194	B1
system	186	B1
wide	186	B1

V. SPEAKING RUBRICS

Unit 1: EXPLORING WORK

Student name:

Date:

Use this rubric to assess each student's speaking. You can add other aspects of their speaking you'd like to assess at the bottom of the rubric, or use the space for more explanation.

4 = Excellent
3 = Good
2 = Satisfactory
1 = Needs improvement

Discuss what makes a good job	4	3	2	1
Content and Organization • Explains the job ranking. • Gives clear reasons for the ranking. • Offers ideas and keeps the discussion going.				
Language Use and Fluency • Language is easy to understand and follow. • Uses a variety of words, including words taught in the unit. • Speaks smoothly with few hesitations or breaks.				
Body Language and Voice • Makes good eye contact and uses natural gestures. • Speaks loudly enough for everyone to hear. • Speed is not too fast or too slow.				

Unit 2: GOOD TIME, GOOD FEELINGS

Student name:

Date:

Use this rubric to assess each student's speaking. You can add other aspects of their speaking you'd like to assess at the bottom of the rubric, or use the space for more explanation.

4 = Excellent
3 = Good
2 = Satisfactory
1 = Needs improvement

Present a special object or photo	4	3	2	1
Content and Organization • Gives a description of the object or photo. • Tells a clear story about it. • Says why it is special and explains feelings about it. • Structures the presentation clearly.				
Language Use and Fluency • Language is easy to understand and follow. • Uses a variety of words, including words taught in the unit. • Speaks smoothly with few hesitations or breaks.				
Body Language and Voice • Makes good eye contact and uses natural gestures. • Speaks loudly enough for everyone to hear. • Speed is not too fast or too slow.				

Unit 3: THE MARKETING MACHINE	Present an advertisement	4	3	2	1
Student name: **Date:** Use this rubric to assess each student's speaking. You can add other aspects of their speaking you'd like to assess at the bottom of the rubric, or use the space for more explanation. 4 = Excellent 3 = Good 2 = Satisfactory 1 = Needs improvement	**Content and Organization** • Gives a complete description of the advertisement: what it's for, where it appears, what it looks like, and the message. • Explains why it does or doesn't work well. • Works well with other members of the group. • Structures the presentation clearly.				
	Language Use and Fluency • Language is easy to understand and follow. • Uses a variety of words, including words taught in the unit. • Speaks smoothly with few hesitations or breaks.				
	Body Language and Voice • Makes good eye contact and uses natural gestures. • Speaks loudly enough for everyone to hear. • Speed is not too fast or too slow.				

Unit 4: WILD WEATHER	Present a process	4	3	2	1
Student name: **Date:** Use this rubric to assess each student's speaking. You can add other aspects of their speaking you'd like to assess at the bottom of the rubric, or use the space for more explanation. 4 = Excellent 3 = Good 2 = Satisfactory 1 = Needs improvement	**Content and Organization** • Gives a clear description of the process. • Describes the steps logically. • Structures the presentation clearly. • Uses slides effectively.				
	Language Use and Fluency • Language is easy to understand and follow. • Uses a variety of words, including words taught in the unit. • Speaks smoothly with few hesitations or breaks.				
	Body Language and Voice • Makes good eye contact and uses natural gestures. • Speaks loudly enough for everyone to hear. • Speed is not too fast or too slow.				

Unit 5: FOOD ON THE MOVE

Student name:

Date:

Use this rubric to assess each student's speaking. You can add other aspects of their speaking you'd like to assess at the bottom of the rubric, or use the space for more explanation.

4 = Excellent
3 = Good
2 = Satisfactory
1 = Needs improvement

Present an argument about food	4	3	2	1
Content and Organization • Explains the argument and includes three reasons. • Structures the presentation clearly. • Uses an effective hook and call to action.				
Language Use and Fluency • Language is easy to understand and follow. • Uses a variety of words, including words taught in the unit. • Speaks smoothly with few hesitations or breaks.				
Body Language and Voice • Makes good eye contact and uses natural gestures. • Speaks loudly enough for everyone to hear. • Speed is not too fast or too slow.				

Unit 6: HOUSING FOR THE FUTURE

Student name:

Date:

Use this rubric to assess each student's speaking. You can add other aspects of their speaking you'd like to assess at the bottom of the rubric, or use the space for more explanation.

4 = Excellent
3 = Good
2 = Satisfactory
1 = Needs improvement

Plan a new city	4	3	2	1
Content and Organization • Describes ideas for the new city, including location, energy, transportation, population, etc. • Explains reasons for the ideas. • Offers ideas, encourages others, and keeps the discussion going. • Works well with other members of the group.				
Language Use and Fluency • Language is easy to understand and follow. • Uses a variety of words, including words taught in the unit. • Speaks smoothly with few hesitations or breaks.				
Body Language and Voice • Makes good eye contact and uses natural gestures. • Speaks loudly enough for everyone to hear. • Speed is not too fast or too slow.				

Unit 7: THE HUMAN BODY

Student name:

Date:

Use this rubric to assess each student's speaking. You can add other aspects of their speaking you'd like to assess at the bottom of the rubric, or use the space for more explanation.

4 = Excellent
3 = Good
2 = Satisfactory
1 = Needs improvement

Discuss pros and cons of future situations	4	3	2	1
Content and Organization • Describes 2–3 pros and cons of the situation. • Gives clear examples of the pros and cons. • Says how likely the situation is. • Offers ideas, encourages others, and keeps the discussion going.				
Language Use and Fluency • Language is easy to understand and follow. • Uses a variety of words, including words taught in the unit. • Speaks smoothly with few hesitations or breaks.				
Body Language and Voice • Makes good eye contact and uses natural gestures. • Speaks loudly enough for everyone to hear. • Speed is not too fast or too slow.				

Unit 8: LEARN TO LOVE ART

Student name:

Date:

Use this rubric to assess each student's speaking. You can add other aspects of their speaking you'd like to assess at the bottom of the rubric, or use the space for more explanation.

4 = Excellent
3 = Good
2 = Satisfactory
1 = Needs improvement

Have a class debate	4	3	2	1
Content and Organization • Gives two arguments for their idea. • Gives details or examples for those arguments. • Says why they disagree with the other group. • Works well with other members of the group.				
Language Use and Fluency • Language is easy to understand and follow. • Uses a variety of words, including words taught in the unit. • Speaks smoothly with few hesitations or breaks.				
Body Language and Voice • Makes good eye contact and uses natural gestures. • Speaks loudly enough for everyone to hear. • Speed is not too fast or too slow.				

Unit 9: OUR RELATIONSHIP WITH NATURE

Student name:

Date:

Use this rubric to assess each student's speaking. You can add other aspects of their speaking you'd like to assess at the bottom of the rubric, or use the space for more explanation.

4 = Excellent
3 = Good
2 = Satisfactory
1 = Needs improvement

Give a presentation about the natural world	4	3	2	1
Content and Organization • Describes the part of the world and says why it is important. • Describes 3-4 key points and gives details. • Says why we should protect the area. • Structures the presentation clearly and uses an effective hook.				
Language Use and Fluency • Language is easy to understand and follow. • Uses a variety of words, including words taught in the unit. • Speaks smoothly with few hesitations or breaks.				
Body Language and Voice • Makes good eye contact and uses natural gestures. • Speaks loudly enough for everyone to hear. • Speed is not too fast or too slow.				

Unit 10: HOW WE COMMUNICATE

Student name:

Date:

Use this rubric to assess each student's speaking. You can add other aspects of their speaking you'd like to assess at the bottom of the rubric, or use the space for more explanation.

4 = Excellent
3 = Good
2 = Satisfactory
1 = Needs improvement

Present a form of communication	4	3	2	1
Content and Organization • Describes the technology clearly. • Gives two advantages and two disadvantages for the technology. • Structures the presentation clearly and uses an effective hook. • Invites and responds to questions effectively.				
Language Use and Fluency • Language is easy to understand and follow. • Uses a variety of words, including words taught in the unit. • Speaks smoothly with few hesitations or breaks.				
Body Language and Voice • Makes good eye contact and uses natural gestures. • Speaks loudly enough for everyone to hear. • Speed is not too fast or too slow.				

ACKNOWLEDGMENTS

The Authors and Publisher would like to acknowledge the educators around the world who participated in the development of the third edition of *Pathways Listening, Speaking, and Critical Thinking*.

A special thanks to our Advisory Board for their valuable input during development.

Advisory Board

Baher F. AlDabba, Amideast Gaza; **Hossein Askari**, Houston Community College; **Dilara Ataman Akalin**, TOBB University; **Andrew Boon**, Toyo Gakuen University; **Fatih Bozoğlu**, Antalya Bilim University; **Julie Cote**, Houston Community College; **Kristen Cox**, Global Launch at ASU; **Patricia Fiene**, Midwestern Career College; **Ronnie Hill**, Royal Melbourne Institute of Technology; **Greg Holloway**, University of Kitakyushu; **Ragette Jawad**, Lawrence Technological University; **Elizabeth Macdonald**, Sacred Heart University; **Daniel Paller**, Kinjo Gakuin University; **Kes Poupaert**, INTO Manchester; **Juan Quintana**, Instituto Cultural Peruano Norteamericano; **Anouchka Rachelson**, Miami Dade College; **David Ruzicka**, Shinsu University; **Gabrielle Smallbone**, Kingston University; **Debra Wainscott**, Baylor University

Global Reviewers

Asia

John Paul Abellera, San Beda College-Alabang; **Andrew Acosta**, Udonpittayanukoon School; **Jherwin Adora**, Department of Education Philippines; **Mubarak Ali**, Unilever; **Joan Arado**, TESDA PTS-Misamis Occidental; **Frederick Bacala,** Yokohama City University; **Katherine Bauer**, Clark Memorial International High School; **Richard Bent**, Kwassui Women's University; **Teresa Bolen**, Ryukoku University; **Johnny Burns,** Kansai Daigaku; **Darine Chehwan**, Rest-art Studio; **Simon Cornelius**, Kansai University; **Aurelio Da Costa**, UNICEF/Senai Language Centre; **Carlos Daley**, London Institute; **Maria del Vecchio,** Nihon University; **Ria De Ocera**, Udomsuksa School; **Michael Donzella**, Kaichi International University; **David Groff,** Meiji University; **Akiko Hagiwara,** Tokyo University of Pharmacy and Life Sciences; **Sisilia Halimi**, Humanities Universitas Indonesia; **Jane Harland,** Fukoka University; **Makoto Hayashi,** Nagoya University; **Patrizia Hayashi**, Meikai University; **Andrea Noemie Hilomen**, Private teacher; **Ha Hoang**, Au Chau Language School; **Ana Sofia Hofmeyr,** Kansai University; **Stephen Hofstee,** Kanto Gakuin University; **Stephen Howes,** Tokyo Seitoku University Fukaya Junior High School; **Yuko Igarashi**, Ritsumeikan University; **Mari Inoue**, Tokyo University of Science; **David Johnson,** Kyushu Sangyo University; **Sarita Joyaka**, Nongkipittayakhom; **Chong Jui Jong**, Universiti Sains Malaysia; **Yuko Kawae,** Kindai University; **Megumi Kobayashi,** Seikei University; **Mutsumi Kondo**, Kyoto University of Foreign Studies; **Gomer Jay Legaspi**, Caraga State University; **Indah Ludij,** Academic Writing Center, Universitas Indonesia; **Kelly MacDonald**, Fukuoka University; **Anh Mai**, Van Lang University; **Tiina Matikainen**, Tamagawa University; **Eiko Matsubara**, Rissho University; **Jason May**, Den-en Chofu Gakuen; **Sean Collin Mehmet**, Matsumoto University; **Mabell Mingoy**, Teach for the Philippines; **Mari Miyao,** Kyoto University of Foreign Studies; **Wah Mon**, Private teacher; **Masaki Mori,** Aoyama-Gakuinn University; **Gerald Muirhead**, Tohoku Gakuin University; **Charlotte Murakami,** Kurume University; **Duong Nguyen**, APU; **Ly Huyền Nguyễn**, FPT High School; **Vinh Nguyen**, Hanoi University; **Ngan Nguyễn**; **Thảo Nguyễn**, Gia Việt English Center; **MaiKhoi NguyenThi**, Danang Architecture University; **Takeshi Nozawa**, Ritsumeikan University; **Naomi Ogasawara,** Gunma Prefectural Women's University; **Mari Ogawa**, Meiji University; **Megumi Okano**, Keio University; **Hisako Osuga,** Meiji University; **Gellian Ostrea**, Manolo Fortich National High School; **Tina Ottman,** Doshisha University, Bukkyo University; **Ardy Paembonan**, SMA El-Shaddai Jayapura; **Anthony Paxton**, Ibaraki Prefectural Takezono High School; **Hong Pham**, Brendon Primary School; **Huong Pham**, Foreign Languages Specialised School, University of Languages and International Studies; **John Plagens** Lutheran College; **Javeria Rana**, The City School; **Rebecca Reyes**, Captain Albert Aguilar National High School; **Florencio Salmasan**, School of the Holy Spirit; **Sherri Scanlan**, Toyama Prefectural University; **Naoki Senrui**, Komazawa University; **Nanik Shobikah**, IAIN Pontianak; **Coleman South,** Saga National University; **Yukiko Sugiyama**, Keio University; **Pavloska Susanna**, Doshisha University; **Eri Tamura**, Ishikawa Prefectural University; **Yuko Tokisato**, Kansai University; **Saeko Toyoshima**, Tsuru University; **Janssen Undag**, Darunapolytechnic Technological College; **Carl Vollmer,** Ritsumeikan Uji Junior and Senior High School; **Isra Wongsarnpigoon**, Kanda University of International Studies

Europe

Ana Maria Andrei, Liceul Teoretic de Informatica; **Regina Bacanskiene**, Kaunas School; **Janice Bain,** Glasgow International College; **Oana Banu**, LPS; **Daniela Berntzen; Sarah Bishopp**, Kaplan International College London; **Anna Broumerioti**; **Cath Brown**, The University of Sheffield; **Laura Cannella**, Kaplan International College London; **Barbara Cavicchiolli**, INTO Manchester; **Ioana Mirela Cojocaru**, Liceul Tehnologic Anghel Saligny; **Viorica Condrat**, USARB; **Astrid D'Andrea**, I.I.S. Croce-Aleramo; **Liesl Daries**, English with Liesl; **Kurtis De Souza-Snares,** Kaplan International Pathways; **Elona Dhepa**, 7 Marsi; **Maral Dosmagambetova,** Lingua College; **Camelia-Adriana Dulau**, Simion Bărnuțiu; **Ruthanna Farragher**, Kaplan; **Olesia Fesenko**, Vyshhorod Lyceum "Suziria"; **Cristina Foltmann**, ITCS Abba Ballini; **Laura Gheorghita**, Scoala Gimnaziala Grigore Geamanu Turcinesti; **Marian Gonzalez**, Liceo de Idiomas Modernos; **Paulina Holesz**, Private teacher; **Lindsey Hollywood**, Universtiy of Liverpool International College; **Sarah Hopwood**, University of Nottingham International College; **Barbara Howarth**, Glasgow International College; **Barbara Howarth**, Glasgow International College; **Jana Jilkova**, ICV & Pedagogical Faculty;

Alina Loata, Colegiul National Dimitrie Cantemir; **Ia Manjgaladze**, Access Program Teacher; **Christiana Mili**, Private teacher; **Laura Morrison**, Glasgow International College; **Robert Pinkham-Smith**, University of Essex International College; **Yuliya Pokroyeva**, Private teacher; **Eva Rodaki**, Private teacher; **Alina Rotaru**, Twinkle Star; **Carme RR**, CEIP Joan Mas Pollença; **Tatiana Silvesan**, Centrul Scolar de Educatie Incluziva; **Bianca Somesan**, Palatul Copiilor Targu Mures; **Elena Strugaru**, Britanica Learning Centre; **Mina Vermot**, Miduca; **Matthew Wilson,** Brunel University London; **Emily Wright**, Arden University

Latin America and the Caribbean

Maria Aguilar, Universidad Nacional de La Rioja; **Karina Aldana**, Colegio la Asuncion; **Mariela Amarante,** Sunshine Academy; **Auricéa Bacelar**, Top Seven Idiomas; **Verónica Bonilla**, Universidad Anáhuac de Puebla; **Lucila Caballero**, MEDUCA; **Milagros Calderón Miró,** Colegio San Antonio IHM; **Maria Carrizo**, Nores; **Erika Ceballos**, Escuela Nacional Preparatoria; **Johana Coronel**, Private teacher; **Marcelo D'Elia**, Centro Britanico Idiomas; **Sophia De Carvalho**, Inglês Express; **Corina Diaz**, CCSA; **Isabela Dias**, Inglês Express; **Joseph Duque**, Unidad Educativa Leibnitz; **Esperanza Espejo**, Iteso; **Susana Espinosa**, ICPNA; **Carolina Ferreira**, Private teacher; **Matheus Figueiredo**, Private teacher; **Andrea Garcia Hernandez**, Bilingual School; **Alessandra Gotardo**, IYEnglish - Language & Culture; **Santo Guzmán**, JFK Institute of Languages, Inc.; **Cecibel Juliao**, Meduca / Udelas; **Letícia Kayano**, Private teacher; **Sandra Landi**, Private teacher; **Patricia Lanners**, Universidad de las Americas Puebla; **Arenas Laura**, ITESO; **Diana Lopez**, ITSE; **Mario López Ayala**, Universidad Autónoma de Sinaloa; **Rosa Awilda Lopez Fernandez**, Universidad Acción Pro-Educación y Culturalic Dominicana; **Fabricio Romeo Mejia Lopez**, Academia Europea; **Silvia Luna**, Universidad Evangélica; **Manuel Malhaber Diaz**, Colegio Nacional San Juan De Chota; **Daniel Martins Aragão**, Private teacher; **Victor Hugo Medina Soares**, Cultura Inglesa Belo Horizonte; **Angélica Parada**, CBA; **Adela Perez del Viso**, Fundación E.S.Y.C.; **Byron Quinde**, Unidad Educativa Particular de la Asunción; **Maria Alejandra Quirch**, Instituto San Roman; **Joselyn Ramos Cuba**, UNMSM; **Jorge Reategui**, Universidad Continental; **Jazmin Reyes**, La Dolorosa; **Iliana Rivas**, ITESO; **Sheirys Hidalgo Ruiz**, Ministerio de Educacion Publica; **Adelina Ruiz Guerrero**, Instituto Tecnológico y de Estudios Superiores de Occidente; **Maribel Santiago**, Colegio de Bachilleres; **Margaret Simons**, English Center; **Margaret Simons**, English Center; **Sheily Sosa García**, ICPNA; **Jane Stories**, Private teacher; **María Trigos**, ITSX; **Henrique Ucci**, Liverpool English Institute; **Ana Carolina Vargas Arreola**, Colegio Vizcaya; **Laura Zurutuza**, ITESO

Middle East and Africa

Merve Akyiğit, Adana Doğa Schools; **Yousef Albozom**, America-Mideast Educational and Training Services; **Rehab Alzeiny**, IPS; **Rais Attamimi**, UTAS-Salalah; **Ezgi Avar**, Tuzla Doğa Lisesi; **Pınar Çakır,** Doğa Koleji; **Burçe Çimeli,** Doğa Koleji; **Christelle Gernique Djoukouo Talla**, Government Bilingual High School Ekangte; **Canan Dülger**, Doğa Koleji; **Manal ElMazbouh,** American University of the Middle East; **Fatma el-zahraa El-sayed zaki nassef**, Damietta Official Language schools; **Necmi Ersungur**, İtü Eta Vakfı Doğa Koleji; **Mary Goveas,** University of Bahrain; **Farhad Hama**, Sulaimani University; **Michael King,** Community College of Qatar; **Georgios Kormpas**, Al Yamamah University; **Volga Kurbanzade**, Okan University; **Eni Ermawati Lasito**, Lusail University; **Gonca Mavuk**, Atasehir ITU Doga College; **Amina Moubtassim**, ALC; **Doaa Najjar**, PISOD; **Mohammad Esmaeel Nasrabadi**, Private teacher; **Naki Erhan Ozer**, Doga Schools; **Rehab Raouf**, Al Safwa School; **Nurhayat Şenman**, Özlüce Doğa Koleji Lise; **Choukri Serhane**, CHSS; **Hussam Tannera**, America-Mideast Educational and Training Services; **Pedro Vemba**, Liceu do Soyo; **Cüneyt Yüce**, Istanbul Okan University

USA and Canada

Galyna, Arabadzhy, St. Cloud State University; **Elizabeth Armstrong,** Midwestern Career College; **Judy Bagg**, Pierce; **Karin Bates**, Intercambio Uniting Communities; **Mandie Bauer**, ASC English; **Elisabeth Bowman,** Schoolcraft College; **Teresa Cheung**, North Shore Community College; **Colleen Comidy**, Seattle Central College; **Jacquelin Cunningham,** Harold Washington College; **Jean Danic**, Hillsborough Community College; **Rosalia dela Cruz**, NorQuest College; **Christine Dick**, Arizona State University; **Yvonne Dunham Slobodenko**, University of Tennessee at Chattanooga; **Karen Eichhorn**, International English Center; **Thomas Fox,** Dallas College; **Diana Garcia**, Union County College; **Bertha George**, Union County College; **Thomas Germain**, University of Colorado Boulder; **Debra Gibes**, Mott Community College; **John Glover,** Old Saybrook High School; **Christine Guro**, University of Hawaii at Manoa; **Carrie Hein-Paredes**, MATC; **Deanna Henderson**, Language Consultants International; **Tom Justice,** North Shore Community College; **Evan Kendall,** Los Angeles City College; **Michael Kelley,** Hillsborough Community College; **Karen E. Kyle**, Aims Community College; **Laura Lamour**, Florida International University; **Maureen Lanseu**r, Henry Ford College; **Heidi Lieb**, Bergen Community College; **Layla Malander**, PLACE/Colorado State University; **Tim Mathews**, Nashville State Community College; **Richard McDorman**, Language On; **Susan McElwain**, Mohawk College of Applied Arts and Technology; **Jason McKenzie**, Apex Language and Career College; **William Miller Jr.**, H.EN; **Lilia Myers Van Pelt,** Colorado State University Pueblo; **Sandra Navarro**, Glendale Community College; **Linda Neuman**, Anne Arundel Community College; **Susan Niemeyer**, Los Angeles City College; **Mariah Nix**, Lumos Language School; **Cheryl Pakos**, Union County College; **Jim Papple**, York University; **Cora Perrone**, Southern CT State University; **Deborah Pfeifer,** Fort Hays State University; **Loretta Quan**, Schoolcraft College; **Thomas Riedmiller,** University of Northern; **Lisa Rivoallon**, Gavilan College; **Noele Simmons**, George Mason University; **Pamela Smart-Smith**, Virginia Tech; **Kelly Smith**, English Language Institute, UCSD Extension; **Brandt Snook**, University of Louisiana – Lafayette; **Shoshanna Starzynski,** Global Launch, Arizona State University; **Kirsten Stauffer**, Immigrant and Refugee Center of Northern Colorado; **JoAnn Stehly**, North Orange County Community College District; **Karen Vallejo**, University of California, Irvine; **Sharifeh Van Court**, Dallas College; **Melissa Vervinck**, ESL Institute at Oakland University; **Christy Williams**, INTO USF; **Paula Yerman,** Los Angeles City College

CREDITS

Illustrations: All illustrations are owned by © Cengage.

Cover ©Sara Zanini/Getty Images; **ii** (tl) The Asahi Shimbun/Getty Images, (cl1) © Ami Vitale/National Geographic Image Collection, (cl2) Sipa USA/Alamy Stock Photo, (cl3) Frank Rumpenhorst/DPA/Getty Images, (bl) Ariyani Tedjo/Alamy Stock Photo; **iv** (tl) © Paul Brouns, (cl1) Thomas Barwick/DigitalVision/Getty Images, (cl2) Dan Kitwood/Getty Images News/Getty Images, (cl3) © George Karbus, (bl) © John Stanmeyer/National Geographic Image Collection; **vi** (t) © Pete McBride/National Geographic Image Collection, (cl) Skynesher/E+/Getty Images, (cr) © Jason Treat / National Geographic Image Collection; **vii** OR Images/DigitalVision/Getty Images; **1** The Asahi Shimbun/Getty Images; **2-3** (Spread) © Iwan Baan; **4** (cr) © Frans Schepers/National Geographic Image Collection, (br) © Ricardo Moreno/National Geographic Image Collection; **6** (t) © Annie Griffiths, (cl) © Mark Thiessen; **9** Jung Getty/Moment/Getty Images; **11** Hajarah Nalwadda/Xinhua News Agency/Getty Images; **12** Tom Werner/DigitalVision/Getty Images; **15** © © Disney/National Geographic Image Collection; **19** Hobo_018/E+/Getty Images; **21** © Ami Vitale/National Geographic Image Collection; **22-23** (Spread) © Robin D. Moore/National Geographic Image Collection; **25** Jon Tyson/Unsplash.com; **26** Skynesher/E+/Getty Images; **29** Betsie Van der Meer/Stone/Getty Images; **31** © Every Life is a Story, LLC., 2017; **32** Fizkes/Shutterstock.com; **34** Courtesy of Dr. Wilma A. Bainbridge; **37** Marco Bottigelli/Moment/Getty Images; **39** MoMo Productions/DigitalVision/Getty Images; **41** Sipa USA/Alamy Stock Photo; **42-43** (Spread) Phynart Studio/E+/Getty Images; **44** Kristoffer Tripplaar/Alamy Stock Photo; **46** (tl) Mary Balchos/Alamy Stock Photo, (tr) Nature and Science/Alamy Stock Photo, (bl) Lanier/iStock Unreleased/Getty Images, (br) Kisler Creations/Alamy Stock Photo; **49** Redpixel.PL/Shutterstock.com; **50** Courtesy of The Advertising Archives; **51** Monopoly919/Shutterstock.com; **54** Klaus Vedfelt/DigitalVision/Getty Images; **59** The Asahi Shimbun/Getty Images; **61** Frank Rumpenhorst/DPA/Getty Images; **62-63** (Spread) © Marco Korosec; **65** Abdul Momin/F MetS/Bav Media/Shutterstock.com; **66** (tl) Totajla/Shutterstock.com, (tr) Christianpinillo/Shutterstock.com, (bl) Koto_feja/E+/Getty Images, (br) Kreml/Shutterstock.com; **70** (tr1) U.S. Department of the Interior (USGS), (tr2) NSIDC, WDC/Science Photo Library/Science Source; **71** © Tracie Alexis Seimon; **72** Monkey Business Images/Shutterstock.com; **74** Jean-Philippe Ksiazek/AFP/Getty Images; **76** Cmannphoto/E+/Getty Images; **79** (c) Skynesher/E+/Getty Images; **80** (tr) Alina.Kalinina/Shutterstock.com; **81** Ariyani Tedjo/Alamy Stock Photo; **82** (tr)Thanasis/Moment/Getty Images, (bl) Ravsky/Shutterstock.com; **82-83** (Spread) Anson_iStock/iStock/Getty Images; **83** (tl) LauriPatterson/E+/Getty Images, (tr) AGCuesta/Shutterstock.com, (bc) Ruslan Semichev/Shutterstock.com; **85** Danny Lehman/The Image Bank/Getty Images; **86** Vitte Yevhen/Shutterstock.com; **91** Eclipse_images/E+/Getty Images; **94** (tl) Anne Stephneson/EyeEm/Getty Images, (tr) O_Solara/Shutterstock.com, (bl) Mariia Zotova/Moment/Getty Images, (br) WildStrawberry/Shutterstock.com; **97** Dave Stamboulis/Alamy Stock Photo; **99** Daniel Reiter/Alamy Stock Photo; **101** © Paul Brouns; **104** Barone Firenze/Shutterstock.com; **106** © Michael Yamashita/National Geographic Image Collection; **109** World Discovery/Alamy Stock Photo; **111** Tony Watson/Alamy Stock Photo; **112** Xinhua/Alamy Stock Photo; **115** Robertharding/Alamy Stock Photo; **117** Shadow of light/Alamy Stock Photo; **119** Sturti/E+/Getty Images; **121** Thomas Barwick/DigitalVision/Getty Images; **122** (b1) Fonikum/DigitalVision Vectors/Getty Images, (b2) Fonikum/DigitalVision Vectors/Getty Images; **122-123** (Spread) © Pete McBride/National Geographic Image Collection; **124** © Charlotte Stanford/National Geographic Creative/National Geographic Image Collection; **127** Pascopix/Alamy Stock Photo; **128** (t) Khaled Desouki/AFP/Getty Images, (bl) Gorodenkoff_iStock/Getty Images, (br) Kilito Chan/Moment/Getty Images; **131** © Jason Treat / National Geographic Image Collection; **132** Double Brain/Shutterstock.com; **134** Sciepro/Science Source; **137** Spencer Grant/Alamy Stock Photo; **139** OR Images/DigitalVision/Getty Images; **141** Dan Kitwood/Getty Images News/Getty Images; **142-143** (Spread) MediaNews Group/East Bay Times via Getty Images/Getty Images; **145** Laura Storm/Alamy Stock Photo; **147** Brent Stirton/Getty Images News/Getty Images; **148** Tom Dulat/ZUMA Press/London/England/United Kingdom/Newscom; **149** (tc) Duncan1890/DigitalVision Vectors/Getty Images, (tr1) VII-photo/E+/Getty Images, (tr2) Gelatoplus/DigitalVision Vectors/Getty Images, (br) Vovalis/Shutterstock.com; **150** (tl) Hemis/Alamy Stock Photo, (tr) Valerija Polakovska/Shutterstock.com, (bl) Duncan1890/DigitalVision Vectors/Getty Images, (bc) VII-photo/E+/Getty Images, (br) Gelatoplus/DigitalVision Vectors/Getty Images; **151** Randy Duchaine/Alamy Stock Photo; **152** © Jodi Cobb/National Geographic Image Collection; **155** Justin Ng/Photoshot Images/London/England/UK/Newscom; **156** Mint Images RF/Getty Images; **159** Amanda Ahn/Alamy Stock Photo; **161** © George Karbus; **162-163** (Spread) © One Planet Network; **164** Yenwen/iStock Unreleased/Getty Images; **166** (cr) © Lorenzo Meloni, (b) © Melanie Wneger/National Geographic Image Collection; **168** (bl) © Joel Sartore/National Geographic Photo Ark, (br) © Joel Sartore/National Geographic Photo Ark /National Geographic Image Collection; **170** (bl) DircinhaSW/Moment/Getty Images, (br) Ed Freeman/Stone/Getty Images; **171** © Michael Forsberg/National Geographic Image Collection; **172-173** (Spread) Anup Shah/Stone/Getty Images; **175** © Willis D. Vaughn/National Geographic Image Collection; **177** John Warburton-Lee Photography/Alamy Stock Photo; **179** Stefan Cristian Cioata/Moment/Getty Images; **181** © John Stanmeyer/National Geographic Image Collection; **182-183** (Spread) R.M. Nunes/Alamy Stock Photo; **185** © Ken Banks/National Geographic Image Collection; **186** © Ken Banks; **189** VTT Studio/iStock/Getty Images; **191** Aleksandr Davydov/Alamy Stock Photo; **192** Tayutau/Moment/Getty Images; **195** Robert Nickelsberg/Archive Photos/Getty Images; **196** Bloomberg/Getty Images; **199** FreshSplash/E+/Getty Images.